The Modern
FAMILY
GARDEN BOOK

By

Roy E. Biles

J. G. Ferguson and Associates, Publishers -- Chicago
1948

Contents

Copyright 1941, 1940, 1935, Roy E. Biles
Copyright 1943, M. E. Biles
Copyright 1948, J. G. Ferguson and Associates

TYPOGRAPHY, PRINTING, AND BINDING IN THE U. S. A. BY
KINGSPORT PRESS, INC., KINGSPORT, TENNESSEE

CHAPTER VII: TREES AND SHRUBBERY 39

TREES

The parts of a tree, 39; the growth of trees, 40; the enemies of trees, 40; breathing and transpiring, 40; age, 40; some popular trees, 40; selection of material, 40; time of planting, 42; planting, 42; cultivation and care, 43; insects and disease, 44; birds, 44; cats, 44; repair work, 44; cavities, 46; crooked trees, 46.

SHRUBS

Selection of shrubs, 46; planting, 46; pruning, 46.

CHAPTER VIII: VINES 49

Selection, 49; planting, 49; ivies, 49; euonymus, 50; carpeting plants, 50; flowering vines, 50; annual vines, 51.

CHAPTER IX: ROSES 52

Selection, 52; location, 52; soil, 52; planting time, 52; planting, 52; pruning, 54; disease, 54; mulching, 54; climbers, 55.

CHAPTER X: BULBS, CORMS, TUBERS, AND ROOTS . . 56

SPRING-FLOWERING BULBS

Crocus, 57; glory of snow, 57; snowdrop, 57; spring snowflake, 57; grape hyacinth, 58; squills siberica, 58; scilla hispanica, 58; scilla bifoloa, 58; winter aconite, 58; star of Bethlehem, 58; narcissus, 58; tulip, 58; hyacinth, 58.

SUMMER-FLOWERING BULBS

Autumn crocus, 58; cluster amaryllis, 58; calla, 59; canna, 59; dahlia, 59; elephant's-ear, 59; gladiolus, 59; summer hyacinth, 61; bearded iris, 61; oriental iris, 62; water iris, 62; lily, 62; madonna lily, 63; other popular lilies, 64; montbretia, 64; mariposa, 64; peony, 65; planting peonies, 66.

CHAPTER XI: FLOWER BORDER 68

Site, 68; arrangement, 68; time, 70; preparation of the bed, 70; selection of plants, 70; annuals, 72; care of the border, 72; winter protection, 73; lists of perennials, 74–77; annual flowers, 78–86; what to plant for garden color (chart), 87; annual flower chart, 88–89.

CHAPTER XII: FLOWER ARRANGING 90

Selection, 90; containers, 90; arrangement, 90; how to keep cut flowers, 92; forcing flowering branches, 93.

CHAPTER XIII: THE ROCK GARDEN 95

Site, 95; stones, 95; soil, 95; plants, 96; plants for rock gardens, 96–97.

CHAPTER XIV: WINDOW BOXES 98

Size and material, 98; soil requirements, 98; fertilizer, 98; plants, 98.

CHAPTER I

Planning

The kiss of the sun for pardon,
The song of the birds for mirth.
I am closer God's heart in a garden
Than anywhere else on earth.

A LANDSCAPE gardener of wide experience once said, "Folks are interested in plants, but not in planting." The reason why many people become discouraged in garden planning is that the instructions are sometimes very confusing. One authority will say that shrubbery borders, perennial beds, etc., should be in straight lines upon a small lot. Others will say that the curved line lends beauty and informality. These so-called authorities will then set forth an ideal garden plan; but as the amateur studies it, he will find many things in the plan to be at variance with his past experience.

For instance, some plans may have shrubbery borders and perennial beds located in dense shade; others may have lily pools located under trees. When he reads these plans the amateur may become so confused that he will abandon all pretense of planning or will attempt to make the plan according to his own past experience. The result is that he clutters up his garden with many things which do not belong there, and it becomes a number of disconnected features and plants rather than a harmonious plan.

Now it would be a fine thing if we could afford the services of a competent landscape gardener to plan our lot. This is no doubt money well spent and will add to the permanent satisfaction and value of a home. However, if the gardener is unwilling to make this original outlay and wishes to do the planning himself, he should take the attitude of the architect about to design a house. He should decide what features are to go into the garden, what are the needs of each feature, and then try to fit them together in a coherent plan. This plan should assure that each feature will, so far as possible, get the proper location.

Open lawn. It has been said that the lawn is the canvas upon which you paint your garden picture. Nothing sets off the beauty of the features of your garden like a stretch of well-kept, weedless lawn. Keep it open in the

What careful planning can do. Here we have a vista from the house, a pool which does not cut up the plan and shrubbery and flowers which grow in proper locations. Rhododendrons flourish in the isolated soil close to the house and recreation space is provided within easy reach.

center, and use it as a setting for the various other things of which your garden is composed. Except in extremely small plans, the lawn should dominate all other features. It should be at least two or three times the width of the borders opening on it.

Foundation planting. Planting around the foundation of the house is primarily for the purpose of adding to or correcting house proportions. Most small homes are two stories high, and the fact that they cover a very small ground area makes it hard for the architect to get the correct proportions between its height and its other dimensions. Then, too, the contractor, because he can save on the cellar excavation, sometimes sets the house higher than is necessary. Therefore, we plant about the foundations of the house to make it look lower and wider, as well as to soften lines or to add a touch of decoration.

Because foundation planting is a year-round feature, we use mostly evergreens and such shrubbery as will harmonize with them in summer, yet at the same time give the decoration of their bark or berries in winter.

Perennials and annuals. While some of these flowers will grow in semishade, the most generally successful location is open sunlight. On the small plan they are usually planted as a border along the property lines. The bed should be at least five feet wide (eight feet is better if you have room) and at least two or three times as long as wide.

Dahlias. Almost every gardener wants a few dahlias. However, these plants require quite a bit of room and the tall stalks upon which the blossoms are borne are usually not very decorative. Many people handle them in a garden to themselves, much as a vegetable garden. Sometimes this garden can be located behind some low-growing shrubbery or other plants, so that the tops of the dahlias bearing the blossoms can be seen without exposing the stalks.

Iris. There are so many kinds of iris that it is very difficult to place them under one heading. However, the most easily grown and generally used varieties are adaptable either in semishade or in the open. Better results are obtained in the open. Iris may be used as fill-ins between beds or borders, as edgings for a drive or walk, or as a temporary planting between young shrubbery while waiting for it to obtain its proper growth. By using various kinds of iris, the blooming period may be extended over several months. Many varieties have the advantage that their foliage stays green and sightly until severe frost.

Bulbs. There are so many varieties of bulbs, each variety requiring somewhat different positions and flowering at different times, that we advise the planner to read the entire chapter on bulbs (Chapter X) before attempting to locate them in the garden scheme.

Rose garden. The best site for a rose garden is an open space on the southerly slope sheltered to the north and east by higher ground, walls, or hedges. The bed must not be too close to the wall or hedge, must have sunlight for at least half the day, and must have air all around it. Roses need a well-drained soil. The beds must not be too wide or it will be necessary to tramp upon them to cut the blooms or attend to them, thus undoing the effects of cultivation.

Climbing roses. An area of at least three square feet of ground should be assigned to each climbing rose. The same ground conditions apply as in the rose garden. For suc-

cessful growth they should have the sunlight upon them for at least two-thirds of the day or most of the time.

Rock garden. If you have on your grounds a small natural slope, fairly well exposed to the light and sun, this is the place to locate your rock garden. A few stones placed as outcroppings will make it look like a natural formation. However, if this slope is not available, construct the rock garden at the edge or boundary of the lot, backing up on the fence or shrubbery. It is seldom that a rock garden can be artistically located in the shape of a mound in the center of the yard.

Water garden. Water plants are easily grown and very adaptable. All they need is sunlight and food. Unless you wish to confine your efforts to very small blooms or to the plants which are rampant growers, the water garden must be in the sunlight all day. A little shade on the north may be used for background, but any shading directly over the pool will interfere with the number, size, and health of the lilies themselves. Do not be misled by the many plans published showing the pools in the semishade. This is not the place for a water garden. Informal pools may be used in connection with almost any feature but formal pools must be located very carefully so that they are in complete balance with the rest of the plan.

Vines. Vines may be grown almost anywhere. Many creepers will grow in the densest of shade. Ground-carpeting plants will grow where no other plant can live. Therefore, if you want to blot out any certain view or to cover any object, you have only to select the kind of vine which will grow in this location.

Flowering shrubbery. Flowering shrubbery is best planted as a border on the edge of the garden. Beds should be six to eight feet deep and at least two or three times as long. Flowering shrubbery can be selected to grow in either shade or sunlight. The most popular varieties, however, grow best when they have sunlight at least half the time.

Fruit trees. Fruit trees of the larger size, of course, require a considerable area. However, many dwarf fruit trees can be included at the edge of the vegetable garden or in the borders. They have the advantage of the blossoms in the spring and, given proper care, they will yield a fair amount of full-sized fruit.

Shade trees. Shade trees have many uses. They may be used to shade the front yard, to frame the house, or for the outdoor living room. In planting shade trees, always remember that in five or six years they will grow considerably and try to imagine what your yard will look like when they are fully grown.

The outdoor living room. The outdoor living room is becoming increasingly popular. Formerly the house was considered the home, and everything outside the house was the out of doors. This idea we get as children and it is sometimes very hard to break away from it. The first requisite of the outdoor living room is privacy. It should be completely screened by shrubbery from the entrance walk or drive. It may be located under trees, an arbor, or a pergola. It should contain a hammock and easy chairs. A waterproof box seat may be used to hold cushions or the hammock when not in use. If it is located in shade where grass will not grow, pave it or cover the ground with stone chips or pea gravel (sometimes called torpedo sand).

A play yard for children. A place for the children will save a lot of wear and tear on the rest of the garden. A sandbox may be provided. Sufficient room for enough play space should be provided for the children. Screen this off with a little shrubbery, within easy calling distance of the house. It will be a very attractive feature.

Drying yard. In families where washing is done each day many plans feature an outside drying yard. There are removable metal clothes posts which drop into sockets in the lawn to make this suitable for drying.

Terraces. A terrace is usually located in connection with the home and has access to it by a door opening on the terrace from the dining room or living room. It is slightly raised to overlook the garden and may be paved with stone or tile and equipped with furniture similar to that used in an outdoor living room.

A garden service plot. In Chapter II is described a garden laboratory or kitchen which contains a vegetable garden, tool house, manure pit, cold frame, propagating bed, and other features. Of course any part of the laboratory may be adapted or the features may be worked in separately.

A propagating bed. A propagating bed for growing a variety of plants will be found helpful and economical. In the spring it may be used for the raising of annuals which are to be transplanted to other locations, after which summer planting of perennials is comparatively simple.

Vegetable garden. Many people omit the vegetable garden because they think that it is not worth while or that it is too much trouble. A small green garden is very handy and convenient for the cook. The vegetable garden should, of course, be a thing to itself. Place it in a corner, or at the end of the lot behind some low-growing shrubbery. Although it is not a part of the garden scene, it need not be unsightly. Grass walks may surround the beds for convenience in weeding in wet weather. Use a formal or semiformal plan. A few ornaments or flowers judiciously placed can make this feature a thing of beauty.

Ornamental accessories. Ornamentals should not be in competition for attention with plants or planting. They are not the main part of the garden; they are the accessories. They accentuate the beauty of the garden much the same as jewelry adds to personal appearance. Overdressing in the garden, like overdressing in clothes, shows bad taste. Accessories should represent something connected with the garden. As lawn ornaments, the iron stag and the hunting dog went out of fashion with the gingerbread ornamentations of the American home in vogue shortly after the Civil War.

Walks and steps should lead somewhere. Gates should be an entrance or exit. A seat should be placed where some one will sit on it, overlooking some garden feature. It should be a place where the gardener can take a short rest from his labors. If the seat is of the more permanent or comfortable variety, it should be located in the shade, and be inviting. A trellis should be used for the display of vines. Statuary must be used sparingly and be appropriate to the woodland or the garden. Sun dials, reflecting globes, bird baths, fountains, etc., may be placed by themselves. They are usually placed upon pedestals and care should be taken to place them substantially and usefully. A sun dial should be readily accessible as we must get very close to it in order to tell the time.

Fountains are placed largely in relation with mirror pools or water gardens. If a fountain is used on a pedestal in connection with the bird bath or similar bowl, the rule

for locating the sun dials, globes, and bird baths will apply to it. Bird houses are designed more for the purpose of attracting our feathered friends than for ornamentation. Any location of them in the plan should be made with a view to the maximum use by the birds. A mirror pool is a small pool usually located flush with the surface of the garden or lawn. A true mirror pool has few or no water plants growing in it, but is supposed to reflect the sky and the surrounding foliage. It acts in the garden much as the reflecting globe. This pool, of course, may be located in the shade or semishade, where water lilies will not grow well.

Making the plan. Now let us carry farther into our garden planning the idea of an architect. First of all he has an idea of how the finished house will look. Then he sits down at his drawing board and draws plans to scale. This means that for every foot there will be in the length of a room, he will draw (let us say) one-quarter of an inch or one-eighth of an inch on his drawing. This may sound very intricate to the amateur but if you are sporty enough to try it, you will find that the awkwardness you feel when you first use the common ruler for this purpose will soon wear away.

For example, if your back yard is fifty by sixty feet and you wish to draw it to one-eighth inch scale, you will draw a rectangle $6\frac{1}{4}$ inches wide by $7\frac{1}{2}$ inches long. You will find that this will go nicely on a sheet of ordinary letter paper. You next take a few pieces of cardboard and out of these cut small pieces to represent the various beds and borders which you are about to use in your garden.

If you have decided that your shrubbery border will be five by ten feet, you will cut it out of cardboard, making it $\frac{5}{8}$ inch wide by $1\frac{1}{4}$ inches long. By shading it a little bit with a pencil, it will appear darker than the outline of your yard which you have just drawn. Proceed to do the same with your perennial beds, water gardens, rockery, and other features. Then move them around on the plan until you have them fitted.

Make it seem as though you were a great giant working out the actual garden itself. Try to imagine what these features will look like when placed side by side. Try to remember differences in the height of the plants, where the sun will be in certain portions of the day, and what plants will be shaded by other plants or existing trees.

Many five- and ten-cent stores and all stationery and school supply stores sell cross-section paper. This paper is ruled into tiny squares, each one of which can represent one

2. Locate the house, garage, and permanent features. Give these matters in detail, showing measurement in scale.

3. Show the approximate spread of the foliage of trees and the approximate path of the shade thrown by them.

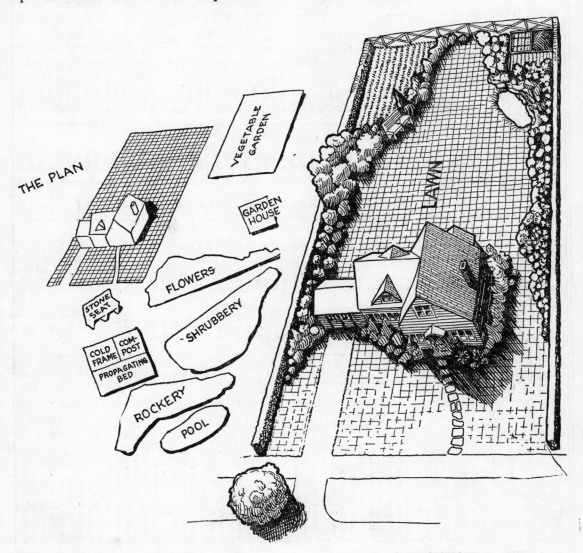

square foot. By counting off the number of feet in width and length of your garden and marking its outlines you can then draw in the various features without the use of a ruler.

Having first carefully selected the features which we want in the garden from the list previously given, and having carefully studied the ideas of design, we now assemble the various features into a harmonious whole. Here is a summary of the things to do to get started:

1. Draw a sketch of your yard in scale.

4. Locate the walks, drives, fences, etc.

5. Decide what views in the neighborhood you wish to screen out, and plan for that planting.

6. Try to arrange for an easy entrance to your rear garden from your house and a handy place for storage of tools and equipment.

7. Mark where shady plants will grow and sun-loving plants will grow.

8. Take some pictures of some various sides

PLANTING LIST OF TREES, SHRUBS, EVERGREENS, AND VINES FOR HOME BEAUTIFICATION

All plant names are taken from "Standardized Plant Names," by the American Joint Committee on Horticultural Nomenclature

Scientific name	Common name	Planting distance, feet	Height in feet	Spread in feet	Exposure	Growth	Flowers		Fruit		Size to Order
							Season	Color	Seas.	Color	
Acer ginnala	Amur Maple	4–6	8–15	5–10	SA	M	April	White	H–C	Red	3–4'
Acanthopanax pentaphylla	Five-leafed Aralia	4	4–5	3–5	SSh	M					3–4'
Berberis thunbergi	Japanese Barberry	3–4	3–4	3–4	SSh	M				Red	18–24"
Buddleia davidi (magnifica)	Butterfly bush	4–5	3–5	5–6	S	F	July	Lilac			2 yr.
Calycanthus floridus	Sweetshrub	4	4	4–5	S	M	May	Red			2–3'
Caragana arborescens	Siberian pea-tree	4–5	6–10	4–5	S†	R	May	Yellow			3–4'
Cercis canadensis	Redbud	5†	15–25	Tree	S†	M	May	Dk. Pink		Seedpod	3–4'
Chionanthus virginica	White Fringetree	6–8‡	5–15	Tree	S*	R	June	White			3–4'
Cotoneaster divaricata	Cotoneaster	4	4–5	4–5	S*	R	May	Yellow	C	Red	3–4'
Cornus alba	Red twig Dogwood	5	6–8	5–7	SSh	M	May	White	E	White	3–4'
Cornus florida	Flowering Dogwood	10	8–20	Tree	A	F	May	White	E	Red	5–6'
Cornus paniculata	Gray Dogwood	5	5–8	5–7	A	M					3–4'
Cornus stolonifera flaviramea	Goldentwig Dogwood	5	5	4–6	A	M	May	White	E	Twigs Yel.	3–4'
Deutzia formosa magnifica	Double White Deutzia	4	5–8	3–4	A	M	May	White			3–4'
Deutzia gracilis (tender)	Slender Deutzia	2–3	2	2	S	R	May	White			12–18"
Deutzia lemoinei	Lemoine Deutzia	3–4	3–4	3	S	M	May	White			18–24"
Euonymus alatus	Winged Euonymus	5	5–6	4–5	S	M	May	Cream	E	Red-Orng.	2–3'
Euonymus europaeus	European Burningbush	5–6	6–10	8–20	S	M	May	Cream	E–H	Red-Orng.	3–4'
Eleagnus angustifolia	Russian Olive	5	15–20	Tree	A	M	June	Yellow	H	Silver	3–4'
Forsythia intermedia spectabilis	Showy Border Forsythia	5	4–6	6–8	S	F	April	Yellow			3–4'
Forsythia suspensa	Weeping Forsythia	4–5	6–8	6–10	A	F	April	Yellow			3–4'
Hibiscus syriacus	Shrub-Althea	4	6–8	3–4	S	M	August	Various			2–3'
Hydrangea paniculata grand.	Peegee Hydrangea	3–4	4–6	3–4	S	M	Sept.	Wh-pink			2–3'
Hydrangea aborescens sterile	Snowhill Hydrangea	3	4	3–4	S	M	July	White			2–3'
Hypericum aureum (tender)	Golden St. Johnswort	3	3–4	3–4	A	M	July	Yellow	E		2–3'
Kerria japonica	Kerria	3	3–4	3–4	S	M	May	Yellow			2–3'
Koelreuteria paniculata	Goldenrain Tree	10	10–20	Tree	S	R	July	Yellow	E–H	Br'n Pods	18–24"
Ligustrum ibolium	Ibolium Privet	4	6–8	4–5	SSh	M	May	Cream			5–6'
Ligustrum ibota	Ibota Privet	5	5–6	4–7	SSh	F	May	Cream	E–C	Blue-Blacks	3–4'
Ligustrum regelianum	Regel Privet, dwarf form.	4	3–4	4–5	SSh*	F	May	Cream	E–C	Blue-Blacks	2–3'
Ligustrum vulgare	European Privet	5	6–8	4–5	A	F	April	Cream	E–C	Black	3–4'
Lonicera fragrantissima	Winter Honeysuckle	5–8	5–6	4–6	A	FF	April	Cream			3–4'
Lonicera morrowi	Morrow Honeysuckle	5–8	6	6–10	SSh	FF	May	Cream	E	Red	3–4'
Lonicera tatarica	Tatarian Honeysuckle, Pink.	5–8	8–15	5–8	SSh	FF	May	Pink	E	Red	3–4'
Lonicera maacki	Amur Honeysuckle	5–6	10–15	5–8	A	F	May	White	H–C	Red	3–4'
Philadelphus coronarius	Sweet Mockorange	3	8–15	4–7	A	M	May	White			3–4'
Philadelphus lemoinei	Lemoine Mockorange	3	3–5	3	A	M	May	White			3–4'
Philadelphus virginal	Virginal Mockorange	3	3–6	6–8	A	F	May	Cream			3–4'
Physocarpus opulifolius aurea	Goldleaf Ninebark	5–8	6–10	5–8	S	M	May	White	E	Red-Green	18–24"
Prunus othello or pissardi	Purpleleaf Plum	5	8–15	3–4	A†	R	April	White	E	Purple	18–24"
Prunus glandulosa (Amygdalus)	Flowering Almond	3	3–4	4–5	S	M	May	Pink-Wh.			3–4'
Rhodotypos kerrioides	Jetbead	4	4–5	2–3	A	M	May	White	E–C	Black	18–24"
Rhus canadensis	Fragrant Sumac	3	3–5	5–8	A	M	April	Yellowish		Red	2–3'
Rhus glabra	Smooth Sumac	3	5–8	5–10	S	M	July	Greenish	E–H	Scarlet	3–4'
Rhus typhina laciniata	Cutleaf Sumac	5	6–12	5–8	S	M	July	Greenish	E–H	Crimson	3–4'
Ribes alpinum	Alpine Currant	3	4	3	SSh	M	April	Greenish			2–3'
Ribes odoratum (aureum)	Golden Flowering Currant	5–8	5–6	5–7	SSh	M	May	Yellow	E	Black	2–3'
Rosa hugonis	Hugonis Rose	3	4–5	4–5	S	F	June	Yellow			3–4'
Rosa wichuriana	Wichurian Rose	5–8	1–2	10	S	F	Jun–Jul.	White			2–3'
Sorbaria aitchesoni (Spirea)	Kashmir False-spirea	4–5	5–6	4–6	S	MF	July	Cream			3–4'

Table (column headings cut off at top of page). Reading order: Common Name | Botanical Name | (numeric) | (numeric) | (numeric / rate) | Exposure | Growth | Bloom month | Bloom color | Season of fruit | Color of fruit | Size for planting

Common Name	Botanical Name				Exp.	Gr.	Bloom	Color	Fruit	Fruit Color	Size
Anthony Waterer Spirea	Spiraea anthony waterer	3	2-3	3-3	A	R	June	Pink			12-18"
Frobel Spirea	Spiraea froebeli	4	3	3	A	M	June	Pink			18-24"
Thunberg Spirea	Spiraea thunbergi	4	3-4	3-4	S	M	April	White			18-24"
Van Houtte Spirea	Spiraea vanhouttei	5	5-6	5-6	S	F	May	White			3-4'
Cutleaf Stephanandra	Stephanandra flexuosa (tender)	3	3-4	3	S	R	June	White			2-3'
Snowberry	Symphoricarpus racemosus	3-4	3-4	3	SSh	M		Pksh.-wh.	E-H	White	3-4'
Coralberry	Symphoricarpus vulgaris	3	6-10	6-8	S	M	May	White	E-C	Red	3-4'
Chinese Lilac	Syringa chinensis (rothom'gn's)	5	6-12	6-8	S	M	May	Lilac			3-4'
Com. Lilac (use French hyb.)	Syringa vulgaris	5	8-10	6-8	S	M	June	Various			2-3'
Late Lilac	Syringa villosa	5	6-10	6-8	S	MF	July	Lilac			3-4'
Tamarix	Tamarix pentandra (hisp. aest.)	3-4	3-5	3-4	S	MF	June	Pink			3-4'
Withe-rod	Viburnum cassinoides	4	5-8	3-5	SSh	M	June	White	H	Blue-Black	3-4'
Arrowwood	Viburnum dentatum	5	5-6	5-6	SSh	M	May	White	E	Red-Black	3-4'
Wayfaring Tree	Viburnum latana	5	6-10	5-6	SSh†	MF	May	White	E-H	Blue-Black	3-4'
Nannyberry	Viburnum lentago	5-6	10-15	6-8	A†	M	May	White	E-C	Red	3-4'
European Cranberrybush	Viburnum opulus	5	6-8	5-6	A	M	June	White	E	Red-Black	2-3'
Doublefile Viburnum	Viburnum tomentosum	4	6-8	5-6	A	M	June	White			2-3'
Japanese Snowball	Viburnum tomentosum plicatum	4	3-5	4-5	S	M	June	Red			2-3'
Eva Rathke Weigela	Weigela eva rathke	5	6-8	5-6	S	M	June	Red			2-3'
Pink Weigela	Weigela rosea	5	6-8	5-6	S	M	June	Pink-wh.			2-3'
Trees											
Sugar Maple	Acer saccharum	50	50	35	SSh	M		White			2"
Norway Maple	Acer platanoides	40	40	35	S	R					2-4"
Horsechestnut	Aesculus hippocastanum	50	50	35	S	M	May	White			1"
Hackberry	Celtis occidentalis	50	50	35	S	M					2-4"
Tuliptree	Liriodendron tulipifera	40	50	35	SSh	M	May	Yellow			1-2"
Pin Oak	Quercus palustris	6-15	40	4-8	S	F					1-2"
Bolleana Poplar	Populus bolleana	50	35	50	S	R					8-10'
Red Oak	Quercus rubra	25	50	20	SSh	R					1"
Laurel Willow	Salix pentandra	50-75	30	50	S	M					1-2"
American Elm	Ulmus americana	3	75	50	S	M					2-4"
Evergreens											
Pfitzer Juniper‡	Juniperus chinensis pfitzeriana	6-10	3-6	6-10	SSh	F					2 yr.
Cannart Juniper	Juniperus virginiana cannarti	5	15	4	A	M					12-18"
Norway Spruce‡ ††	Picea excelsa	10-20	50	20-30	S	M					
Austrian Pine‡ ††	Pinus nigra	10-20	30	20-30	S	R					
Douglas Fir‡	Pseudotsuga douglasi	3-5	50	10-20	A	R					
Japanese Yew‡	Taxus cuspidata	3-10	20	5-10	SSh	R					
Arborvitae	Thuja occidentalis	6-20	50	15-30	S	R					
Hemlock‡	Tsuga canadensis	4	4		SSh	R					
Wintercreeper	Euonymus radicans				SSh	R					
Oregon Grape	Mahonia aquifolia	3	3-4	2-3	SSh	R					
Vines											
Virginia Creeper‡	Ampelopsis quinquefolia	10	15-35	Vigor.	SSh	F		Wings	E-H	Black	2 yr.
Japanese Creeper (Boston)	Ampelopsis tricuspidata (veitchi)	10	10-50	Good	A	M					2 yr.
Dutchmans-pipe	Aristolochia sipho	15	35	Good	S	M					3 yr.
Trumpetcreeper	Bignonia radicans	20	50	Vigor.	A	F	June	Orange	E-H	Br'n Pods	2 yr.
Japanese Clematis	Clematis paniculata	6	15	Fair	S	R	August	White			2 yr.
Bittersweet	Celastrus scandens	10	25	Good	SSh	M	May	White	H-C	Or'ng-Red	2 yr.
English Ivy	Hedera helix	6	25	Fair	A	R				Evergreen	2 yr.
Hall Japanese Honeysuckle	Lonicera halliana	10	25	Vigor.	A	F	June	Cream			2 yr.
China Fleecevine, Silverlacev.	Polygonum auberti	10	25		A	M	Summer	White			2 yr.
Chinese Wisteria (grafted)	Wisteria sinensis	20	50	Vigor.	S	F	May	Lavender			2 yr.
Common Yucca	Yucca filamentosa	2			S	F	June	Cream			
Periwinkle (myrtle)	Vinca minor	1			A	M	Summer	White			
Japanese Pachysandra	Pachysandra terminalis	2			S	F	May	Lavender		Evergreen	

SYM- { Growth: F—Fast; M—Medium; R—Slow
BOLS { Preferred exposure; A—Partial shade; S—Sun; Sh—Shade; SSh—Sun or shade
{ Season of fruit: E—Summer; H—Fall; C—Winter

USED { * For wet ground. † For dry ground. ‡ Specimen plant. †† Windbreak.

(From Ohio State Bulletin 73—by Victor H. Ries.)

of your house. Study them and visualize how you would like the planting to look in regard to the house.

9. Determine the kind of garden features you are going to have, whether formal or informal planting.

Now, having cut your various features to scale, attempt to fit them into a plan.

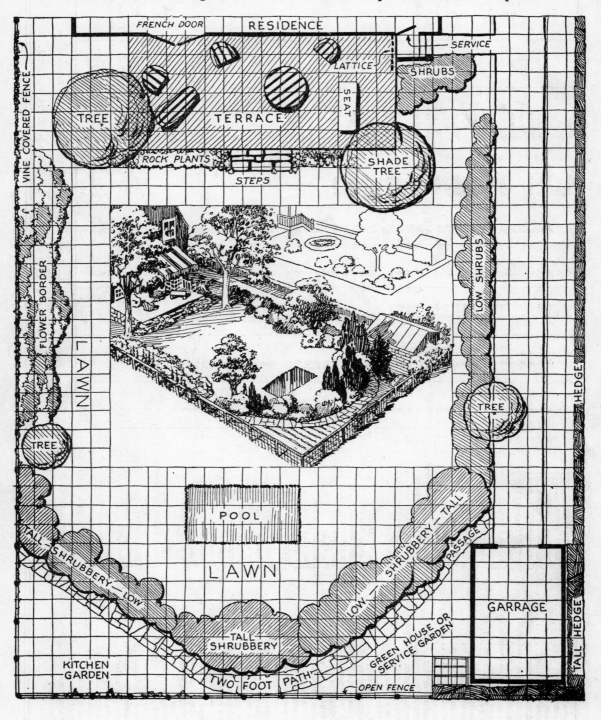

CHAPTER II

Equipment

The failures of life sit around and complain,
That the gods haven't treated 'em right.
They've lost their umbrellas whenever it rains
And they haven't their lanterns at night.

Kinds of tools. The illustration shows a number of garden tools. A planting shovel (1) is small and very handy around the garden. The spading fork (2) is much easier to handle and does better work than a regular spade. A speedy cultivator (3) will help keep the perennial beds and the rose garden in shape with very little labor. The bow rake (4) has two uses: it takes the roughage off the lawn and is much handier than the regular rake in garden cultivation. The weed spud (5) should be used for plantain, dock, and other surface-rooted weeds which can be eradicated with one removal. This tool is not good for dandelions, unless they are worked over a dozen or more times a season. The dandelion will sprout from the old root and make more plants when cut. The broom rake (7) should be used to remove rubbish from the lawn; do not use it to remove grass clippings, but allow them to go back into the soil, replacing vegetable matter. Shears (8) should be used by every gardener, since proper pruning makes good plants. A home-made tamper (9) is fine to smooth out the newly dug garden bed or to level up the lawn in the spring. Dozens of uses can be found for it about the garden. The hand fork (12), the trowel (10), and the hand cultivator (13) should be kept in the hand box at all times within easy reach to remove weeds or to break up the soil around the backward plant. The hand sprayer (11) may be enough for you to use, but the knapsack sprayer (24) can be pumped up and carried about the garden with a generous supply of spray. A good edging sickle (14) is now sold which utilizes old razor blades, keeping a keen edge at all times. Nothing is more neglected about the garden than the hose (15). The sprinkler (16) is absolutely necessary in any garden. Thorough soaking always brings better results, if only done occasionally, than frequent light

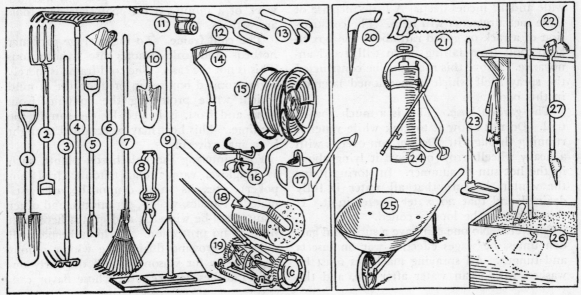

sprinkling. The roller (17), sprinkling can (18), and mower are well known. The dibble (20) is for planting seeds and seedlings. The potato hoe (23) is fine for deeper cultivation. The lawn edger (27) will keep your walks looking trim at all times. The rest of the tools are so well known as to need no comment.

Care of tools. Of course the most desirable place to keep tools is in a rack especially constructed for them. The illustration shows a box of sand over which has been poured some oil. Crank-case drainage will do for this if it is strained through a cloth to remove the carbon or lamp-black which will stain the hands. Mix about a third or half as much sand as you require, and gradually add dry sand to the mixture until it has a dry, oily feeling. Too much oil should not be used as it will make the tools greasy and hard to handle. There should never be enough oil on the tools to soil clothing.

Tools plunged into this oily sand are not exposed to the air and consequently do not rust. In addition, there is a constant film of oil upon them and they are easily cleaned after use. Sickles, scythes, shears, etc., will stay sharp much longer if they are not rusty.

Of course tools which have working parts, such as the lawn mower, must be kept free from sand. Only the blade of the shears should be forced into this sand and sand must not get into the pivot or friction surface of the shears. Keep this pivot well oiled and wipe sand from the shears before using.

This box should be not less than 12 inches wide and 12 inches deep. A little increase of these measurements will help. The construction of a rack or guard rail above the box to keep tools from falling down will avoid annoyance. Above this rack may be constructed the spray shelf which is mentioned later on in this book.

The garden hose. This is a much abused tool. Do not allow it to kink while water is running through it. Do not run over it with a heavy wheelbarrow or leave it lying about in the hot sun of summer. In storing it for the winter, be sure that all water is fully drained and that no water freezes in it. It should always be loosely coiled.

Sprayers. No one can have a successful garden unless he wages effective war on insects and fungus. All spraying machines must be washed with clean water after use, and the nozzle should be examined to get the particles of grit which is bound to choke them.

The lawn mower. The care of the lawn mower is sometimes disheartening. The circular blade of the mower rotates against the bottom knife, which is fixed. These blades should barely touch the lower knife evenly all along. The revolving blades, driven by gears located on the inside of the driving wheels which roll upon the ground, frequently become full of dirt or dust, making them hard to operate. Loosen the screw on the center of these wheels and remove them one at a time. After removing the wheel, flush out the interior with kerosene which you can apply with a regular squirt oil can.

When the mower leaves ridges of uncut grass, it needs adjustment. If the blades seem to be dull, they can be sharpened by applying coarse valve-grinding compound on the stationary blade, and then running the mower backwards. Some mowers cannot be reversed. The knives may be touched up a bit with a file, but care is needed to avoid filing them unevenly. If the blades are badly worn or nicked, it is best to take them to a professional sharpener. Bronze or aluminum paint applied with a small brush is the thing for this. The wooden roller determines how long or how short the grass shall be cut. This may be raised to make a longer cutting and lowered for a shorter one.

The hand tool box. Good tools are useless if they are not handy. In our trips of inspection, a snip here, a little spraying or dusting there, or even tying up a plant is but the work of a minute if the materials and tools are with us.

The cold frame. To the average gardener hotbeds and cold frames are synonymous This is not the case. The cold frame is merely a glass-topped box set in or upon the ground which, while protecting the contents from wind and frost, is heated by the sun in the daytime. This heat may be retained at night by a mat covering.

For wintering the half hardy plants, such as foxglove, campanula, tritonia (red hot poker), etc., its value cannot be over estimated. Pansies, violets, geraniums, and other plants may be wintered and grown here with little or no protection. No housekeeper will object to growing during the winter onions and parsley for seasoning, and the early onions, radishes, lettuce, etc., whose flavor cannot be duplicated in stores. Seeds started early may be hardened to outdoor conditions and chances of success are multiplied many times.

A practical selection of plants which can easily be started in cold frames in March would include China aster, black dahlia, coreopsis, cardinal flower, chrysanthemum (annual), early cosmos, larkspur (annual), phlox (annual), snapdragon, stock (ten weeks), sweet william, etc. Your own experience will find many more.

Location of hotbeds and cold frames. Both hotbeds and cold frames should be located in a sheltered place, where they will be protected from north and northwest winds. They should also be placed on ground with a southern and an eastern exposure, so that the plants will receive the maximum amount of light and heat. The soil in and about the frame should be well drained. Water supply should be close to the frame, for watering is an essential factor in the production of good plants. Be careful not to place the frame in a damp spot unless it has first been thoroughly drained with farm tile.

Construction. Do not be in too big a hurry to construct the frame out of concrete. A wooden one will last for years. The frame may be constructed on top of the ground, but a better way is to dig a pit extending the wooden frame to the bottom; then, after conditioning the soil, replace it in the pit.

The frame should be made of tight boards and it is better to bank the soil around as a further protection. The sashes come in standard size, three feet wide and six feet long. Half size—3 x 3 feet—are also made for small

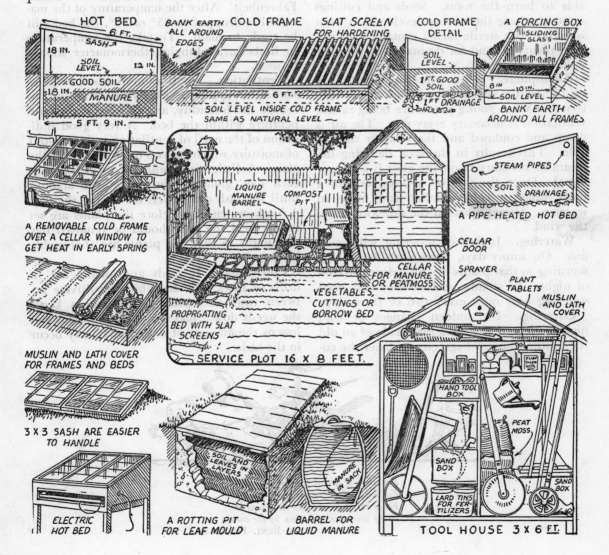

HOT BED · BANK EARTH ALL AROUND EDGES · COLD FRAME · SLAT SCREEN FOR HARDENING · COLD FRAME DETAIL · A FORCING BOX

6 FT. · 18 IN. · SASH · 12 IN. · SOIL LEVEL · GOOD SOIL · 18 IN. · MANURE · 5 FT. 9 IN.

SOIL LEVEL INSIDE COLD FRAME SAME AS NATURAL LEVEL

SOIL LEVEL · 1 FT. GOOD SOIL · 1 FT DRAINAGE

SLIDING GLASS · 8 IN. · 10 IN. · SOIL LEVEL · BANK EARTH AROUND ALL FRAMES

A REMOVABLE COLD FRAME OVER A CELLAR WINDOW TO GET HEAT IN EARLY SPRING

LIQUID MANURE BARREL · COMPOST PIT

STEAM PIPES · SOIL · DRAINAGE · A PIPE-HEATED HOT BED

PROPRGATING BED WITH SLAT SCREENS

VEGETABLES, CUTTINGS OR BORROW BED

CELLAR DOOR · CELLAR FOR MANURE OR PEATMOSS · SPRAYER · PLANT TABLETS · MUSLIN AND LATH COVER

SERVICE PLOT 16 X 8 FEET.

MUSLIN AND LATH COVER FOR FRAMES AND BEDS

3 X 3 SASH ARE EASIER TO HANDLE

SOIL AND LEAVES IN LAYERS · MANURE IN SACK

ELECTRIC HOT BED · A ROTTING PIT FOR LEAF MOULD · BARREL FOR LIQUID MANURE

HAND TOOL BOX · PEAT MOSS · SAND BOX · LARD TINS FOR FERTILIZERS · SAND BOX · TOOL HOUSE 3 X 6 FT.

frames. They can be purchased ready made, which is cheaper than having them made to order. They must be painted each year and stored on end, in the shade, where it is fairly dry, when not in use, as the sun and continual moisture rot them.

The sashes are made as light as possible for handling and because of this sag quickly. They must be supported by a 2 x 4 on edge at each end of the frame and by 2 x 4 bars set flat between each sash. The sashes are allowed to rest upon these bars one inch on either side. Upon the bars are nailed one-inch strips to keep the sashes from interfering when moved and to make them fit tight. Close fitting is essential, as a slight draft at the wrong time will harm the plants.

Soil. A well-developed plant usually thrives in rich soil but in the younger plant it is liable to burn the roots. Seeds and cuttings must first have their roots developed in what is known as a sterile media, usually poor soil with plenty of sand for drainage and peat for holding moisture.

Atmosphere. When wintering plants in a cold frame the sash may be left on most of the time but when young plants are being raised, ventilation is necessary every day. The air is damp and confined and the weather changeable. This results in the fatal damping off. Steam or moisture upon the glass is a danger signal. Open the sash on a tiny crack for a short time in cold weather and more in warmer. Always open on the side away from the wind.

Watering. Indiscreet watering will cause loss. On sunny days, water each day in the morning so that plants dry off before the cold of night. In cloudy weather they may need watering only once every two or three days.

Covering. For sudden changes or cold nights it is well to have a mat made of an old rug, quilted burlap bags, etc., to cover the en-tire frame. Tie it down but be sure to re-move it during the daytime. These mats can be purchased.

Filling the hotbed. In filling the hotbed, place the manure in the bed in layers six inches deep. The bed will settle less if the manure is well firmed before the soil is placed in the frames. When the pit has been filled to the level of the ground, with well-tramped layers of manure, the sash should be placed on until the manure has thoroughly heated. The soil should then be placed in the pit to a depth of six inches, if crops are to be grown to maturity, while four inches of soil will be sufficient for starting early plants. The soil should be a finely pulverized garden loam, which has been well leveled and packed.

Temperature. The temperature rises rapidly for several days, often going above 125° Fahrenheit. After the temperature of the manure has dropped to 85° or 90°, the bed will be ready to plant. To take the temperature in hotbeds, a plunging thermometer should be used.

Ventilation. Ventilation is absolutely essential to supply the plants with fresh air, to reduce the humidity, and to control the temperature within the bed. A very good indication of the need of ventilation is the amount of moisture which collects on the inside of the glass. A little air should be given the beds each day, gradually increasing the amount until the sash can be left off during the day. A week or ten days before the plants are set in the field the sash should be removed day and night so that the plants are thoroughly hardened.

Cultivation. If seeds and plants are in drills or rows, it is desirable to cultivate between rows and plants. Cultivation keeps the weeds down, makes a surface mulch, and lessens the amount of disease that may occur in the beds.

For want of a nail the shoe was lost,
For want of a shoe the horse was lost,
For want of a horse the rider was lost;
Being overtaken and slain by the enemy.
—BENJ. FRANKLIN

CHAPTER III

Fertility

In the spring when seeds are sprouting,
  Stir the land.
In the summer, nothing doubting,
  Stir the land.
Stirring helps each little seed,
Stirring kills each little weed,
Stirring—let this be your creed:
  Stir the land.

GOOD growing soil consists not only of the tiny crumbs of soil but of minute air spaces between them. The soil crumbs are made up of finely ground rock and decomposing vegetable matter, or humus. The water which the roots absorb is held in the spongelike humus and in a thin film surrounding the oil particles and attached to them largely by capillary attraction.

How plants grow. The miracle by which plants grow is illustrated in the picture. The root hairs absorb the elements which make sap from the soil, where it is formed by means of air, capillary water, etc. In the center of the tree is the stationary part, called "heartwood." The sap rises in the layer about this through the sapwood. It then passes out

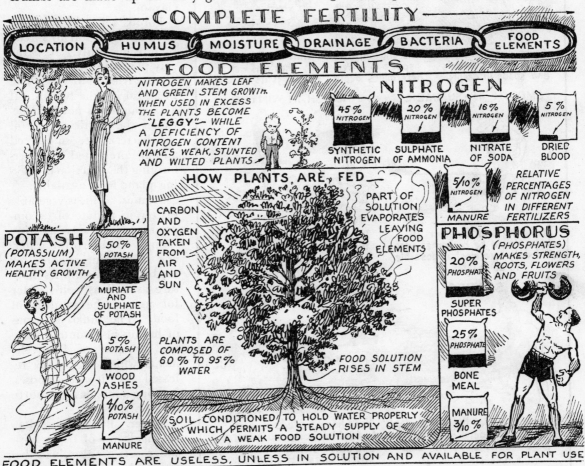

COMPLETE FERTILITY

LOCATION — HUMUS — MOISTURE — DRAINAGE — BACTERIA — FOOD ELEMENTS

FOOD ELEMENTS

NITROGEN MAKES LEAF AND GREEN STEM GROWTH. WHEN USED IN EXCESS THE PLANTS BECOME "LEGGY"—WHILE A DEFICIENCY OF NITROGEN CONTENT MAKES WEAK, STUNTED AND WILTED PLANTS.

NITROGEN

45% NITROGEN — SYNTHETIC NITROGEN
20% NITROGEN — SULPHATE OF AMMONIA
16% NITROGEN — NITRATE OF SODA
5% NITROGEN — DRIED BLOOD
5/10% NITROGEN — MANURE

RELATIVE PERCENTAGES OF NITROGEN IN DIFFERENT FERTILIZERS

HOW PLANTS ARE FED

CARBON AND OXYGEN TAKEN FROM AIR AND SUN

PART OF SOLUTION EVAPORATES LEAVING FOOD ELEMENTS

PLANTS ARE COMPOSED OF 60% TO 95% WATER

FOOD SOLUTION RISES IN STEM

POTASH (POTASSIUM) MAKES ACTIVE HEALTHY GROWTH

50% POTASH — MURIATE AND SULPHATE OF POTASH
5% POTASH — WOOD ASHES
4/10% POTASH — MANURE

PHOSPHORUS (PHOSPHATES) MAKES STRENGTH, ROOTS, FLOWERS AND FRUITS

20% PHOSPHATE — SUPER PHOSPHATES
25% PHOSPHATE — BONE MEAL
MANURE 3/10%

SOIL CONDITIONED TO HOLD WATER PROPERLY WHICH PERMITS A STEADY SUPPLY OF A WEAK FOOD SOLUTION

FOOD ELEMENTS ARE USELESS, UNLESS IN SOLUTION AND AVAILABLE FOR PLANT USE along the branches and through the leaf stem to the leaves, where by the action of the sun and light, carbonic acid gas is absorbed from the under side of the leaf, and oxygen and water are expelled from the upper side. The solution, changed in the laboratory of the leaves, flows back for storage and assimilation through the outside of or growing layer of the bark. Some of it goes down into the roots to feed them.

When it is considered that about one hundred pounds of water must be used by the plant to form one pound of solid plant material, it is easy to see the necessity for large quantities of usable water. Also we see that most of our garden favorites will suffer or die from an overabundance of water.

Fertilization. We cannot always control location and weather but we can change soil. Almost no soil is so poor that we cannot make it grow plants which are suited to our climate and environment. We talk of fertilizers and buy this kind and that when the thing our soil really needs is proper structure. Actually a very small amount of chemical plant food is necessary. Air and water in the soil are far more important. Bacteria cannot live without them, and most plants cannot grow without bacteria.

Manure. This has long been a favorite application for plants. It is usually regarded as a fertilizer but in reality its chief value lies in the fact that it conditions soil by supplying humus. Manures usually hold about one half of one per cent nitrogen and a much smaller amount of other plant foods. Yet cow manure binds sandy soil together, and horse manure is valuable because it separates clay soil.

Porous soil. Most plants need an open soil to spread their roots easily. Also the tiny plants in the soil which are the friendly bacteria live in and upon the humus. If a gaseous air is not held between the particles of soil the bacteria are smothered and are prevented from performing the function of making plant food available.

Humus. This is vegetable matter in a state of decomposition. It acts as tiny sponges to absorb the water, and in forming a home for the bacteria, it supplies moisture as well as holds water for use in the solution of food. The different forms of humus also contain varying amounts of food elements which are slowly released as it decomposes, forming a long-lasting source of supply.

Water. Plants themselves are made up of 60 to 90% water. It is also held between the crumbs of parti-

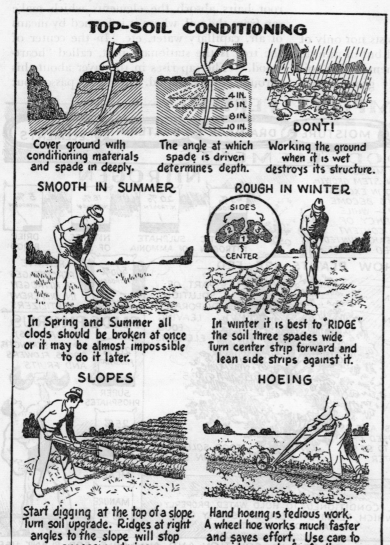

TOP-SOIL CONDITIONING

Cover ground with conditioning materials and spade in deeply.

The angle at which spade is driven determines depth. 4 IN. 6 IN. 8 IN. 10 IN.

DON'T! Working the ground when it is wet destroys its structure.

SMOOTH IN SUMMER

In Spring and Summer all clods should be broken at once or it may be almost impossible to do it later.

ROUGH IN WINTER

SIDES 2 3 1 CENTER

In winter it is best to "RIDGE" the soil three spades wide Turn center strip forward and lean side strips against it.

SLOPES

Start digging at the top of a slope. Turn soil upgrade. Ridges at right angles to the slope will stop excessive drainage.

HOEING

Hand hoeing is tedious work. A wheel hoe works much faster and saves effort. Use care to avoid spread of infection.

cles of earth, but it should remain only to replenish the supply held in the humus and in capillary form, clinging to or surrounding the soil particles. If it completely fills the spaces for any length of time it becomes stagnant and develops unfriendly bacteria or fungus diseases, often ruining structure. Good gardeners avoid this.

Growing soil. All growing soil is made of small particles of rock and decaying vegetable matter (humus). There are two extremes of density in soils. Since sand is coarsely ground rock, water and air go through too rapidly. Clay is so finely ground and dense that it excludes all air, and water runs off. In swamps or bogs too much water is held, excluding air, which makes it unfertile to all but a certain type of plant.

A good formula for general purpose garden loam is 20% sand, 40% clay, and 40% humus. Many plants prefer other mixtures and many successful gardens are grown with less than this requirement but, in striving for the best, this formula gives something at which to aim. There is seldom any soil used for gardening which is pure clay or pure sand. All soils contain some humus and are mixed. We can only approach the application of corrective materials in a general way. We cannot physically lift the soil to measure it and see that it contains the proper proportions, but must use our own judgment as to how heavy or sticky the clay or how open the sand.

To supply the 20% sand to heavy clay soil, spread a full two-inch layer of medium washed sand over the surface and work it in with a spading fork. Hold the fork straight upward when digging so that it penetrates nine or ten inches deep. Merely spading in the sand will not make the clay crumble until it is mixed completely with every fine particle of the soil. Mix it as finely as possible and then allow it to lie for a while so that nature may attack the lumps for you. Rains and the sun will help during the summer, but spading up the soil late in the fall and allowing it to lie rough over the winter will mix it better than hours of labor. Freezing crumbles the lumps and allows the sand to penetrate. Strange to say that, although we add sand to clay to make it drain, after the sand becomes thoroughly mixed and the soil becomes fine and crumbly, it will actually hold more usable water because of the additional air spaces created.

Digging. Turning ground or ordinary digging is carried out with a spade or garden fork. Ground is turned one spit deep. (A spit means the depth of soil that can be conveniently moved in one spadeful.) In this operation, any ground conditioner, such as humus or fertilizer, should be first spread over the ground and then worked through the soil. If the ground is to lie through cold weather, the clods should not be broken up but should be left rough. All roots, weeds, and stones should be brought together in a basket and a small wooden scraper should be available for cleaning off the spade. When digging on a slope, begin at the higher end and work downhill.

Ridging. Vacant beds may be ridged for winter freezing by throwing the ground into little hills from six to twelve inches high so that the frost may penetrate more of the ground. Freezing breaks up soil into fine particles, leaving it porous for the growth of the plant.

Double digging. This is a lot more trouble but is well worth while in any garden operation. A garden line is stretched across the garden two feet from the end. A trench one spit deep and two feet wide is then dug and this dirt is wheeled to the opposite end of the digging operation. On the bottom of the open trench may be thrown sand, coal ashes, cinders, or similar rubbish, together with all the leaves, straw, manure, or other conditioning material, and this is spaded into the second spit of ground or subsoil. If this soil is hard clay use plenty of sand or cinders. This makes the soil light so that it may drain well. If the soil is sandy use more humus, leaf mould, peat moss, etc. The garden line is then moved two feet more and the topsoil mixed with suitable conditioning materials as in simple digging, forming a new trench. The process is then repeated until the first soil removed fills the last trench at the end of the garden.

Mulching. Frequent cultivation not only breaks up the particles of soil so that water is held in the spaces between the soil particles but keeps it from drying out by forming a dust blanket or mulch on top of the soil. This soil-loosening also makes it easy for the plant to send out roots, thereby increasing its capacity to feed and grow. Mulching is also done by covering the earth about plants with leaves, straw or manure.

Some fertilizers. *Cow manure:* This is a cold manure rich in the elements which go to make plant food; it is wet, and therefore a first-class manure for light to medium loams.

Horse manure: This is a hot, dry manure which warms up the land and is excellent for heavy, cold, clayey soils. There is, as a rule, a fairly large percentage of litter in it which

Green manure: No scientific gardener will allow his land to stand vacant long. It is immediately sown down with seed of a quick-growing and leafy plant; this is then allowed to grow and in due course is dug in when partly grown. Italian ryegrass, mustard, vetch, rye, soybeans, rape, and turnip make excellent green manure.

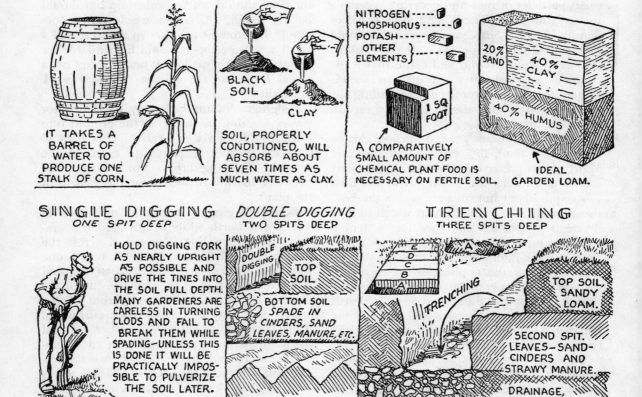

IT TAKES A BARREL OF WATER TO PRODUCE ONE STALK OF CORN.

SOIL, PROPERLY CONDITIONED, WILL ABSORB ABOUT SEVEN TIMES AS MUCH WATER AS CLAY.

BLACK SOIL — CLAY

NITROGEN — PHOSPHORUS — POTASH — OTHER ELEMENTS — 1 SQ. FOOT

A COMPARATIVELY SMALL AMOUNT OF CHEMICAL PLANT FOOD IS NECESSARY ON FERTILE SOIL.

20% SAND — 40% CLAY — 40% HUMUS — IDEAL GARDEN LOAM.

SINGLE DIGGING ONE SPIT DEEP

HOLD DIGGING FORK AS NEARLY UPRIGHT AS POSSIBLE AND DRIVE THE TINES INTO THE SOIL FULL DEPTH. MANY GARDENERS ARE CARELESS IN TURNING CLODS AND FAIL TO BREAK THEM WHILE SPADING—UNLESS THIS IS DONE IT WILL BE PRACTICALLY IMPOSSIBLE TO PULVERIZE THE SOIL LATER.

LEAVE CLODS UNBROKEN & ROUGH ONLY WHEN EXPOSED TO FREEZING

DOUBLE DIGGING TWO SPITS DEEP

DOUBLE DIGGING — TOP SOIL — BOTTOM SOIL SPADE IN CINDERS, SAND LEAVES, MANURE, ETC.

SOIL RIDGING IS USED IN WINTER TO EXPOSE A LARGER SURFACE FOR FREEZING

TRENCHING THREE SPITS DEEP

TRENCHING — TOP SOIL, SANDY LOAM. SECOND SPIT. LEAVES—SAND—CINDERS AND STRAWY MANURE. DRAINAGE, SPADE IN CINDERS—SAND—ASHES—ETC.

SEE THAT TOP SOIL REMAINS ON TOP AND NOT WASTED BELOW REACH OF PLANT ROOTS

also adds to its warming effects. It is best where straw or peat is used for bedding. Such material is good for liquid manure or surface mulching. Even when it is a year old, care must be used with horse manure when working it in around plants. It may burn the root ends if brought in contact with them.

Poultry and pigeon manure: This, when free of litter, is more like a bulky guano than manure in the ordinary sense of the term; it should be stored under cover and kept dry. If it is to be in storage for any length of time, it will benefit considerably if each day's manure is very lightly dusted with lime.

Bone dust and bone meal: These are excellent fertilizers for general use, and have more lasting effect than many; the finer they are ground, the more quickly they act. They contain much phosphate and some nitrogen. Raw bone acts more slowly than steamed bone; therefore we use coarse raw bone for starting trees, shrubbery, peonies, and other plants which are to remain in one place a long time.

Nitrate of soda: Rich in nitrogen, this fertilizer is good where alkalinity is desired. It is a powerful material and will kill many plants if used in any quantity. Dissolve a tablespoonful in a little hot water and dilute to two gallons.

Sulphate of ammonia: This is the most powerful of all nitrogenous manures. It is slightly acid. It is indispensable when fast and good growth is desired. It acts slowly; it may be said that it does not act at all until it has lain on the ground for a short time. It is

is therefore used on such root plants as dahlias, peonies, and gladiola to stimulate growth. It is always well to add an equal amount of the more slowly available bone meal for later fertility.

Wood ashes: Wood ashes are the ashes left after vegetable matter of any kind is burnt. They contain charcoal, a soil sweetener, and

ONE APPLICATION OF CHEMICAL FERTILIZER IS GOOD FOR ABOUT ONE MONTH—BEING READILY SOLUBLE THE FOOD WASHES BELOW REACH OF PLANT ROOTS.

EFFECTIVE AREA FOR PLANT FOOD.

BEST RESULTS FROM BONEMEAL COME 3 MONTHS AFTER APPLYING. IT IS SLOW ACTING AND VERY LITTLE IS WASTED. COTTONSEED, BLOOD, TANKAGE, ETC., ARE QUICKER ACTING BUT LAST LONGER THAN CHEMICALS.

DON'T ADD CHEMICAL FERTILIZER TO SOIL UNTIL ANNUALS SHOW THREE STURDY LEAVES. IT MAY DO MORE HARM THAN GOOD FEED SEVERAL TIMES A SEASON.

SEVERAL TIMES EACH SEASON. WORK IN ½ OZ. (1 TABLESPOONFULL) OF CHEMICAL FERTILIZER AROUND PERENIALS KEEP FERTILIZER OFF OF LEAVES AND ROOTS.

BELOW REACH OF PLANT ROOTS ALL FERTILIZEING MATERIAL IS WASTED—

FLOWER BOXES AND ALL SMALL GARDEN PLANTS. USE 1 SMALL PLANT FOOD TABLET TO EACH PLANT—3 TIMES A SEASON.

FOR A LAWN TREATMENT USE 2 OZ (ABOUT 3 HEAPING TABLESPOONS) OF CHEMICAL FERTILIZER TO A 2 GALLON SPRINKLING CAN OF WATER. THEN WET THOROUGHLY BY WASHING INTO GROUND WITH HOSE—REPEAT MONTHLY.

CULTIVATION IS ONE OF THE BEST FERTILIZERS. IT ENABLES THE SOIL TO HOLD FERTILITY AND MAKES IT ACCESSIBLE TO THE PLANT.

1 LB. TO EVERY 15 FT. 3 OZ TO 2 SQ. FT.

FERTILIZE HEDGES AND SHRUBBERY ONCE A YEAR—3 OZ. (4½ TABLESPOONS) TO EVERY 2 SQ. FT OF SHRUBBERY AND 1 LB. TO EVERY 15 FT. OF HEDGE. APPLY TO TOP SOIL. WORK IN LIGHTLY

ALLOW 3 LBS. OF CHEMICAL FERTILIZER FOR EACH INCH OF THICKNESS OF TRUNK 4 FT. ABOVE GROUND

MAKE HOLES 18" APART, 18" DEEP BY 2" WIDE. FILL HALF FULL OF CHEMICAL FERTILIZER

4 FT.

WIDTH OF CIRCLE SAME AS FULL SPREAD OF TREE.

PEAT MOSS, LEAF MOLD, OR HUMUS PACKING.

not apt to be washed away by rain, as the nitrates are. Beware of letting this manure, which is caustic, come into contact with vegetation.

Sulphate of potash and muriate of potash: This is the form of potash most commonly in use. It is obtained as a white powder and should be applied to the ground a week or two before the growing season or even as a top-dressing to growing crops.

Superphosphate: This material, sometimes called acid phosphate, is more quickly available than the phosphorus in bone meal and

the fine dust has a percentage of potash in a most useful form. Use wood ashes at cropping time or later, as a top-dressing or in plantings.

Using fertilizer. In the use of any fertilizer we must know what we are doing. If we apply nitrogenous material in proper quantities to a bed of lettuce, it will give fine results, for nitrogen makes leaves. If, however, we apply it to beets or root crops, they will all "go to tops" and give the opposite of the desired results. Roots are formed from phosphate and potash.

Over-stimulation is weakening to any plant. Young plants especially must be fertilized with care only after they have attained healthy growth by watering and cultivation.

How then are we to combine all the elements necessary to successful plant growth? First, by the proper selection of location. Second, by the addition of enough vegetable matter or humus. Third, by the addition of any necessary chemicals. Having added the water-holding, soil-conditioning humus, the chemical elements are held in solution for a longer time. Also the humus itself, having a quantity of slowly available chemical elements, helps to provide a source of balance ration for the life of the plant.

Use chemical fertilizers sparingly. Far more material is wasted than can be taken up by the plant. It is readily dissolved in water and is therefore soon washed into the lower soil where plant roots cannot absorb it.

Vitamin B₁. At the present time there is extensive publicity being given to vitamin B₁. It is largely used in the transplanting of plants because the roots grow so quickly that it is easy for the plant to recover. It works well in California and in localities where soil contains little humus. In several states the Nurserymen's Association has stated that experiment showed no good results; while from others have come almost unpredictable results from the use of this vitamin.

Chemical elements. The chemical elements most used and most liable to rapid exhaustion are nitrogen, phosphoric acid (phosphorus), and potash (potassium). There are, of course, other chemical elements but they are used in such small quantities that they are exhausted from the soil only in exceptional cases. These elements are used only by the plant in solution.

Nitrogen makes leaf and stem, promotes quick growth, weight, and bulk, and gives good color to foliage.

Phosphate promotes fruits and flowers, makes strong roots, and stimulates crop maturity.

Potash adds to general health of plant and of flowers, strengthens stems or stalks, and increases size and flavor of fruits.

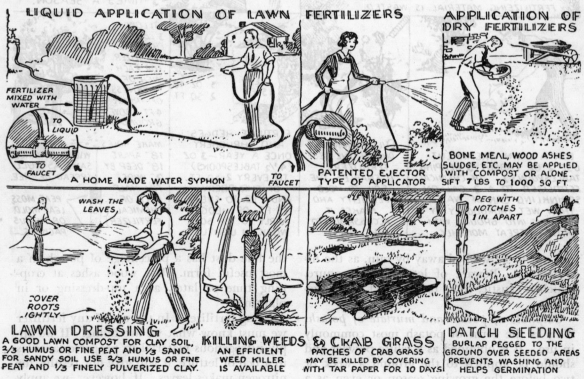

LIQUID APPLICATION OF LAWN FERTILIZERS

FERTILIZER MIXED WITH WATER

TO LIQUID

TO FAUCET

A HOME MADE WATER SYPHON

TO FAUCET

APPLICATION OF DRY FERTILIZERS

PATENTED EJECTOR TYPE OF APPLICATOR

BONE MEAL, WOOD ASHES SLUDGE, ETC. MAY BE APPLIED WITH COMPOST OR ALONE. SIFT 7 LBS TO 1000 SQ FT

WASH THE LEAVES

COVER ROOTS LIGHTLY

LAWN DRESSING
A GOOD LAWN COMPOST FOR CLAY SOIL, 2/3 HUMUS OR FINE PEAT AND 1/3 SAND. FOR SANDY SOIL USE 2/3 HUMUS OR FINE PEAT AND 1/3 FINELY PULVERIZED CLAY.

KILLING WEEDS & CRAB GRASS
AN EFFICIENT WEED KILLER IS AVAILABLE
PATCHES OF CRAB GRASS MAY BE KILLED BY COVERING WITH TAR PAPER FOR 10 DAYS

PEG WITH NOTCHES 1 IN APART

PATCH SEEDING
BURLAP PEGGED TO THE GROUND OVER SEEDED AREAS PREVENTS WASHING AND HELPS GERMINATION

Fertilizers and lawn dressings are especially needed in April. They thicken the grass and exclude weeds as well as prepare for summer. Chemical fertilizers are easily measured and evenly applied in liquid form. Any dry applications to the lawn should be washed off the grass blades to avoid burning and injury to mower blades. Patches in the lawn may be seeded late in the season by covering with cheesecloth or burlap to preserve the necessary moisture. The notched peg permits a gradual exposure to air and sun after germination.

CHAPTER IV

Lawns

*A child said, "What is the grass?" fetching it
to me with full hands;*
*How could I answer that child? I do not know
what it is any more than he.*

*   *   *

I guess it is the handkerchief of the Lord;
*A scented gift and rememberancer, designedly
dropped,*
*Bearing the owner's name somewhere in the
corners, that we may see and remark and say,
Whose?*

—WALT WHITMAN

Grading and drainage. As the first requisite of a lawn is drainage, the ground must have sufficient slope to carry off the surface water. If a slope cannot be obtained or the soil is water-bearing, it must be drained with agricultural tile.

Steep slopes. Many a lawn is impossible because of its grading. Grass is difficult to maintain satisfactorily on steep terraces and grades facing the sun, because water drains from them easily. Slopes should be as gentle as possible and should always be covered with soil well supplied with water-holding material.

We show here the methods of grading for best results. If regrading on a large scale is impractical the slope should be hollowed out to be slightly concave, which makes for slower drainage. Most terraces are rounded upward (convex) which allows them to wash more easily. Also the use of fescue grasses mixed with a small amount of red top will help because they are able to stand dry conditions better than the blue grass. Proper watering is also indicated.

Time. For over one hundred years, experts have been advising fall sowing, but the fact remains that the greater sale of grass seed is in the spring, and the late spring at that.

Every hour of intelligent effort expended during September is worth several hours in the spring.

Weeds treated in the fall must go through the hardship of winter in a weakened condition with little chance for survival. Grass, on the other hand, has the benefit of the fall rains and mild weather (cool, damp nights and warm days) to germinate and mature before winter.

Late August or early September is the ideal time but even a planting in October is better than waiting until spring.

A healthy stand of grass will combat weeds successfully. Once the seed is germinated and established in the fall, the grass uses the warmer days of winter to grow. The more severe weather seems to harden and develop a sturdy root system, ready in the spring to spread into a good thick turf and to combat the weeds.

The most important fact to be remembered in grass-seed germination is that the seeding must be kept wet for three or four weeks. Seed requires from ten to fourteen days to germinate and once allowed to dry the process stops. The difficulty of holding moisture in the late spring or summer precludes any great success at these times.

The foundation. Grass does not grow well either in hard-packed clay incapable of allowing the penetration of air or water, or in thin, sandy soil so porous that no water will remain in it.

Most lawns receive too much water in the spring and fall, which causes them to pack. Unless the drainage is good the grass is killed by the standing water, no matter how much other care has been bestowed on it.

Examine your soil by digging down through it. If it has two to three inches of good friable loam on top and four to six inches of good drainage soil below, you may make it into a fine lawn.

Remove all weeds. Level all bare spots and seed them and the rest of the lawn, using a good fall mixture. Stir the mixture often to keep the smaller seed from going to the bottom, and sow it on a still, dry day.

Roll the lawn smooth and fertilize it, using material (13 cubic feet) will cover from 200 to 500 square feet of lawn.

Making a new lawn. Many lawns started on soil from cellar excavations have little chance to be anything but a nuisance to their owners. If the grass is patchy and the soil is

CONDITIONING THE SOIL
REDUCE TOP LAYER TO FINE TILTH WITH HUMUS, LEAF-MOULD, FINE PEAT-MOSS, ETC.— BREAK UP BOTTOM LAYER WITH SAND, IF NECESSARY, AND ADD MANURE, LEAVES, HUMUS, ETC.— *MUST BE WELL DRAINED.*

DIVIDE LAWN INTO AREAS OF 250 SQ. FT. AND APPLY 1 LB. OF SEED EACH

SOW ½ LB. OF SEED LENGTHWAYS AND ½ LB. CROSSWAYS GOING OVER THE AREA TWICE

ROLL DRY GROUND JUST BEFORE SEEDING. *ROLL WITH A HEAVY ROLLER.*

A BUSHEL OF BLUE GRASS SEED MAY WEIGH FROM 10 LBS. TO 25 LBS. PER BUSHEL— *DON'T BUY CHAFF* — ONLY GOOD SEED, PROPERLY PLANTED, WILL MAKE A GOOD LAWN.

RAKE SEED LIGHTLY INTO GROUND AND ROLL WITH A LIGHT ROLLER TO COMPACT INTO THE SOIL.

WATER WELL AND OFTEN— SEED MUST BE KEPT WET FOR FOUR WEEKS TO MATURE—

chemical lawn food—five pounds for each 1000 square feet. Wash it well into the grass roots to avoid burning. Apply it dissolved in water, using a sprinkling can if you wish.

A still better treatment is to apply a mulch of one-half inch compost, made of one part sand to two parts domestic peat humus, before applying the fertilizer. This will wash under the grass roots during the heaving and thawing of winter and provide soil condition for the following season. It will also help in holding the fertilizer for a longer period and repeated over a period of years will work wonders in building up a good turf. Finely ground peat moss may be used if domestic peat is not available. A full-sized bale of this

hard packed and bare of water-holding humus, it is best to do it over.

The procedure is not intricate when once we understand the reasons for it. First, stake out the area and, beginning at one edge, use a spade to remove a strip of topsoil four feet wide and four inches deep, piling it on lod sacks or carpets outside the staked area. This exposes the bottom ground or subsoil. If this is hard clay, spread over it one inch of sand or two inches of fine ashes or cinders, together with an inch or two of old manure, leaf mould, peat moss, or domestic humus. Any old sods from the topsoil, lawn clippings, or leaves, may also be incorporated if not overdone.

Lime should not be used in the topsoil of the lawns unless a soil analysis shows it will relieve an excess of acidity. Lime encourages weeds in ordinary growing soil and is generally not beneficial. However, it is of great use in breaking up hard-packed clay; if your subsoil is composed of this, use it generously.

Work these materials into the bottom soil, breaking it up finely. This is more easily done with a spading fork. It is essential that this layer not only drains well and quickly but that some moisture is retained at all times.

If the subsoil is sandy or loose, the sand and cinders will not be needed, but a larger quantity of water-holding material (old manure, peat moss, leaf mould, or humus), will be required to prevent drying out due to the easier drainage.

The bottom soil of the first strip is now firmed back into place with a tamper and the topsoil of the second strip is removed. Instead of piling it upon the sacks, remove all roots and lumps by sifting it through a coarse wire screen and deposit it upon the packed bottom soil of the first strip. The subsoil of the second strip is then conditioned as stated before and the process repeated over the entire area. The topsoil piled upon the sacks is used to cover the last strip.

The topsoil over the entire area should be mixed to a fine condition. All grass roots must be removed and the entire top area made into good garden loam by the addition of rotted vegetable matter, commercial humus, leaf mould, fine peat, etc. Good garden loam is made up of 40% clay, 40% vegetable matter, and 20% sand. If the soil is heavy, sand should be added; if it is sandy, more humus.

Cottonseed meal, sewage sludge, tankage, and bone meal may be thoroughly worked into this soil in the proportion of 25 pounds to 1000 square feet. In this case, water well and do not seed for several days. If chemical plant food is used, it is best applied in weak solution after the grass is sprouted.

After the soil is prepared, rake it smooth and roll it firm with a heavy roller while it is still dry. Roll it twice at right angles. Now sow the seed, using one pound to an area of 250 square feet, sowing one-half lengthways and one-half across, and going over the ground twice. Rake in the seed lightly or—better still—cover it with sifted soil; then roll the soil with a light roller to firm the seed in the soil and keep it wet.

The covering of the thoroughly wet seed bed with single burlap or muslin will help keep it wet until the seed has germinated, when the cloth can be raised ten inches high, by stakes, for a day or two to allow the young grass to harden before full exposure. All watering may be done during germination, through the cloth.

The young grass should be allowed to grow six inches high before cutting, which should be done with a grass scythe or a sickle.

Seed. Use the best of seed and see that it is guaranteed to be free of weeds. Heavy grass seed is usually free from chaff and is the most economical in the long run while light cheap seed gives a poor rate of germination.

In the northern section of the United States the following grasses are recommended:

Kentucky blue grass. While Kentucky blue grass is considered the best lawn grass, it has the disadvantages of needing a resting period in midsummer and soiling light clothing and shoes.

It has the advantage of forming a thick turf which will grow in either alkaline or slightly acid soil. It starts slowly but once established puts up a good fight against weeds.

Red top. Second in importance is red top. It makes good with Kentucky blue because they supply each other's deficiencies. Red top is a good beginner, will grow most anywhere, and has its resting period in the fall after the blue grass has recovered. It does not stain and is used for walks and play spots.

Fescue. Chewings fescue is the only fine-textured grass which has been successful in shade. Red fescue and various leaved fescue are sometimes used with lawn mixtures of blue grass and red top. They mature late in the season and are drought-resisting, making a good summer and fall lawn. They grow well in acid soil which is excellent in combating weeds, and will survive some shade as well as dry conditions.

Mixtures. If you must buy ready-mixed seed, get it from a reliable dealer. Four parts Kentucky blue grass to one part red top is a good base mixture. To this you may add the other grasses suited for your conditions.

If you are starting a new lawn in spring, add one part of Italian rye grass and a small amount of timothy. These are annuals which will help start the first year's crop.

Perennial rye grass. This is tough, quick-growing grass which is added to starting mix·

tures. It helps keep out weeds until the lawn is established. It is tough and can stand much traffic; for this reason is used on playfields and exhibition grounds. It is hard to cut, but will yield to the other grasses in a few years.

Shade mixtures. For shade, add to the base mixture some chewings fescue which is fine textured, *poa trivialis* (rough-stalked meadow grass), or *poa memoralis* (wood meadow grass). The denser the shade, the larger the proportion of shade type.

Many shady seedings fail because of the use of cheap seed. Seedsmen don't sell cheap seed because they like it. They sell it because the customer wants to pay a low price. Good shade seed costs money; it is hard to raise and harvest. Don't trust to mixtures—make your own.

White clover. Where a lawn is to be left to shift for itself, white clover may have some uses, but in a well-kept lawn it has many drawbacks and few advantages. It leaves a bare spot to carry through the winter and its texture and large white flowers spoil the velvet appearance of any lawn. It thrives only in alkaline soil and so do weeds. A luxuriant crop of clover usually means plenty of lawn pests. Its only advantage is that it may, in conjunction with blue grass, survive sandy alkaline conditions where red top burns out.

Bent grass. This is a very particular plant. It is very susceptible to drought and pests. It is successful only on the northern Pacific coast, in New York State, and in New England. Unless you live in these areas or are willing to give it a large amount of intelligent care, including almost daily watering, don't attempt the cultivation of bent grass. If you are intrigued by its velvety appearance, ask the manager of a golf course concerning the cost of construction and care of bent-grass putting greens.

Water. To do a lawn any good, water should penetrate four inches. Light sprinklings by hand do harm, not good. They are about the worst treatment you can give your lawn. The idea that watering should not be done in sunlight is wrong; if enough water is applied, it can be done at any time.

Data compiled from golf-course irrigation shows that grass on ordinary clay soil requires at least one inch of water weekly.

It is best to water only once a week on clay soil but the water should be applied so that it is quickly absorbed into the soil. Standing water is harmful. We should bear in mind that since sandy soils dry out more quickly and lighter, they require more frequent waterings.

Rolling. A lawn should be rolled just once or—at the most—twice each year, at the time when the frost is coming out of the ground. Rolling is not supposed to smooth out the lawn; this is done by filling and grading. Rolling is done to push the grass roots back into contact with the soil, after the heaving due to frosts. If it is gone over twice, roll at right angles. If you roll when it is wet enough to puddle the ground, you smother the grass roots by ejecting all the air necessary to the growth of beneficial bacteria. Never roll in dry weather.

Maintenance. Cutting ten to fifteen times each year exhausts the soil. Food and moisture are necessary at all times. These may be maintained by the following methods:

Burning. As elsewhere explained, high cutting in warm weather shades the grass roots and helps the cooling of the soil necessary to nitrogenizing. Many people become discouraged by the burning out of grass or browning of it each summer. This is caused by two conditions: lack of moisture, and the resting period of the grasses of which the lawn is made. By a proper combination of grasses, lawn may be kept green all season if proper food and moisture conditions are maintained.

Moisture. Grass and other leaf crops require large quantities of nitrogen. To be of any use to the grass, this must be in the form of liquid nitrates.

Water is held in the soil only by decayed vegetable matter, which should be placed in the soil when the lawn is made. However, it is good practice to apply a yearly dressing of compost. Compost may be made of a mixture of domestic peat humus from sedge grasses. Shredded peat moss may be used if peat humus is not obtainable. Mix with one-third sand, if your soil is clayey, or one-third finely pulverized clay, if it is sandy. Apply the mulch one-half inch thick and, finely pulverized, to wash into the roots. Any bulk left on the grass will smother and kill it. The heaving caused by thawing and freezing in winter tears the grass roots from the soil. The compost then washes into these spaces and, when compacted by rolling in the spring, remains part of the turf. In applying peat mulches, we discourage weed without harming the grass. Most city water contains some lime which applied to the soil by watering encourages weeds. Peat helps to counteract this condition.

You may also mulch with rotted leaf mould

weather and will prevent weeds and crab grass from seeding. Weeds will not grow in a thick, shady stand of grass and crab grass will not germinate even in semishade.

Mow frequently and let the clippings work

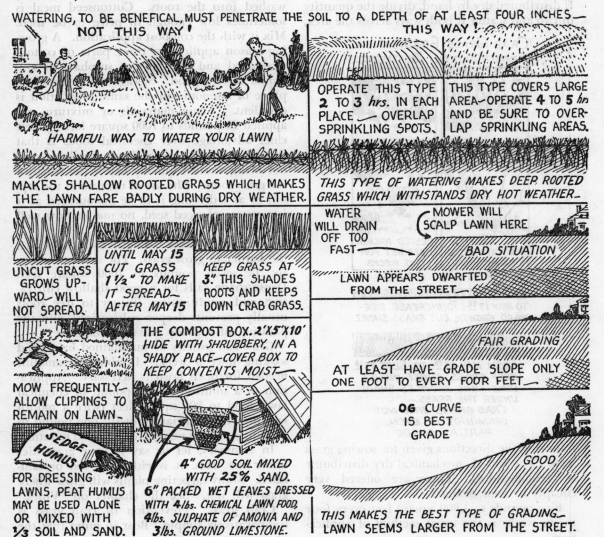

WATERING, TO BE BENEFICAL, MUST PENETRATE THE SOIL TO A DEPTH OF AT LEAST FOUR INCHES —

NOT THIS WAY !

HARMFUL WAY TO WATER YOUR LAWN

MAKES SHALLOW ROOTED GRASS WHICH MAKES THE LAWN FARE BADLY DURING DRY WEATHER.

UNCUT GRASS GROWS UPWARD — WILL NOT SPREAD.

UNTIL MAY 15 CUT GRASS 1½" TO MAKE IT SPREAD — AFTER MAY 15

KEEP GRASS AT 3". THIS SHADES ROOTS AND KEEPS DOWN CRAB GRASS.

MOW FREQUENTLY — ALLOW CLIPPINGS TO REMAIN ON LAWN.

SEDGE HUMUS

FOR DRESSING LAWNS, PEAT HUMUS MAY BE USED ALONE OR MIXED WITH ⅓ SOIL AND SAND.

THE COMPOST BOX. 2'X5'X10' HIDE WITH SHRUBBERY, IN A SHADY PLACE — COVER BOX TO KEEP CONTENTS MOIST —

4" GOOD SOIL MIXED WITH 25% SAND.
6" PACKED WET LEAVES DRESSED WITH 4 lbs. CHEMICAL LAWN FOOD, 4 lbs. SULPHATE OF AMONIA AND 3 lbs. GROUND LIMESTONE.

THIS WAY !

OPERATE THIS TYPE 2 TO 3 hrs. IN EACH PLACE — OVERLAP SPRINKLING SPOTS.

THIS TYPE COVERS LARGE AREA — OPERATE 4 TO 5 hrs AND BE SURE TO OVERLAP SPRINKLING AREAS.

THIS TYPE OF WATERING MAKES DEEP ROOTED GRASS WHICH WITHSTANDS DRY HOT WEATHER —

WATER WILL DRAIN OFF TOO FAST —

MOWER WILL SCALP LAWN HERE

BAD SITUATION

LAWN APPEARS DWARFTED FROM THE STREET —

FAIR GRADING

AT LEAST HAVE GRADE SLOPE ONLY ONE FOOT TO EVERY FOUR FEET —

OG CURVE IS BEST GRADE

GOOD

THIS MAKES THE BEST TYPE OF GRADING — LAWN SEEMS LARGER FROM THE STREET.

or home-made compost, filling out any deficiency of supply with the above-mentioned materials.

Mowing. Grass allowed to go to seed does not spread and causes a spotty lawn. The little seed gained by this process is more than offset by the lack of root increase and unsightly appearance. Grass should be cut quite short until the middle of May. Fertilize it well and try to get a complete ground cover. After this is accomplished, keep it cut as long as possible.

This will shade the grass roots in hot

down to the roots. Short grass clippings are the easiest way to return vegetable matter to the soil. Long grass, however, must be removed, as must leaves, and no compost should be added in hot weather. Grass is easily smothered during this period. All grasses should start through the winter about one inch long.

Fertilizers. Chemical fertilizers offered for lawn foods are usually salts which are easily dissolved, and therefore readily available for plant use. They consist mostly of nitrogen, being composed of ten parts nitrogen to four parts each of phosphate and potash (4:10:4). This fertilizer when properly used lasts about four to six weeks. Once begun, its use should be continued. Several methods of application may be used. Even distribution is essential. If distributed dry by hand, divide the quantity in two and scatter it both ways across the area,

CRAB GRASS ERADICATION
SUMMER AND FALL TREATMENT

PULL UPRIGHT WITH RAKE

MOW AS SHORT AS POSSIBLE

DIG OUT WITH STRAIGHT KNIFE

RESEED AREAS. KEEP WET FOR TWO WEEKS

SPRING CARE

TO MAY 15th.: TO INCREASE SIDE-WARD GROWTH, CUT GRASS SHORT.

FROM MAY 15th. TO SEPT. 15th KEEP GRASS THREE INCHES LONG—THIS PROVIDES SHADE UNDER THE GRASS— CRAB GRASS WILL NOT GERMINATE IN, EVEN, PARTIAL SHADE

following the directions given for sowing grass seed. The use of mechanical dry distributor is recommended. These are offered very cheaply by your dealers.

Five pounds to 1,000 square feet every four to six weeks is the usual method of application.

The same applies to sulphate of ammonia, which is also recommended. It is high in nitrogen, has a slight acid reaction, and discourages weeds when used on alkaline or neutral soils.

Organic fertilizers, such as bone meal, sewage sludge, blood, tankage, and the like, while usually more expensive, work excellently in compost. They are not so quickly exhausted as the chemical foods. Sludge and bone meal are also valuable because of their ground-conditioning effect.

Bone meal applied in the fall is recom-

mended for established lawns. A good fall (September) application is three parts bone meal, three parts wood ashes, and one part sulphate of ammonia. This applies seven pounds to 1000 square feet. It should be washed into the roots. Cottonseed meal is sometimes low enough in price to be used. Mix it with the compost application. A growing season application three parts of cottonseed meal and one part of sulphate of ammonia is very good. Sewage sludge and sulphate of ammonia in the same proportion is excellent. These materials or mixtures are applied 25 pounds to 1000 square feet. Their chief advantage over chemical foods is that they last longer, being slowly available and not being washed quickly below the reach of the grass roots. The use of manure in the topsoil or as a dressing is to be discouraged as it is a source of weed seed, no matter how well rotted.

Grass under trees. The denser the shade, the harder to grow grass. For shade sow five, six, or seven pounds to 1000 square feet. Dense shade calls for a good shallow cultivation and conditioning (injury to tree roots usually prevents deeper cultivation) and the planting of a shady grass-seed mixture.

Grass can usually be maintained by a good soaking once a week. Double the amount needed for open lawn is necessary. Application of a solution of one pound of chemical lawn food to 200 square feet twice a month will insure a luxuriant growth; one pound to 100 square feet is necessary if applied monthly.

In summary, let us say if your grass dies under the trees, it is either starved or famished. Many carpeting plants will grow where grass will not. See the chapter on "Vines."

Crab grass. Prevention of crab grass is comparatively simple. Bear in mind that the plant is an annual. It originates from seed only during June. Its roots are killed by frost each fall and are of no further danger. It will not grow in even partial shade and is seldom if ever seen in the shadow of a tree or building.

After it has sprouted it is a rampant grower. Five shoots spread out like fingers of a hand, rooting at every joint to repeat the process of sending out five more shoots. In this way it is able to cover large areas, smothering the other grasses and leaving bare spots when it is killed by frost.

In the spring, until May 15, the grass should

be cut short to develop a strong root system and to encourage it to spread sideways into a thick turf. From May 15 until September 15 it should be kept cut three inches high. No crab grass will grow in this shade and in addition, this shading will keep the grass from burning during hot weather. It may be necessary to make alterations to your mower to cut three inches high, but it is a sure way of getting rid of this lawn pest.

Another effective way of killing it is by shading it with tar paper pegged down tightly by long, heavy-wire staples. Ten days usually finishes it in hot weather. The blue grass will be browned and perhaps killed but will start again from the roots. In either case (weeding or covering) start on the plants early in July, while they are small and easy to kill and you will not have the lawn discolored by large bare spots.

Weed Control. Of course, the best way to have a weedless lawn is to make the soil conditions so attractive to grass, and to establish such a fine thick stand of turf that weeds cannot get a foothold. But sometimes they do, and it may be easier to get rid of them than start over again and build a better lawn. If the invader is crab grass, there does not seem to be yet an easy way to victory; just read the directions on page 28 and make up your mind to fight it out to a finish. But if you have dandelions, plantain, or any of a number of broadleaved weeds to fight, you can rejoice that "something new has been added" to the gardener's arsenal, namely the selective weed-killing material 2,4-D. That name is a convenient label for one of the hormone, or growth-regulating, substances about which much has been heard of late years. Called by chemists 2,4-dichlorophenoxyacetic acid, it was discovered some years ago; but only recently was it found that, in certain concentrations, it serves not to promote plant growth, but to induce such a rapid consumption or depletion of a plant's food reserves as to bring about its death in from two to four or six weeks. Furthermore, properly used, it affects different kinds of plants in varying degrees, so that, when sprayed on a weedy lawn, it will destroy many if not all of the broad-leaved weeds, but leave the desirable grasses uninjured. Since these facts have been revealed, a number of proprietary materials containing 2,4-D as their active agent have been put on the market under various trade names. Because they vary in composition and are offered in various forms, they require careful handling, and the directions accompanying the package should be carefully read and explicitly followed. As with other recently discovered chemicals useful in horticulture, all the facts about 2,4-D are not yet known, even to scientists, so it is impossible to make com-

KILLING WEEDS—

DANDELIONS: IN LARGE AREAS THEY CAN BE KILLED BY SPRAYING WITH 2.4-D FIRST BRUISE LEAVES WITH BACK OF RAKE—

ALL CREEPING WEEDS: CHICKWEED, GROUND IVY, ETC., CAN BE EASILY ERADICATED WITH A 2.4-D SPRAY.

KILL SCATTERED DANDELIONS WITH 2.4-D APPLICATION.

PLANTIANS AND OTHER WEEDS YIELD READILY TO THE WEED SPUD.

plete and positive statements about it. Gardeners should watch for the latest authoritative announcements. However, on the basis of known facts the following summary and recommendations would seem to be in order:

1—A solution containing as little as $1\frac{1}{3}$ oz. of 2,4-D in 10 gallons of water (1 to 1000 by weight) when used as a spray is deadly to many species of broadleaved plants including: Dandelion, plantain, lawn pennywort, Japanese honeysuckle, false-strawberry, annual morning-glory, daisy, heal-all, chickweed, pokeweed, ragweed, curled dock, burdock, pigweed, wild mustard, wild lettuce, and annual sow thistle. Others, including some perennials and even woody plants such as poison-ivy, are known to be more or less affected and will doubtless in time be found to succumb to solutions of the proper strength.

2—Bent grasses appear susceptible to injury,

and white and other clovers are killed by it. In the concentration advised, it does not affect other grasses, including, unfortunately, crabgrass, quackgrass, Johnson grass, sedges, etc.

3—The solution should be applied as a spray in sufficient quantity to wet the foliage thoroughly; on lawns, 4 to 5 gallons per 1000 sq. ft. are recommended. Treatments should be made in late spring or early fall when the grass is growing vigorously; if a spring treatment is not wholly successful, a second application can be made after two or three months. When a bad infestation is destroyed, it is advisable to topdress and fertilize the lawn and reseed the thin spots so as to develop a thick sod that will resist future weed invasion.

4—While 2,4-D is apparently harmless to human beings and animals, non-toxic to the soil, and not corrosive to spray equipment, it is *not* selective as to broadleaved plants. Hence care must be taken to prevent the spray from reaching vegetable crops, flowering plants, shrubs and other desirable materials. Also, since a very small amount remaining in a sprayer may be sufficient to injure or kill plants when, later, a protective spray is applied with the same equipment, the sprayer should be rinsed several times with water and a soda solution after 2,4-D has been used in it. Better still, a sprayer should be bought and kept solely for this purpose, using other equipment for applying insecticides and fungicides.

Tests made in New York State indicate that 2,4-D sprayed on ragweed in August will prevent the development of pollen. If this is so, and if patches of this pest can be treated without jeopardizing valuable plants in the vicinity, results of great importance to hay-fever sufferers should result.

Other Weed Killers. For some time salt brine, borax, and various acids, especially crude sulphuric, have been used, but always with certain risks and disadvantages. Where caustic herbicides are applied to drives, tennis courts, etc. there is always a chance that they may be carried in solution to the roots of surrounding grass, flowers or shrubs. And a soil made sterile to the growth of weeds, needs a long period of reconditioning before desirable plants can be grown in it. The development of various chlorate preparations which, when dusted or sprayed on the foliage of poison-ivy, Japanese honeysuckle and other undesired growth, are absorbed and carried to all parts of the plants, killing them without af-

fecting the soil, was therefore hailed as a great advance. Then followed the development of another chemical, ammonium sulfamate (now sold as Ammate), with the same properties but the added advantage of not presenting the fire hazard involved in that materials wet with chlorates become inflammable. Both types of materials have a place in weed extermination, if used with care and judgment. However, they are no respecters of desirable plants, since they have none of the selective attributes of the newest munitions in the field.

Pests. *Grubs and earthworms.* Grubs and earthworms may be destroyed by the application of five pounds of arsenate of lead mixed with a bushel of slightly damp sand, and applied to 1000 square feet when the grass is thoroughly dry. It may be necessary to repeat yearly for several years.

Sod webworms. Sod webworms are indicated by small brown patches of grass which gradually become larger. They may be found hidden in their webs among the grass roots. Apply arsenate of lead seven or eight pounds to 1000 square feet either with sand, as above described, or very lightly with a dust gun. Distribute evenly, dust in with a broom, and wash into the soil with a hose, nozzle removed.

Ants. Ants may be killed by squirting carbon bisulphide into the holes with an oil can. Cover the hills with wet newspapers. Another method of killing ants is to soak hills with kerosene or gasoline and set them afire; this method will destroy the grass.

Moles. Moles can be killed with a trap sold for that purpose or by fumes from an automobile exhaust. Fumes may be conveyed to the holes by a garden hose. Allow the motor to run twenty minutes or more and retard the spark if possible. Calcium cyanide is sold to be placed in the holes at five feet intervals. It gives off a strong poisonous gas and must be handled carefully. Close all openings to the runways before fumigating. Poisoning by opening the shells of several peanuts and inserting a crystal of strychnine in each has been recommended, as has shelled corn soaked in arsenic.

Sometimes moles may be drowned by flooding runways with a hose. They usually work in these burrows between 7 and 8 A.M. By watching at that time, armed with a pitchfork, they can be killed as they are seen moving the earth going through runways.

CHAPTER V

Propagating

*Old Mother Nature doesn't fret
When skies are gray and fields are wet;
Old Mother Nature always knows
What's underneath the wintry snows.*
—DOUGLAS MALLOCH

Indoor seeding. By sowing the seeds indoors early in the spring we are able to gain from four to six weeks over those sown outdoors directly in the beds where they are to bloom. Almost any sort of receptacle will do for starting the plants. If you have only a few seeds a large flowerpot or bulb pan is the best and most easily handled receptacle, although any pot or kettle which is pierced with holes for a ready drainage is permissible.

If the pots are new they must be soaked in water for a couple of days before using; boiling them for an hour will serve the same purpose. First cover the holes of the flowerpot with several pieces of broken pot and add an inch or two of coarse gravel or small cinders for drainage. Many people prefer to place over this a shallow covering of peat moss and then add the carefully prepared soil for the planting of the seed.

Soil should consist of good garden loam, clean sharp sand, and peat moss, humus, or leaf mould in equal parts. If you do not have a good garden soil buy a bushel or so for the

purpose from a florist. The soil should be screened through a one-half inch wire riddle and firmed down into the pot with the bottom of another pot until it is about one inch from the top. The pot is now watered thoroughly and the best way to do this is to set it in a pan of water so that the pot is submerged two-thirds its depth.

Wait until the dampness begins to appear on the surface of the soil, then set it aside for an hour or two until the surface has dried somewhat. Water should always be at room temperature. The seed may be planted in rows or broadcast, being careful not to have it too thick. Fine soil is then sifted over the seeds through a piece of fly screen.

The usual rule is to cover with soil about three times the diameter of the seed, but many of the finer seeds may be pressed into the soil and not covered at all except with some paper to keep them from drying out. One of the best means of preventing the seed from drying is to cover the pot with a piece of cloth.

Flats are boxes of almost any size but are handiest when nine inches wide, 12 inches long, and 3 inches deep. They may be made of almost any scrap lumber if the bottom is thoroughly pierced for drainage. A very good and inexpensive way to make them is to use two pieces of 7/8" board for the ends, which

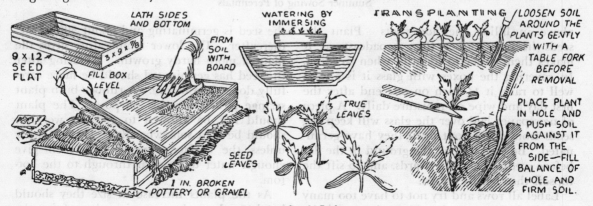

Planting Seeds Indoors

should be 9" x 3". The balance of the flats is composed of lath, spaced ¼" apart. No holes for drainage will be necessary in this case.

The bottom of the flat should be covered with broken flowerpots or fine cinders about ½ to 1 inch thick and proceed as instructed

which will mature for transplanting at the same time. It cuts down general care.

As soon as a fair number of seedlings appear it is necessary to remove the paper as well as the glass, and place the container in the light, but out of the direct rays of the sun. The temperature should be about 70° while

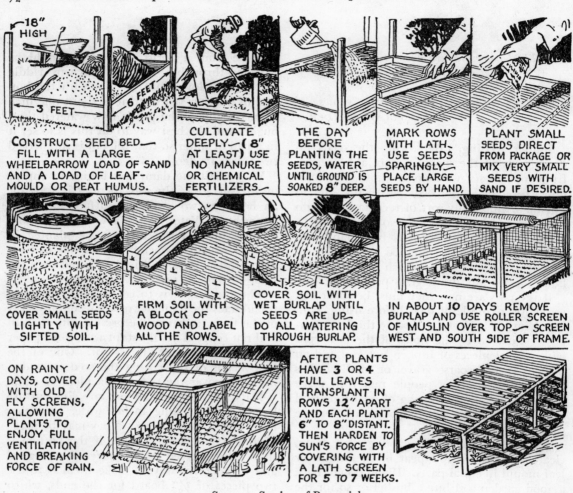

CONSTRUCT SEED BED— FILL WITH A LARGE WHEELBARROW LOAD OF SAND AND A LOAD OF LEAF-MOULD OR PEAT HUMUS.

CULTIVATE DEEPLY—(8" AT LEAST) USE NO MANURE OR CHEMICAL FERTILIZERS—

THE DAY BEFORE PLANTING THE SEEDS, WATER UNTIL GROUND IS SOAKED 8" DEEP.

MARK ROWS WITH LATH— USE SEEDS SPARINGLY— PLACE LARGE SEEDS BY HAND,

PLANT SMALL SEEDS DIRECT FROM PACKAGE OR MIX VERY SMALL SEEDS WITH SAND IF DESIRED.

COVER SMALL SEEDS LIGHTLY WITH SIFTED SOIL.

FIRM SOIL WITH A BLOCK OF WOOD AND LABEL ALL THE ROWS.

COVER SOIL WITH WET BURLAP UNTIL SEEDS ARE UP— DO ALL WATERING THROUGH BURLAP.

IN ABOUT 10 DAYS REMOVE BURLAP AND USE ROLLER SCREEN OF MUSLIN OVER TOP— SCREEN WEST AND SOUTH SIDE OF FRAME.

ON RAINY DAYS, COVER WITH OLD FLY SCREENS, ALLOWING PLANTS TO ENJOY FULL VENTILATION AND BREAKING FORCE OF RAIN.

AFTER PLANTS HAVE 3 OR 4 FULL LEAVES TRANSPLANT IN ROWS 12" APART AND EACH PLANT 6" TO 8" DISTANT. THEN HARDEN TO SUN'S FORCE BY COVERING WITH A LATH SCREEN FOR 5 TO 7 WEEKS.

Summer Sowing of Perennials

above in filling the flowerpots. Plant the seeds in rows rather than broadcast, as it makes them easier to identify when weeding. In covering the boxes with glass it is always well to raise it ¼ inch on one end after the first day and wipe off moisture daily. A piece of newspaper laid over the glass will keep the seeds from drying out until they have germinated. Be sure to soak the ground in the flat before seeding, not afterwards, and to sift the topsoil through fly screen.

Label all rows and try not to have too many varieties in a receptacle. Plant those varieties

the seed is germinating and about 50° to 60° thereafter. The lower temperature gives the plant a more hardy growth. Watering after the seed has germinated should be more carefully done than before. A rubber bulb plant syringe is best for this purpose. The plant should not be allowed to get too wet but should be kept somewhat dry. Do not water unless the surface appears dry, then give enough water to go clear through to the bottom.

As the plants increase in size they should be thinned out by removing them from the soil. Do not break them off. If the remaining plants show signs of sluggishness, put them closer to the window and thin them out some more.

Damping-off is the chief enemy of indoor plant culture. It is a fungus growth caused by too much moisture and lack of ventilation. A light sprinkling of sand or powdered sulphur sometimes helps to keep this in check. Sometimes soil sterilization is used to prevent it. The seedlings should not be exposed to the direct rays of the sun until well advanced, after which they may be hardened gradually, being shaded from the direct noonday rays of the sun.

Contrary to popular belief, transplanting helps the development of the young plant. Transplanting to new pots, pans, or flats indoors will help harden the plant for its outdoor debut. Soil may be prepared much in the manner as for planting seed. Do not fertilize the young plant until it has a good hearty start. Plants may be lifted from the soil with a pointed stick, teaspoon, or kitchen fork, and the ground should be fairly moist in order to enable some soil to be lifted with them.

Never transplant into soil too rich in humus or into pure humus, as this will cause a fungus growth. Sand in the soil induces rapid drainage which is the best preventive of fungus.

Plants should not be transplanted until they have developed their first pair of true leaves. Do not become confused with the seed leaves which some plants put out, and above all, do not mistake them for weeds. Be sure to firm the soil carefully about the roots. Loose planting is dangerous.

After the plants have obtained some growth, cultivate them. They may be hardened by placing the flats in a cold frame before moving outdoors. Do not be afraid to transplant them two or three times before reaching their permanent location. Poppies, candytufts, sweet alyssums, cornflowers, and portulacas (moss roses) are flowers which must not be transplanted, but sown directly where they are to bloom.

Outdoor seeding. Every garden should have a propagating bed in which plants raised indoors are hardened before being set in permanent locations. Annuals may be planted directly here in the spring, following somewhat the instructions given for indoor sowing, but covered with burlap instead of glass to conserve moisture during germination.

Many uses will be found for the propagating bed, as explained later, but not the least of these is raising perennials and biennials by summer sowing. Perennials are raised during the summer for blooming the following season and a number of seasons thereafter. Some, if sown in the spring, will bloom the same year if planted early enough, and for this reason are handled as annuals by good gardeners.

Biennials differ from perennials in that they bloom the second year from seed, but only for a single season.

While perennial seed may be successfully planted any time between June and September, most authorities consider June the best month. This gives them time to establish hardy clumps before winter and they will be ready to bloom the following spring.

The most essential things are shade, moisture, and drainage. Dry seeds will not propagate. Rich soil is not necessary. In fact, an excess of nitrogen may be harmful, as it causes a soft, quick top growth which will not transplant well.

After the plant has appeared above the ground it is necessary to protect it from the sun and from drying out but ventilation is necessary to prevent damping-off. If the following rules are followed success is reasonably sure.

First secure a sunny fence corner. Measure a bed about three feet wide by six feet long or smaller. This will raise a lot of plants and yet be easy to reach to tend them. If the bed is of ordinary lawn soil, dump on it one wheelbarrow load of sand and one of sifted leaf mould, sedge peat humus, or finely granulated, well-weathered peat moss. Do not use coarse peat moss as it comes from the bales. It should sift easily through a $\frac{1}{4}$-inch sieve. If the soil is bad clay these materials must be increased enough to make it friable, yet able to hold moisture. It must break up easily even when wet. Some gardeners make the top three inches of the bed of a compost of equal parts soil, sand, and humus. This insures proper moisture condition. Also it is good policy to raise the bed four to six inches above grade.

Cultivate the soil deeply and be sure it drains well and finishes fine and level. Construct a frame as illustrated providing various degrees of shade for special conditions. Do not think it is complicated; it is not.

The day before planting seeds soak the bed until it penetrates eight inches deep. Allow it to remain uncovered until the topsoil is readily friable and then sow the seed in rows four to six inches apart.

ten days most of the seedlings will appear; then remove the burlap and cover the frame with muslin roll, watering the seedlings gently each day with fine spray.

As soon as the seedlings have three to four leaves, transplant them to a nursery bed of well-drained soil prepared with sand-rotted

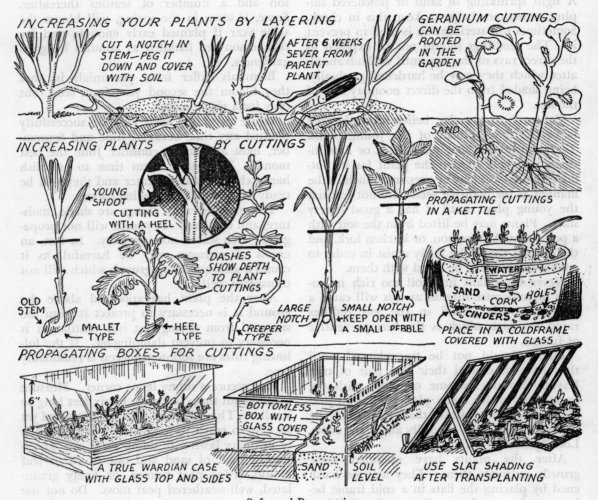

INCREASING YOUR PLANTS BY LAYERING

CUT A NOTCH IN STEM—PEG IT DOWN AND COVER WITH SOIL

AFTER 6 WEEKS SEVER FROM PARENT PLANT

GERANIUM CUTTINGS CAN BE ROOTED IN THE GARDEN

SAND

INCREASING PLANTS BY CUTTINGS

YOUNG SHOOT

CUTTING WITH A HEEL

DASHES SHOW DEPTH TO PLANT CUTTINGS

OLD STEM

MALLET TYPE

HEEL TYPE

CREEPER TYPE

LARGE NOTCH

SMALL NOTCH KEEP OPEN WITH A SMALL PEBBLE

PROPAGATING CUTTINGS IN A KETTLE

WATER

SAND   CORK   HOLES

CINDERS

PLACE IN A COLDFRAME COVERED WITH GLASS

PROPAGATING BOXES FOR CUTTINGS

6"

A TRUE WARDIAN CASE WITH GLASS TOP AND SIDES

BOTTOMLESS BOX WITH GLASS COVER

SAND   SOIL LEVEL

USE SLAT SHADING AFTER TRANSPLANTING

Softwood Propagation

Seeds large enough to be handled may be sown two to three inches apart. Most gardeners sow small seed too thickly and waste it by the necessary thinning which follows. Mix the seed with fine sand if necessary, but make it cover. Sowing in rows enables you to tell seedlings from weeds in the care of the plants.

Sift soil lightly over the seeds. Firm it well with a smooth block. Water lightly and cover with burlap pegged down to the soil. Water this burlap often but lightly. In about

manure or other vegetable matter. Care should be taken to remove plants when soil is damp but not wet. A little soil around the seedling roots will retain the fine feeding roots.

Nursery rows should be about 12 inches apart and plants six to eight inches apart. Fill each hole with water before planting and cover with dry dirt. Plants should be protected from direct, prolonged sun by the slatted screen until they are about six or seven weeks old. Cultivate these transplants often and fertilize lightly until well established.

Do all watering in early morning or late evening during hot weather.

Plants from summer cuttings. While raising plants from seed is the normal, easiest, and most satisfactory way to propagate, it sometimes becomes necessary to propagate by cuttings and root division. Many plants reproduced by seed will not flower true to the color, size, and growth characteristic of the parent plant. This is due to cross pollination or other causes, but cuttings and roots are not so affected and will come true to variety.

If but a few new plants are desired, many of the plants in your garden and rockery can be increased by layering. This is the process of rooting a branch without detaching it from the parent. Many plants propagate themselves by this method.

A branch is notched and this notch held open by a small pebble or by bending the stem. It is then stapled to the ground by bent pieces of heavy wire and well covered with earth. Kept watered, it is severed from the main plant when well rooted. Plants which may be easily layered are dianthus, nepeta, sedum, thyme, veronica, forsythia suspensa, climbing roses, and most other creeping plants.

When making cuttings for propagation cut the shoots from sturdy plants which have finished blooming. Iberis and arabis may be taken with a piece of the old stem (mallet-shaped); other plants, if large enough, may be cut with a heel which is a small oval piece of the covering of the old stem about one-half inch long. This is cut with a straight knife and must not be torn or pulled away from the stem of the new shoot. Roots form very quickly from heel cuttings. Small creeping plants may be cut eight or ten joints long and buried two-thirds. Care must be taken not to get shoots too long as weak leggy plants will result. The best length for softwood cuttings is three to six inches. About half the leaves and all flower buds should be removed, cut carefully without tearing.

Rooting seems best carried on in a slightly acid medium; so first water the sand with a weak solution of vinegar (acetic acid)—one teaspoon of vinegar to each gallon of water.

Now set the plants about two inches apart each way, carefully label, and water. Seal the top of the box with a piece of glass. Shade the box with paper or cloth and keep closed for about ten days, opening it to give light and fine spray sprinklings *only* if the top of the sand shows signs of drying out.

After ten days the glass is raised during the mornings, shade being maintained and the sand being kept moist at all times. If there is any sign of damping-off or fungus, water with a solution of three tablespoons of formalin to one-half gallon of water or with a weak solution of potassium permanganate, using just enough to color the water pink.

When plants show signs of growth, remove the glass but maintain the shade until a good root system is established. Transplant to growing soil composed of two parts of finely sifted garden loam and one part of rotted leaf mould or sedge humus. Be sure to get soil firm around roots. Shade for a day or two and then apply semishade by slatted covering until they can stand full sun.

Water well and keep soil loosened on top. Apply weak chemical fertilizer (one tablespoon to one gallon of water) to the plants after they have three or four new leaves. Do this only in August so that new growth will not be stimulated late in the season.

Hardwood cuttings. Hardwood cuttings are usually taken eight inches long when the plant is dormant, but not during freezing weather. The wood should be one year old, firm, strong, and free of leaves. Each should have two or more eyes or nodes and be plump and thick. Thin branches have little food in them. There should be an eye at the top of each cutting. The soil and care for planting outdoors should be followed substantially as previously described for softwood transplants. All shrubbery should be transplanted several times before placing in permanent location.

CHAPTER VI

Planting and Pruning

He who plants a tree
Plants a hope.

PLANTING

TRANSPLANTING is a violent shock to the plant. Because its food supply is curtailed by the cutting of its roots, we must cut down the demand on the roots by pruning the top growth. These two processes constitute a severe operation and, as in the case of an operation on a person, should usually be performed when the plant is nearest asleep or when the chances of immediate recuperation are most favorable.

General rules. General rules are always dangerous because there are usually many exceptions. Among the perennials, oriental poppies are best moved soon after their blooming (when foliage has withered) in order to avoid loss of bloom the following season, while wind flowers, chrysanthemums, and a few fall bloomers do not do well at all unless allowed to get a start before moving the following spring.

November, just after the first good ground freeze, is considered best for deciduous trees and shrubs, yet silver maple and poplars move better in the spring. Magnolias transplant best just before their blossom-buds begin to form. Snowball, butterfly bush, tamarix, sumac, strawberry shrub, and a few others do not seem to stand the winter's cold when weakened by fall transplanting. Coniferous evergreens transplant best in August or September.

One of the most important things to know about a plant is spacing, that is, how much room it will need to develop when matured. The result of too close a planting is an overcrowded condition which makes for unhealthy plants and the loss of flowers or fruit. Most plants need air all around them as well as through the center. If planted too close, the branches intertwine and, except in the case of hedges of specially selected plants, the result is not a beautiful thing. Many amateurs plant younger stock too closely, expecting to thin it out at some future time. Very few of them have the nerve to do the ruthless thinning when the time comes.

Shrubs usually mature and fill up the gaps in two to three years; trees in eight to ten years; and perennials in two seasons. When we consider how many years they will grow if properly planted we should be willing to wait this length of time for the effect.

There are several other things which we must consider in selecting planting material. We must visualize its appearance when fully grown, and we must figure out whether it will fill the space which we have selected for it, whether it will grow in shade or in sun, and whether it will fit itself to the soil in which we wish to plant it.

Planting seldom should be done in frozen ground. Sometimes big trees are moved when the ground is frozen in order to get a large solid ball to insure protection to the fine roots. In this case a supply of unfrozen ground is provided for filling around the ball in order to get rid of any air pockets.

Transplanting is best done on a dull moist day rather than on a bright one. The drying out of roots is extremely bad for almost any plant. Winds are equally as injurious as sunlight. It is always best to protect the roots by a covering of wet sacking or other cloth.

Foliage is often more important than flower. We may have a plant which has beautiful blooms for a few weeks and is an eyesore for the rest of the season.

In selecting a location remember that there is considerable difference in the shade cast by a building and that cast by a tree or shrub. The tree lets in air and some light.

Mulching. An important part of planting is mulching. Mulching, as previously explained, is the covering of the soil about the plant to prevent alternate freezing and thawing in winter or to conserve moisture in summer.

Mulching is not done to keep the plants warm; it is designed to keep them cold. The

plant and thin the mulch out considerably.

Soil. The character of the soil has much to do with the time of transplanting in the spring. Light soils warm up more quickly than clay soils, and for this reason planting can be undertaken earlier.

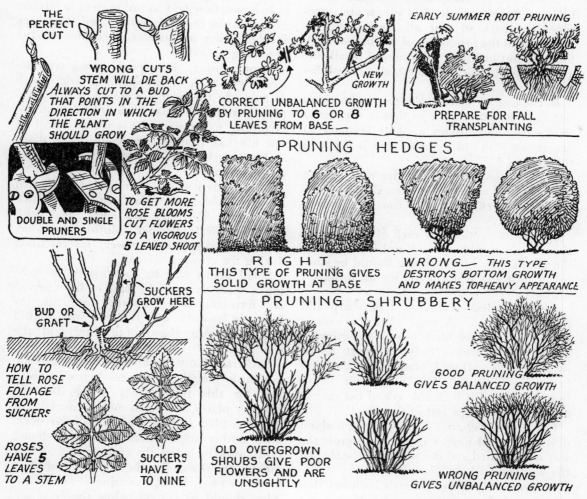

THE PERFECT CUT

WRONG CUTS STEM WILL DIE BACK ALWAYS CUT TO A BUD THAT POINTS IN THE DIRECTION IN WHICH THE PLANT SHOULD GROW

CORRECT UNBALANCED GROWTH BY PRUNING TO 6 OR 8 LEAVES FROM BASE

NEW GROWTH

EARLY SUMMER ROOT PRUNING

PREPARE FOR FALL TRANSPLANTING

DOUBLE AND SINGLE PRUNERS

TO GET MORE ROSE BLOOMS CUT FLOWERS TO A VIGOROUS 5 LEAVED SHOOT

PRUNING HEDGES

RIGHT THIS TYPE OF PRUNING GIVES SOLID GROWTH AT BASE

WRONG — THIS TYPE DESTROYS BOTTOM GROWTH AND MAKES TOP-HEAVY APPEARANCE

BUD OR GRAFT

SUCKERS GROW HERE

PRUNING SHRUBBERY

HOW TO TELL ROSE FOLIAGE FROM SUCKERS

ROSES HAVE 5 LEAVES TO A STEM

SUCKERS HAVE 7 TO NINE

OLD OVERGROWN SHRUBS GIVE POOR FLOWERS AND ARE UNSIGHTLY

GOOD PRUNING GIVES BALANCED GROWTH

WRONG PRUNING GIVES UNBALANCED GROWTH

heaving of most soils during sudden changes in weather breaks roots. A parasol of leaves is used to prevent this. If it is desired to fertilize at the same time, new strawy manure will do it. This is turned under in the spring.

Special mulches are indicated for less hardy perennials and other plants in their respective chapters. These plants many times cannot stand wet-packed mulching.

In the use of straw do not make it too thick as it may form a nesting place for mice, which feed upon the bark of shrubs and trees, often killing them. If you find indications of bark chewing, dust the mulch with red pepper from a kitchen shaker around the base of the

PRUNING

Pruning produces good habits in plants. Planting and pruning go hand in hand because it is necessary to maintain a balance between the upper plant and its roots. The roots take up the moisture and with it the food from the soil and distribute it to the upper part. The leaves evaporate the excess moisture, leaving the food elements in the chemical laboratory of the plant, where they are changed into cell-building material.

After the plant has grown we may prune it again to limit its height or secure some desired form. It is also pruned to remove diseased, injured, or dead branches.

In the case of some roses and many shrubs and vines the blossoms are borne upon new wood only. In this instance we remove the worn-out branches to stimulate the growth of the new ones.

Where exceptionally large specimen or exhibition flowers are desired, plants are sometimes cut back so that all their energy is thrown into the producing of the blossom. A modification of this is the removal of all but a few flower buds. This method is called disbudding.

In the case of a sickly plant it is sometimes necessary to cut it back so that it may get a new start. Oftentimes a plant becomes so overgrown with old branches that it is cut to the ground.

Hedges, evergreens, or specimen plants are often pruned or cut with shears to some desired form or effect. This is usually known as shearing.

Special instructions for each of these operations is given with the cultural directions of the plants themselves. These should be studied, as pruning is not a job for an unskilled workman.

General rules. Tools must be sharp and properly selected. A single-bladed pruner is best. Cut with the blade toward the growing plant. This bruises only the part to be thrown away. Double-bladed pruners may bruise both parts. Use a saw on larger branches and if it is double edged use care to avoid damage to the rest of the plant.

Cut near a vigorous bud. The new shoot developing will have a tendency to grow the way it is pointed and the plant may be shaped the way you wish it.

A vigorous bud on a branch indicates that there is vitality at that point. If you cut close to the bud and in a slanting direction down from it, the wound will soon callus over before withering or decay can take place. This idea should also be carried to the cutting of flowers for vase arrangement. See the illustrations of how to cut a rose. Proper cutting allows for future blooming on the same joint. All cuts on larger branches should be coated with liquid asphaltum to keep out air and disease.

The cutting out of the heads or leading branches of many trees will cause them to become bunchy and ugly at that point as well as make an opening where disease may enter.

It is generally best to prune trees in winter, evergreens in the early spring, and shrubbery in the spring or summer, according to the blooming period.

Root pruning. Root pruning is good practice if you wish to transplant a large shrub or tree. In the spring, a trench is dug completely around the plant at a suitable distance according to its size. This forms a ball of fine fiberlike feeding roots close to the plant and will help it to get started again after transplanting.

Fill the trench with compost or earth rich in water-holding material. Do not use manure which will burn root ends. Soak with weak chemical fertilizer solution (a tablespoon to two gallons of water) several times during the growing season.

Small plants may be root-pruned by driving a spade around the ball to be removed and fertilizing closely around the plant. At least six months of growing time should elapse between the root-pruning and the transplanting.

Suckers. Many of our flowering plants are not hardy enough to grow on their own roots, and for this reason they are grafted on stronger plants, known as mother stock. For instance, lilacs may be grafted on briar stock. The mother stock often throws off shoots, called suckers, below the graft or bud. These suckers are shown by the character of their leaves in roses, lilacs, flowering almonds, etc. They should be cut off below the graft several times each season to avoid absorbing the energy needed for the growth of flowering plant.

Bleeding. Prune maples and elms in the fall or late summer, but not in early spring, as they may "bleed." If it is necessary to cut them back in spring, wait until they are out in full leaf.

CHAPTER VII
Trees and Shrubbery

*Jock, when ye hae naething else
to do, ye may be aye sticking in a
tree; it will be growing, Jock,
when ye're sleeping.*

—WALTER SCOTT

TREES

THE difference between trees and shrubs is not very clearly marked. A tree has been described as having but one stem or trunk while a shrub has several stems or trunks. This is a rather poor definition, but as many cultural directions are similar we may study them together with some profit.

Man cannot get along without trees. Apart from their practical value, they make for better manhood and womanhood by inspiring cleaner thoughts and higher ideals. The spiritual value of loving them and being with them is beyond estimate.

The parts of a tree. When we look at a tree we can recognize in its makeup three principal parts. They are the roots, the stem, and the crown. Our common trees have two general types of root systems, namely, shallow-rooted and taprooted.

Roots anchor the trees to the ground, absorb water from the soil, and transport water to the stem. Without roots, trees could not stand up. Without roots, trees would starve, for they supply water and food to the stem, branches, twigs, leaves, and other parts of the crown. The principal work of the big roots near the stem is to help the trees stand up, while the fine root hairs at the end of the rootlets are the ones that absorb the water from the soil.

The stem of a tree, also called the trunk or bole, is the main axis extending from the roots to the crown. Tree stems range from long to short, straight to crooked, and from erect to prostrate. An examination of a cross-section of a stem will show three principal parts—bark, wood, and pith. In the central part of the stem is the pith. About it is the wood. Between the wood and bark is a thin layer known as the cambium. This is the most vital part of a tree, for it is here that all new wood and bark are made. When a tree is girdled, the ring of cambium is severed. This kills the tree, for the thin cambium layer is the life-giving part of the stem. The most valuable part of a forest tree is the stem, for in it is produced the wood that is used so extensively by man. The principal functions of the stem are (1) support of the tree crown; (2) transportation of food and water; and (3) storage of food. During the winter months considerable food is stored in the stem for use early in spring when growth starts.

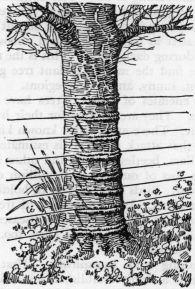

The growing bark of the tree (cambium) protects it from insects and disease. Anything driven into it wounds this membrane and is an invitation to trouble. Here we show a tree trying to overcome the effects of a wire fence nailed to it.

The growth of trees. We know that trees grow. The raw material out of which trees make their food comes from two sources— the soil and the air. The rootlets with their many small root hairs absorb water and with it many food substances are held in solution. During the growing season there is a continuous flow of sap from the roots through the stem to the leaves, where it is converted into nutritious tree food. When the sunlight plays upon the granules of leaf green, tree food is manufactured. To make the food, water is brought from the stem through the leafstalks into the leaves. Then a complex chemical process takes place. This is the reason why leaves have been called "the laboratory of the trees" The principal product derived from this process, known by the technical name of photosynthesis, is starch. As rapidly as the food is manufactured in the leaves, it makes its way down through the cells of the twigs, branches, and the stem. A continuous stream of nutritious sap is moving downward. The thin layer of cambium cells which encircles the tree then draws upon this food supply to build up new wood bark and other tree tissue. When there is an excess of food material it is stored for later use in the roots, stems, branches, and twigs.

It is interesting to know that in making the starch, oxygen is a by-product. Leaves prepare food only in daytime, their output being the greatest in full sunlight, and almost negligible during dark nights. This is the reason why we find the most luxuriant tree growth in moist, sunny, and warm regions.

The enemies of trees. Trees have many enemies They are fighting for their lives all the time. There are 200,000 known kinds of insects that attack trees. It is estimated that caterpillars, beetles, borers, and other insects cause a loss of one hundred million dollars every year. Birds help us a lot in holding insects in check. When we think of tree enemies we must not overlook tree diseases, such as blights, rusts, and rots. They, too, are a serious menace.

Breathing and transpiring. That trees breathe is a firmly established scientific fact. Year after year, during night and day, in summer and in winter, trees breathe from the time they are seeds until they die. Trees also transpire, that is, give off water. When an excess amount of water is delivered to the leaves it is given off through the small sto-

mata, the same openings through which the trees breathe. This excess water is given off as an invisible vapor.

Age. A definite age limit cannot be set for each kind of tree, but for general use our common trees may be said to be long-lived or short-lived. Of our native trees, the white oak, buttonwood, white pine, and hemlock are long-lived trees, and the poplars, willows, some cherries, and a few oaks are short-lived. Some of the sequoias of California are over 3,000 years old.

Some popular trees. If a little forethought is exercised in their planting, trees will repay all the care that is given them. All trees are not lawn trees but some are most attractive because of graceful habit, pleasing foliage, or showy bloom. Some of the finest small lawn trees belong to the group of ornamental crabs Two of our popular native trees are the redbud or Judas tree, producing lavender rose flowers before the leaves appear, and the flowering dogwood. The various sorts of hawthorns usually have more or less horizontal branches so that they have a distinctive appearance in a planting. Of the larger trees for lawns, the elms and maples have few rivals.

Selection of material. The first thing which a gardener must decide is whether he is to plant nursery or collected stock. Most amateurs have been disappointed at some time or another with the results from a tree which they had attempted to transplant from the field or woodland.

Plants in their natural state have great sprawling root systems, and when we attempt to transplant them we must cut off the major portion of the roots. This shock usually results in unsuccessful transplanting.

Nursery stock has already had its root system restricted several times by root-pruning. The top growth is also pruned to strengthen the roots so that the plant reaches you ready to go to work in the small place usually prepared for it.

Material taken from natural growing conditions should first be root-pruned, and in the case of larger plants this takes at least two years. We illustrate trenching. A part of the circle is completed one spring and the balance of the trench is dug out the following spring. This causes the tree to make a fine growth close to the trunk and when it is finally moved the ball is filled with fine roots.

The tree is then pulled over and the bottom roots cut, and in this way the root shock is divided into three parts. The moving of large trees is a job for experts or someone the nursery, and includes such nut-bearing trees as hickories, walnuts, chestnuts, and oaks.

It is better for an amateur to buy small

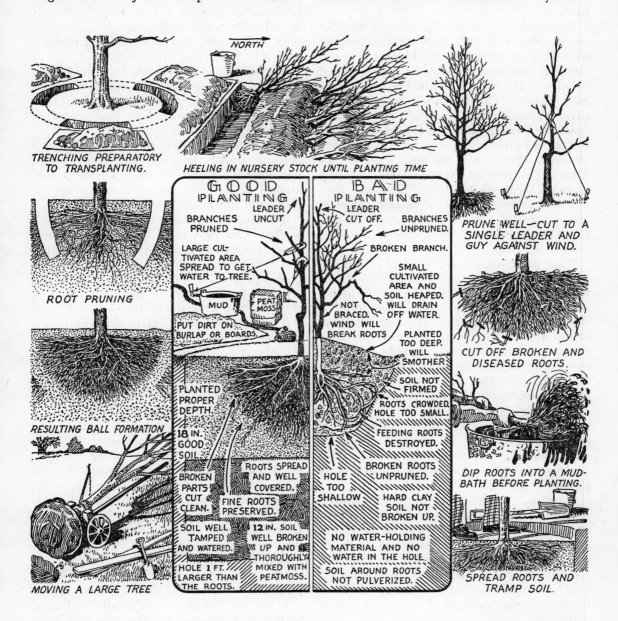

TRENCHING PREPARATORY TO TRANSPLANTING.

HEELING IN NURSERY STOCK UNTIL PLANTING TIME

ROOT PRUNING

RESULTING BALL FORMATION

MOVING A LARGE TREE

GOOD PLANTING

NORTH

BRANCHES PRUNED
LEADER UNCUT
LARGE CULTIVATED AREA SPREAD TO GET WATER TO TREE.
MUD PEAT MOSS
PUT DIRT ON BURLAP OR BOARDS.
PLANTED PROPER DEPTH.
18 IN. GOOD SOIL
BROKEN PARTS CUT CLEAN.
ROOTS SPREAD AND WELL COVERED.
FINE ROOTS PRESERVED.
SOIL WELL TAMPED AND WATERED.
12 IN. SOIL WELL BROKEN UP AND THOROUGHLY MIXED WITH PEATMOSS.
HOLE 1 FT. LARGER THAN THE ROOTS.

BAD PLANTING

LEADER CUT OFF. BRANCHES UNPRUNED
BROKEN BRANCH.
SMALL CULTIVATED AREA AND SOIL HEAPED. WILL DRAIN OFF WATER.
NOT BRACED. WIND WILL BREAK ROOTS
PLANTED TOO DEEP. WILL SMOTHER
SOIL NOT FIRMED
ROOTS CROWDED. HOLE TOO SMALL.
FEEDING ROOTS DESTROYED.
HOLE TOO SHALLOW
BROKEN ROOTS UNPRUNED.
HARD CLAY SOIL NOT BROKEN UP.
NO WATER-HOLDING MATERIAL AND NO WATER IN THE HOLE.
SOIL AROUND ROOTS NOT PULVERIZED.

PRUNE WELL—CUT TO A SINGLE LEADER AND GUY AGAINST WIND.

CUT OFF BROKEN AND DISEASED ROOTS.

DIP ROOTS INTO A MUD-BATH BEFORE PLANTING.

SPREAD ROOTS AND TRAMP SOIL.

with a great deal of patience, and requires the preparation of a hole of great width and depth.

In addition, there are a number of trees which can be transplanted successfully only when they are very young. These are the ones with a "tap" root, that is, the strong center root which grows straight down. This type usually receives special root treatment in

stock and to expend the balance of the money in preparing the ground. Properly planted, even "switches" or "whips," as the nurserymen call them, will outgrow a larger tree for which proper preparation has not been made.

Remarkable growth will be made by small trees if the soil is enriched and water is plentifully supplied during the growing season. The usual period for establishing small high-class nursery stock in its new location is one to two years, whereas the usual period for establishing collected stock—even though carefully transplanted—may range from three to six years.

In addition to the above, we must consider the suitability of the plant for the purpose for which we are to use it. It must fit a certain soil and then be adapted to a specified location. If the soil is alkaline, it will fit most plants. Quick-growing trees, such as silver maples, willows, and poplars, should be considered as temporary and used only until the slower-growing, permanent trees have matured. These trees are usually dirty; they litter a lawn throughout the season, and their branches break off during a windstorm. Poplars and willows are also a nuisance in clogging up drains. Silver maples are more useful, but they should be followed by more permanent planting.

Time of planting. The time of planting is determined somewhat by the selection of material. Almost all woody deciduous plants are easily transplanted from the beginning of the dormant period in the fall until the time of sap activity in the spring, providing temperature conditions are favorable. Because the spring is crowded with other tasks, the best time is considered to be just after the first thorough ground freeze in the fall. The outstanding exceptions to this rule are the magnolia, birch, tulip-tree, and poplar. If the planting is done in spring it is best to wait until the soil warms up a little. No planting should be done when the ground is lumpy or frozen.

Planting. Care in handling and planting of the material is real economy and the least expensive way in the long run of obtaining good results. In the purchase of the stock, insist that it be properly packed to keep the roots from drying out. It should be heeled into a vacant flower bed as soon as you receive it where it may be kept as long as it is dormant.

When taken from the soil it is best to dip it into a bath of mud. This dipping is called "puddling." Puddling protects the roots from exposure to the air before planting, and also from any air pockets which may exist after planting.

We have already spoken of the importance of the size of the planting hole. The hole should be excavated two feet deep and should be at least one foot wider each way than the full spread of the roots. Any increase in this size will be repaid by quicker growth and plant health. The bottom of the hole should be broken up with a fork and thoroughly mixed with water-holding material, such as peat, leaf mould, thoroughly rotted manure, etc. The hole must drain readily.

The excavated soil should be placed upon a piece of burlap cloth or boards with the best soil separated. Manure should be used with care. No matter how well rotted, it will burn the growing roots.

Remember you have but one chance to cultivate under the plant and that is when you plant it. Later you may cultivate ground around it, but you cannot then dig up the plant and put nourishment under it.

The balance of the soil should be well worked with peat moss, humus, etc. Sometimes it is well to abandon the soil altogether and bring in some good garden loam for the planting. Having filled the hole to the depth required by the roots of the plant, flood it with water to settle the bottom soil, and when this has drained away, place the tree in the position in which it is to grow and work the soil about it. Be sure that there are no air pockets; use a stick or shovel handle, as well as your hands and feet, to work the soil under and around all roots. Use care in doing this to see that they are not injured.

Plant the tree at approximately the same depth as it grew in the nursery. Lay the roots out naturally. When the hole is two-thirds filled tramp it firmly with the feet and again flood it with water. Now place the balance of the soil loosely in position. Do not tramp or firm it, but grade it so that any water will drain toward the trunk of the tree. The tree should now be cut back sharply, at least one-third. Chapter VI explains how to do this. It should have only one leader or principal stem and this should not be topped.

If the tree has any size it should be braced with wire, using care to protect the bark from injury. The larger the cultivated area around the tree, the more quickly it will recover. The writer has found it excellent practice to mulch the area with two inches of new strawy manure. On younger trees it is good practice to do this each fall, cultivating into the soil in the spring. If the planting is done in the spring, a mulch of straw or leaves will hold the moisture in the ground. Strawy manure is good, but the odor may be objectionable.

Cultivation and care. It is essential that young trees and shrubs obtain a ready supply of moisture, and excellent results can be obtained from placing a piece of tile in the planting hole. A hose may be placed in this

use almost all moisture which falls upon its surface. Part of the rainfall is siphoned down the stem of the leaf upon the branch, and then down the trunk. If the ground is properly graded, this water flows deep into the soil where it is held for the use of the taproots during dry weather. The water

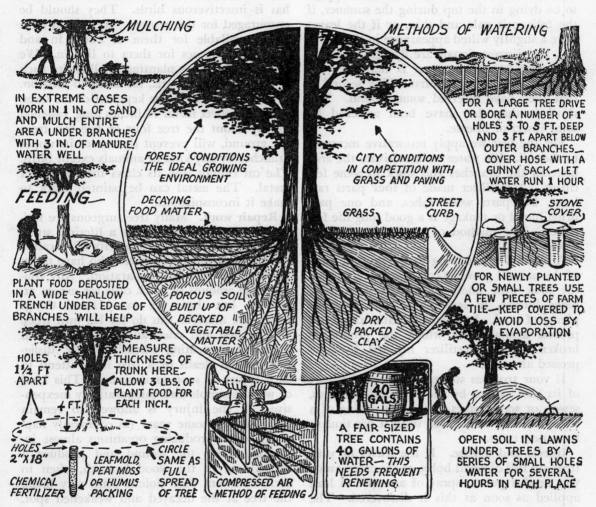

MULCHING

IN EXTREME CASES WORK IN 1 IN. OF SAND AND MULCH ENTIRE AREA UNDER BRANCHES WITH 3 IN. OF MANURE. WATER WELL

FEEDING

PLANT FOOD DEPOSITED IN A WIDE SHALLOW TRENCH UNDER EDGE OF BRANCHES WILL HELP

HOLES 1½ FT APART

← 4 FT. →

MEASURE THICKNESS OF TRUNK HERE— ALLOW 3 LBS. OF PLANT FOOD FOR EACH INCH.

HOLES 2"x18"

CHEMICAL FERTILIZER

LEAFMOLD, PEAT MOSS OR HUMUS PACKING

CIRCLE SAME AS FULL SPREAD OF TREE

COMPRESSED AIR METHOD OF FEEDING

FOREST CONDITIONS THE IDEAL GROWING ENVIRONMENT

DECAYING FOOD MATTER

POROUS SOIL BUILT UP OF DECAYED VEGETABLE MATTER

CITY CONDITIONS IN COMPETITION WITH GRASS AND PAVING

GRASS

STREET CURB

DRY PACKED CLAY

40 GALS

A FAIR SIZED TREE CONTAINS 40 GALLONS OF WATER— THIS NEEDS FREQUENT RENEWING.

METHODS OF WATERING

FOR A LARGE TREE DRIVE OR BORE A NUMBER OF 1" HOLES 3 TO 5 FT. DEEP AND 3 FT. APART BELOW OUTER BRANCHES— COVER HOSE WITH A GUNNY SACK—LET WATER RUN 1 HOUR

STONE COVER

FOR NEWLY PLANTED OR SMALL TREES USE A FEW PIECES OF FARM TILE—KEEP COVERED TO AVOID LOSS BY EVAPORATION

OPEN SOIL IN LAWNS UNDER TREES BY A SERIES OF SMALL HOLES WATER FOR SEVERAL HOURS IN EACH PLACE

and the subsoil supplied with water. Allow it to run for ten or fifteen minutes slowly or, better still, put a "Y" in your hose and supply several trees at the same time. Chemical fertilizer can also be supplied by pouring it in solution into this hole.

Few people realize the spread of the roots of a tree. Fifty feet is not unusual for a root to travel to reach water and nourishment.

Many feeding roots, however, are just under the edge of the branches where the drip of the water falls upon them. Nature has arranged the tree to conserve for its own

which drips off the edge of the leaves falls directly upon the feeding roots where it may be used by the tree at once.

Most people know that the tree breathes through its leaves, but few people realize the necessity for air around its feeding surface roots. In the forest, trees are fed under natural conditions by a decaying litter of leaves returning to the soil food and water-holding material previously taken from it.

Under city conditions, trees are brought into competition with grass from which all leaves are carefully raked. They must be fed by artificial means and if they show signs of distress, the soil should be loosened under their branches to prevent the smothering of the feeding roots by tight, heavy clay. In dry weather the lawn should be kept well watered and if the soil is heavy, sand should be worked in with a mulch. If the trees appear to be dying in the top during the summer, if the foliage is pale and thin, or if the leaves have a slightly wilted appearance in the morning, the distress signals are flying. The first and most probable reason is that they are dying of hunger and thirst. The second is that they have received some wound. The third is that they have been attacked by some insect or disease.

For the first we apply restorative measures to the soil. We water well, cultivate the area beneath the branches and work in some fertilizer. A fertilizer made of four parts raw bone, five parts wood ashes, and one part dried blood or tankage is a good long-life fertilizer. The method of application is illustrated.

A method of restoring to the ground some of the natural growing conditions is to mulch the area with finely pulverized peat moss, sedge humus, or leaf mould, and work in plenty of sand. In almost all cities there is a process available by which the ground is broken up and fertilizer injected by compressed air.

If your tree has suffered the loss of a part of its root system by the installation of gas, sewer, or water pipes, or by the paving of a street or walk, feed it well until it has time to form new roots.

Insects and disease. If the leaves of your trees are full of small holes, or are eaten away, you need a poison spray of arsenate of lead applied as soon as this is discovered. The chewing insect eats this stomach poison with the leaves. If tiny insects (scale) form along the trunk and branches they are best eradicated by an oil spray or with lime sulphur in the spring before the buds start to open. Burn out all web insects with flaming rags soaked with kerosene and tied to long poles.

Borers sometimes attack the trunk and branches, leaving holes—and many times sawdust—where they enter. Borers will scarcely ever enter a healthy tree. They usually appear on a young tree which has been over-fertilized, or they enter through some injury caused by carelessness with a pruning saw or long-handled hook. The easiest way to prevent borers, therefore, is to avoid injury to the tree.

Never cut a branch if it can be avoided. Coat all wounds with liquid asphaltum or tar. Do not coat the entire trunk.

Birds. One of the best friends that the tree has is insectiverous birds. They should be encouraged for this reason. We should have water available for them to bathe in and drink, and houses for them to live in. We can include in our planting small fruits, such as berries, cherries, etc., for them to feed on.

Cats. Cats should be kept out of the trees. A strip of sheet metal 18 inches long, fastened loosely about the tree four or five feet from the ground, will prevent the use of its upper branches by any kind of animals except birds. The cat cannot sink its claws into the sheet metal. The metal can be painted black to make it inconspicuous.

Repair work. Many tree surgeons are university men who have made a lifetime study of trees. However, the majority of so-called tree men are merely butchers who have taken up this line with no preparation. Any considerable amount of work calls for expert attention, but there are many small things which the amateur can do for his own trees.

"The best and safest and most economical means of preventing extensive decay, disfigurement, or death of a tree is to attend to each injury as soon as it occurs. This kind of work is simple and comparatively inexpensive. If the injury is allowed to remain untreated for some years (as commonly happens), decay-producing organisms almost invariably enter the wound and produce a rotted area in the wood beneath, often to such an extent that violent wind may break the tree at the decayed and weakened spot. Uninjured bark or an injured area promptly and properly treated usually prevents the entrance of decay organisms." The foregoing quotation from a bulletin of the United States Department of Agriculture sums up the tree surgery idea perfectly. We quote further: "In repair work a few fundamental principles must be observed in order to secure permanently good results. These may be summarized briefly as follows:

" (1) Remove all dead, decayed, diseased, or injured wood or bark. When on a limb this can often be done by removing the entire limb; on a large limb or on the trunk it may mean at times digging out the decayed matter so that a cavity is formed.

" (2) Sterilize all cut surfaces.

" (3) Waterproof all cut surfaces.

" (4) Leave the work in the most favorable condition for rapid healing; this may some-

work should never be allowed to work on trees. Nails and leather soles and heels on shoes often cause injury. Rubbersoled tennis shoes, or 'sneakers,' or some similar soft-soled shoes that will not slip should be used in tree-surgery work."

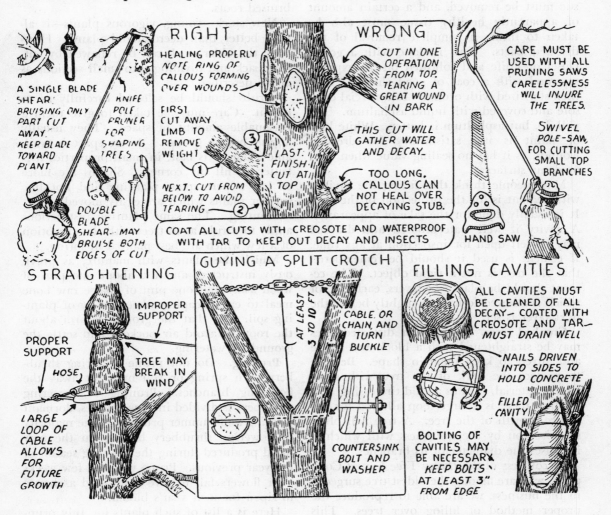

RIGHT

WRONG

HEALING PROPERLY NOTE RING OF CALLOUS FORMING OVER WOUNDS

CUT IN ONE OPERATION FROM TOP. TEARING A GREAT WOUND IN BARK

A SINGLE BLADE SHEAR BRUISING ONLY PART CUT AWAY. KEEP BLADE TOWARD PLANT

KNIFE POLE PRUNER FOR SHAPING TREES

FIRST CUT AWAY LIMB TO REMOVE WEIGHT

LAST: FINISH CUT AT TOP

THIS CUT WILL GATHER WATER AND DECAY

TOO LONG. CALLOUS CAN NOT HEAL OVER DECAYING STUB.

NEXT: CUT FROM BELOW TO AVOID TEARING

CARE MUST BE USED WITH ALL PRUNING SAWS CARELESSNESS WILL INJURE THE TREES.

SWIVEL POLE-SAW, FOR CUTTING SMALL TOP BRANCHES

DOUBLE BLADE SHEAR. MAY BRUISE BOTH EDGES OF CUT

COAT ALL CUTS WITH CREOSOTE AND WATERPROOF WITH TAR TO KEEP OUT DECAY AND INSECTS

HAND SAW

STRAIGHTENING

GUYING A SPLIT CROTCH

FILLING CAVITIES

IMPROPER SUPPORT

PROPER SUPPORT

HOSE

TREE MAY BREAK IN WIND

LARGE LOOP OF CABLE ALLOWS FOR FUTURE GROWTH

AT LEAST 3 TO 10 FT

CABLE OR CHAIN, AND TURN BUCKLE

COUNTERSINK BOLT AND WASHER

ALL CAVITIES MUST BE CLEANED OF ALL DECAY- COATED WITH CREOSOTE AND TAR- MUST DRAIN WELL

NAILS DRIVEN INTO SIDES TO HOLD CONCRETE

FILLED CAVITY

BOLTING OF CAVITIES MAY BE NECESSARY KEEP BOLTS AT LEAST 3" FROM EDGE

times necessitate filling or covering deep cavities.

" (5) Watch the work from year to year for defects, and if any appear, attend to them immediately.

"The careless use of a long pruning hook or other implement to break off small dead twigs should be avoided, as every bruise may become the point of entrance of disease or decay. Climbing spurs produce wounds that are very easily and frequently infected. Spurs should never be used except on a tree that is to be removed or destroyed. A man who insists on using climbing spurs in tree-surgery

If the amateur will learn some simple rules he will be able to solve any tree problem for himself. As previously stated several times, the bark keeps out insects and disease; therefore we wish to keep the bark membrane (the cambium) as healthy as possible. The removal of branches must be done so that this bark, called a callus, may be completely healed over the wound before decay sets in.

It is important that all wounds drain so that any cut upon a tree should be perpendicular, and as close to the bark as possible without injuring it.

As previously stated, trees should not be

allowed to grow with two leaders. If you have a tree in this shape you may prevent it from splitting by guying it with a chain or cable and a turn buckle as illustrated.

Cavities. The filling of cavities is a job to be handled with great care. All diseased tissue must be removed, and a certain amount of apparently healthy tissue must also be taken to insure a complete removal of the diseased parts. This is done with a gouge chisel or knife and followed on all exposed sapwood with a coat of good shellac. It is then sterilized with ordinary commercial creosote and covered with liquid asphaltum. Tar will do, but asphaltum is better. White lead or paint is not satisfactory for dressing wounds, as it has no sealing value when used on damp surfaces.

Most people think that filling the cavities with cement is for the protection of the tree. It is usually done for the sake of appearance. A cavity if well waterproofed and drained may be left for inspection at any time. If cement is used it should be remembered that the tree is not a rigid object. The cement should be placed in layers, each one of which is allowed to harden slightly before the next layer is set.

Crooked trees. Crooked or distorted trees may be straightened with a block and tackle and guyed to keep them in shape. Be sure to protect the bark of the tree with some heavy material, such as an old tire casing, and see that there is a large loop allowed for the future growth of the tree. A tree will often surprise you by the quickness with which it increases the diameter of its branches.

By courtesy of the Davey Tree Expert Company, who are among the oldest tree surgeons in the business, we are able to reproduce the proper method of filling over trees. This should never be done unless absolutely necessary, for the tree roots will be smothered by putting clay upon them.

SHRUBS

Like trees, shrubs need careful selection and should be purchased, freshly dug, from reliable firms. One advantage of fall planting is that the nursery stock is more likely to be fresher.

Selection of shrubs. Select only those plants which grow well in your locality. Buy the best of them and be sure that they are hardy. You may be able to replant your shrubbery border by dividing the old bushes which have outgrown their location. They may be cut up with a hatchet and pruned both as to roots and top. The oldest wood should be removed as should all broken or bruised roots.

New stock—young, vigorous plants—is always better than decrepit old plants. However, the older stock can be renewed by cutting back and dividing into small sections as above described.

Shrubs should be selected carefully as to height. Care must be taken to give them a reasonable amount of space. They usually appear best in groups. Where space is available a border is best; in small properties it is better to fill the corners. Shrubs are more or less a permanent planting and not like smaller plants which are easily moved.

Planting. The same planting instructions apply to shrubs as to trees with the exception of a few which are best planted in spring.

Mulch the plants with manure, as previously instructed, and use about one pint of wood ashes and one pint of coarse raw bone meal to each heaping wheelbarrow of planting soil. See that the ground is firm about the roots to avoid air pockets, and settle the ground by watering.

Pruning. Do not prune flowering shrubbery each spring or you may cut away the flowering branches. Pruning of flowering shrubbery is divided into two classes, dormant pruning and summer pruning. The majority of flowering shrubbery blooms on the new wood produced during the growing season of the year previous. Prune within a few weeks after flowers fall to give new wood a chance to ripen for next year's bloom.

Here is a list of such plants for July pruning:

White fringe-tree . .	Shorten stray shoots.
Dogwood	Remove old wood.
Japanese quince . .	Trim to preserve form.
Deutzia	Trim sparingly.
Pearlbush	Trim sparingly.
Forsythia or golden bell	Trim severely, July 1 to July 10.
Kerria	Remove dead wood.
Ibota privet	As desired.
Fragrant honeysuckle	Prune lightly in spring and fall.
Standish honeysuckle	Prune lightly in spring and fall.
Magnolia	As little as possible.

Flowering crab . .	Cut back when young.
Tree peony . . .	
Mock orange . . .	Remove dead wood.
Flowering plum . .	Cut budded plants severely.
Flowering peach . .	Cut budded plants severely.
European bird cherry	Cut budded plants severely.
Jetbead	Remove dead wood.
Slender golden currant	Remove dead wood.
Billardi spirea . .	Remove old wood.
Bridal wreath . . .	Remove old wood.
Van Houttei spirea .	Remove oldest wood only.
Common lilac . .	Remove oldest wood only.

The general rule is, trim early-flowering shrubs just after they bloom. Trim late-flowering or berry-bearing shrubs in March.

Temper your shears with brains; do not just lop off a few outer branches. The neglected shrub may seem to be a hopeless mass of branches, but proceed gradually. Dead-wood may be removed at any season. Cut off some of the oldest branches. Always keep some of the old wood and yet have new

LARGE SHRUBS IN REAR
MEDIUM IN CENTER
DWARF IN FRONT
USE ZIG-ZAG ARRANGEMENT. NOT STRAIGHT LINES.
LARGE SHRUBS WHICH GROW IN CLUMPS CAN BE DIVIDED WITH A HATCHET
2 FT. EXCAVATED PREPARED SOIL
BOTTOM SPIT BROKEN UP—BUT NOT REMOVED. SAND, CINDERS, ETC.—FOR DRAINAGE.
2 FT.
1 FT.

Persian lilac . . .	Remove oldest wood only.
Viburnum (flowering varieties) . . .	Prune to keep in form.
Weigelia or diervilla .	Trim sparingly.
Tamarix (early flowering)	Prune severely.

The following plants should be pruned in March:

Indigo bush . . .	Cut to ground.
Butterfly bush . .	Cut to ground.
Shrub althea . . .	Cut back severely.
Hydrangeas . . .	Cut back severely.
Regel privet . . .	Trim sparingly.
Honeysuckles (fruited varieties) . . .	Trim sparingly.
Sweetbrier . . .	Remove old wood.
Anthony water spirea	Cut ½ last year's growth.
Snowberry . . .	Remove old wood.
Coralberry . . .	Remove old wood.

shoots coming from the bottom, not only on the outside of the plant, but in the center. This means that your trimming must admit light and air to the center to support this growth.

Remember, shrubbery does not have to be pruned every year. It is more a process of thinning out than of trimming back. If the plant is hopelessly overgrown, cut it back to the ground next March and start over again. This, of course, is the last resort.

Shrubs for Various Purposes

For low porches or windows:
  Lemoinei Deutzia, Froebel Spirea, Coralberry.
For medium high porches and windows:
  Jetbead, Thunbergii Spirea, Regel Privet, Cotoneaster.
Tall screen plantings:

Mock Orange, Tatarian Honeysuckle, European Privet, Maackii Honeysuckle.

Screen plantings in shady places beneath trees:
European Privet, Flowering Currant, Morrowi Honeysuckle.

Medium height plantings for lower objectionable views and for background:
Ibota Privet, European Cranberry Bush, Japanese Snowball, Van Houttei Spirea.

Screen plantings in shady places:
Viburnums, Privet, Honeysuckle, Snowberry.

Excellent foliage for background plantings:
Fragrant Honeysuckle, Gray Dogwood, Maackii Honeysuckle.

Background shrubs for flower border:
Ibota Privet, Althea, Virginal Mock Orange.

Low hedges—sheared or unsheared:
Regel Privet, Japanese Barberry.

Tall hedges—unsheared:
Ibota Privet, Ibolium Privet, Althea.

Tall hedges—sheared:
Amur Privet, Amur Maple.

Spreading shrubs for covering banks:
Morrowi Honeysuckle, Coralberry, Golden Twig Dogwood.

Low shrubs for shady places:
Fragrant Sumac, Coralberry, Regel Privet, Alpine Currant.

Flowering shrubs for sunny spots:
Weigela, Lilac, Deutzia, Spirea, Buddleia.

Small trees for accent among shrub plantings:
Flowering Crabs, Hawthorns, Golden Rain Tree, Eleagnus.

Winter twig effects:
Coral Dogwood, Yellow Twig Dogwood, Yellow Kerria, Roses.

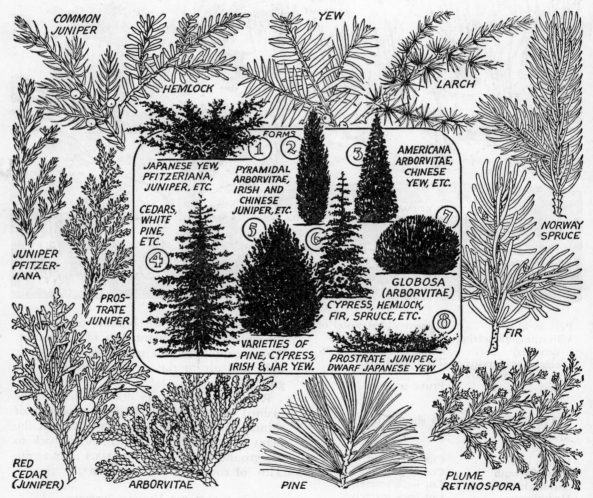

Above are shown the foliage of our most popular evergreens. Also are shown the eight general forms taken by coniferous trees, with the names of some running most true to these forms. Many plants do not run true to these forms, but are combinations of two or more of them.

CHAPTER VIII

Vines

Ordered vines in equal ranks appear,
With all the united labours of the year;
Some to unload the fertile branches run,
Some dry the blackening clusters in the sun.
—HOMER

VINES have a place in garden decoration that cannot be taken by any other plant. They have the ability to produce a large quantity of flowers in the minimum of space and to hide or soften ugly materials or outlines.

Selection. Vines should be selected for the purpose for which they are adapted. Certain groups work well on masonry, others make good ground cover, while some must have artificial support for help in their climbing. Vines are divided into two general classes, annual and hardy. The annual vines, as well as some of the smaller hardy types, grow very well in well-drained soil which has received ordinary digging. The larger hardy varieties, however, are often expected to remain in a single spot for many years, and so merit about one cubic yard of good soil.

Planting. The hole for planting should be at least two feet square and two feet deep, or better, three feet each way. If the soil is hard the ground in the bottom should be broken up and made to drain. The excavation should then be filled with good soil, well supplied with rotten manure and coarse raw bone.

Each plant should have a space three to six feet square in which it will not have to compete for food and moisture with other strong growing plants.

Vines should not be planted where water drips on them every time it rains. This is bad for the foliage but is still worse for the winter plant. Much winter killing is caused by the drip of water on warm days which coats the plant with ice at sundown. The ice-coated vine, swaying in the wind, gets many cracks and wounds which allow the entrance of pests and which cause loss of stem juices in the spring.

Large plants should be dormant if possible and the roots spread to the fullest extent, cutting off all broken or injured ones. Care must be taken to see that wooden supports are made of substantial, long-lasting material.

Plants grown against a sunny wall should receive special watering. They get the heat not only from the sun but also that reflected from the wall. Also at night the wall will reflect the heat long after sundown. Here are listed some of the best known vines and their cultural directions.

Ivies. *Virginia creeper,* sometimes called *woodbine* or *American ivy,* is that plant which we see twining around trees and covering the ground in our woodlands. It has five distinct dark green leaves in a group, but is often mistaken for the three-leafed poison ivy. For covering banks, fences, or buildings it is excellent, but it may become heavy and need thinning out as it becomes older. It grows well in shade, but being the native of woodland, does best in a moist, loose soil. The *Engleman creeper* is a variety of woodbine having a different foliage.

English ivy is sometimes called our most useful vine. Slower in growth, it does not grow well on wooden walls and is too strong a plant to train on trees. In northern sections it must be sheltered from direct winter sun and does best on north exposure. It can be easily propagated as a vine by layering or by selecting cuttings from creeping branches and inserting them in sandy loam.

Boston ivy is the quickest and best for growing, without fastening, over masonry walls. It also grows well on frame structures, doing no harm—public opinion to the contrary. It does not do well on south walls in the country farther north. It kills easily by late frosts after it has started to bud; keep it dormant with mulch if this is necessary.

Euonymus. *Euonymus radicans (Japanese bittersweet)* is a species of evergreen vine that comes in several excellent varieties. Some make good ground cover as well as wall plants, rarely growing over ten feet high. It thrives well on north sides of buildings as well as in exposed location. It will grow readily in semishade and reasonably well in dense shade.

Carpeting plants. For steep banks, shady places under trees, *Japanese spurge (pachysandra terminalis)* has turned many an eyesore into a thing of beauty. Six inches tall, it is about the most easily grown evergreen, enduring both shade and drought, and does equally well in sunshine. Its cuttings root easily and planted in ground properly manured it spreads quickly if the tops are pinched back occasionally. Used as a border

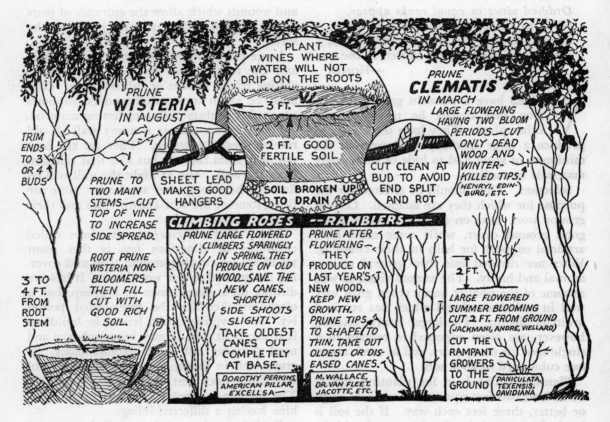

PLANT VINES WHERE WATER WILL NOT DRIP ON THE ROOTS — 3 FT. — 2 FT. GOOD FERTILE SOIL — SOIL BROKEN UP TO DRAIN

PRUNE **WISTERIA** IN AUGUST

TRIM ENDS TO 3 OR 4 BUDS

PRUNE TO TWO MAIN STEMS—CUT TOP OF VINE TO INCREASE SIDE SPREAD.

SHEET LEAD MAKES GOOD HANGERS

ROOT PRUNE WISTERIA NON-BLOOMERS THEN FILL CUT WITH GOOD RICH SOIL.

3 TO 4 FT. FROM ROOT STEM

PRUNE **CLEMATIS** IN MARCH LARGE FLOWERING HAVING TWO BLOOM PERIODS—CUT ONLY DEAD WOOD AND WINTER-KILLED TIPS. (HENRYI, EDINBURG, ETC.)

CUT CLEAN AT BUD TO AVOID END SPLIT AND ROT

CLIMBING ROSES
PRUNE LARGE FLOWERED CLIMBERS SPARINGLY IN SPRING. THEY PRODUCE ON OLD WOOD. SAVE THE NEW CANES. SHORTEN SIDE SHOOTS SLIGHTLY TAKE OLDEST CANES OUT COMPLETELY AT BASE.
DOROTHY PERKINS, AMERICAN PILLAR, EXCELLSA—

--RAMBLERS---
PRUNE AFTER FLOWERING—THEY PRODUCE ON LAST YEAR'S NEW WOOD. KEEP NEW GROWTH. PRUNE TIPS TO SHAPE TO THIN, TAKE OUT OLDEST OR DISEASED CANES.
M. WALLACE, DR. VAN FLEET, JACOTTE, ETC.

2 FT.
LARGE FLOWERED SUMMER BLOOMING CUT 2 FT. FROM GROUND (JACKMANI, ANDRE, VIELLARD) CUT THE RAMPANT GROWERS TO THE GROUND (PANICULATA, TEXENSIS, DAVIDIANA)

The variety *Euonymus radicans vegatus (Scarlet-fruited Japanese evergreen ivy)* is an excellent strain, half shrub, half vine. For low-growing hedges or rounding out corners in the foundation planting it has the advantage of growing under broad eaves, clinging closely to the building but having the appearance of an evergreen shrub. Its glossy green foliage and red berries attract much attention. Once established for a year or so it grows and spreads rapidly but is easily confined to the space desired. Given good soil, it is an economical evergreen. Pinching out the tops during the first year will produce healthy bottom growth in both ivy and euonymus.

for walks, it is easily kept within bounds. Try it where everything else has failed.

Periwinkle, also called *running myrtle (Vinca Minor)*, is another evergreen making excellent ground cover. It grows in shade, is vigorous in growth, and has lilac-blue flowers which bloom all summer. There are also white-flowering varieties.

Flowering vines. *Clematis* has many diversified varieties, but their culture is quite simple. Use rich, well-drained soil with plenty of lime. Bone meal in generous quantities is needed, as is a thick layer of rotted manure or leaf compost. They thrive in peaty soil if it is thoroughly limed; peat alone is too acid. They need shaded roots; and partial shade is also good for the vine. Protect its roots from winter winds by a thick mulch. Cultivation, if at all, must be shallow.

Lack of bloom in *wisteria* is always a question. The answer is correct pruning and planting. When it blooms well it is one of our best vines, having clusters of scented white to purple blossoms in May. It is unequaled for trellis or pergola. It has exceptionally heavy growth and must have stout support. Its branches must not entwine as they will choke one another. Seedlings may not bloom at all. Buy grafted plants from reliable nurseries; they often bloom the second year.

The best of the old-fashioned honeysuckle is *Hall's evergreen (lonicera jap. halliana)* with its exquisitely perfumed white flowers which turn yellow before they fade. It holds its foliage almost all winter and is good alike for banks, arbor, or trellis.

Another excellent type is *coral* or *trumpet honeysuckle,* of heavier and more rampant growth. It is also good for covering and climbing. It has no odor, but a great deal of bright red bloom.

The *trumpet creeper (tecoma bignonia)* is well known for covering stumps, fences, etc. It grows ten feet high with bright orange red flowers.

American bittersweet (celastrus scandens) is valued for its heavy foliage as well as for the orange and crimson berries used so much for winter bouquets. It is comparatively easily cultivated and especially good in semi-shade. It is scarcely ever troubled by disease and sometimes reaches a height of 30 feet. If flowers are desired, prune it well in spring and give it, as near as possible, wood-soil conditions—moisture and fairly loose ground.

ANNUAL VINES

The following is based upon a list from Ohio State University Bulletin 101 (Victor H. Ries), with additions and omissions.

Balloonvine (*Cardiospermum halicacabum*)
Height 8–10'. Plant 12" apart.
Small white flowers, balloon-like seed pods. Prefers a warm situation. Excellent to cover fences.

Balsam-Apple (*Momordica balsamina*)
Height 15–20'. Plant 12" apart.
A handsome vine with good foliage and warty, apple-shaped fruits which expose a brilliant carmine interior when ripe.

Balsam-Pear (*Momordica charantia*)
Height 10'. Plant 12" apart.
Resembles the balsam-apple, but has pear-shaped fruit.

Canary Nasturtium (*Tropaeolum peregrinum*)
Height 15'. Plant 8–12" apart.
A dainty vine with finely cut leaves and sprays of small yellow flowers. Resembles the Nasturtium.

Cardinal Climber (*Quamoclit coccinea*)
Height 10–20'. Plant 12" apart.
A striking vine with bright red flowers, resembling a morning glory. Blossoms all season.

Cup and Saucer Vine (*Cobaea scandens*)
Height 30'. Plant 5' apart.
One of the most rapid growing vines, which is a perennial farther south. Large bell-shaped pink and purple flowers, plum-shaped fruits. Seeds germinate best if planted edgewise rather than flat. Start seeds early indoors.

Cypressvine (*Quamoclit pinnata*)
Height 15–20'. Plant 12" apart.
Very finely cut leaves and large number of small starry flowers in orange, scarlet, or white. Prefers sunny location. Used for small trellis and posts.

Gourd (*Cucurbita*)
Height 8–20'. Plant 24" apart.
The gourds are grown more for their curiously shaped fruits, which may be dried, than for any beauty they possess.

Hyacinth-Bean (*Dolichos lablab*)
Height 15'. Plant 12" apart.
A rapid growing vine with good foliage and profusion of flowers. Daylight, white. Darkness, purple. Good for cut flowers. Twine on strings.

Morning Glory (*Convolvulus* and *Ipomea*)
Height 15–25'. Plant 12" apart.
The "Japanese Morning Glory" prefers a warm, sheltered location. The "Mexican Morning Glory," with its evening blooms of white and pink and the true Moonflower, Calyoniction aculeatum, (Ipomea bona-nox) gives evening charm in the garden, having fragrant six-inch white flowers, opening late in the day and remaining open until the sun strikes them in the morning. The "Heavenly Blue" Morning Glory, with its huge, pale blue flowers. Soak all seeds several days, or better still, notch shell all around with a file.

Nasturtium (*Tropaeolum majus* and *T. lobbianum*) Height 8–15'. Plant 12" apart.
The climbing form, although gaudy, may often be used. The Lobb Nasturtium usually has the best colors.

Scarlet Runner Bean or Fire Bean (*Phaseolus multiflorus*) Height 8–15'. Plant 12" apart.
A mass of brilliant scarlet flowers. Showy, attractive. Blooms all summer. Twiner.

Black-Eyed Susan (*Thunbergia alata*)
Height 3–5'. Plant 12" apart.
For rock gardens, porch boxes or hanging baskets. Covered with numerous white or orange flowers with dark throats. Sow seed early in the cold frame.

Roses

Who loves not roses, knows not Beauty's
smile;
Romance hath spurned him—
Poetry passed him by

*   *   *   *

Roses, all roses, bloom for the soul's delight.

—ROCKWELL

ROSES are really very simple of culture and no flower is more adapted to as many uses. If you will follow these six simple rules, success is assured.

1. Buy good bushes.
2. Select a location where you have sun at least half of the day and then protect them from foraging roots of other plants.
3. Plant them properly.
4. Prune them early in the spring.
5. Start weekly cultivation and dusting early in the spring.
6. Protect them in the winter.

Selection. Most bush roses do not possess the vigor to reproduce themselves direct and are grafted on to what is known as foster stock, which is usually a hardy briar. It is not advisable, therefore, for the amateur to attempt to propagate his own roses from cuttings. A good northern-grown rose from open ground will endure for years.

Location. The best site for a rose garden is an open space on a southerly slope, sheltered to the north and west by higher ground, walls, or hedges. The bed should not be too close to the walls or hedge and should have some sunlight and plenty of air all around it. Confined gardens are productive of disease. If you must place roses close to a hedge or wall, use care to see that they have direct sunlight a little more than half the day. You must see, also, that they are kept free from the roots of trees or other shrubbery. If the site must be close to these other plants, cut down into the ground near the bed the full length of the spade several times each year to see that the roots do not grow into the bed itself. Poplars and willows of all kinds are extremely dangerous to rose beds. Roses should not have to compete with tree roots for food moisture. Do not make the beds too high or too wide. If the beds are more than four feet wide, it will be necessary to walk on them and undo the effect of cultivation.

Soil. A medium-heavy soil, well supplied with humus, and having plenty of drainage, is necessary. Every kind of soil, capably handled, will furnish roses. The secret is deep cultivation. The top twelve inches of soil in the bed should contain the plant food. Generous quantities of humus, well-decayed manure, if you have it, and plenty of bone meal should be added. Do not force the plants too fast with chemical fertilizer, and above all do not fertilize late in the season. Chemical fertilizer applied at this time will make new growth late in summer and the plant may not winter well.

Planting time. The best time to plant is in September. This will allow the roots to obtain a good start and the plants will bloom sooner the following year. If you plant in the spring, do it as early as you are able to dig in the ground.

Planting. Take the tree from the package on receiving it from the grower. If it is out in leaf, free it from all buds and most of the foliage. Shorten the longshoots that offer resistance to the wind so as not to disturb the roots. Cut off damaged or broken roots and cut the thick ones back six inches from their starting point. Preserve as much as possible the tiny fibrous roots, as these are the important ones. Heavy roots may take up a little water, but the fibrous roots feed the plant. If a root has a crack in it, cut it off sharply, as it will breed disease. If the bark is shriveled when the plants are received, bury them under six inches of moist soil for a few days. If there are signs of mildew, dip the tree in a solution of one ounce of liver of sulphur (potassium sulphide) to one gallon of soft water. Spread the roots to the fullest extent laterally and do not plant too deeply. Combine your headwork with footwork. Make the soil firm as the hole is filled. Use your hands and doubled fists. As soon as there is sufficient earth around the roots to prevent damage, step on it and rock backward and forward to make the soil very firm.

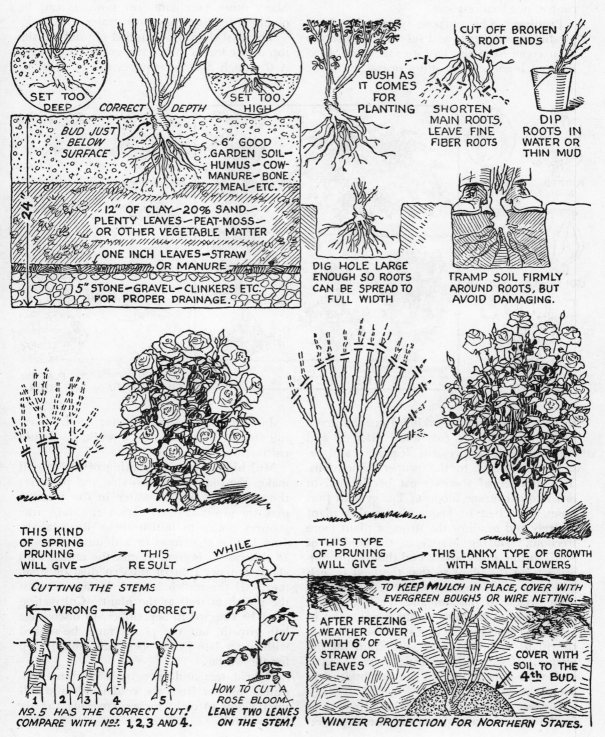

SET TOO DEEP — CORRECT DEPTH — SET TOO HIGH

BUD JUST BELOW SURFACE

6" GOOD GARDEN SOIL — HUMUS — COW MANURE — BONE MEAL — ETC.

24"

12" OF CLAY — 20% SAND — PLENTY LEAVES — PEAT-MOSS — OR OTHER VEGETABLE MATTER

ONE INCH LEAVES — STRAW OR MANURE

5" STONE — GRAVEL — CLINKERS ETC. FOR PROPER DRAINAGE.

BUSH AS IT COMES FOR PLANTING

CUT OFF BROKEN ROOT ENDS

SHORTEN MAIN ROOTS, LEAVE FINE FIBER ROOTS

DIP ROOTS IN WATER OR THIN MUD

DIG HOLE LARGE ENOUGH SO ROOTS CAN BE SPREAD TO FULL WIDTH

TRAMP SOIL FIRMLY AROUND ROOTS, BUT AVOID DAMAGING.

THIS KIND OF SPRING PRUNING WILL GIVE → THIS RESULT

WHILE

THIS TYPE OF PRUNING WILL GIVE → THIS LANKY TYPE OF GROWTH WITH SMALL FLOWERS

CUTTING THE STEMS

← WRONG → CORRECT

1 2 3 4 5

NO. 5 HAS THE CORRECT CUT! COMPARE WITH NOS. 1, 2, 3 AND 4.

CUT

HOW TO CUT A ROSE BLOOM — LEAVE TWO LEAVES ON THE STEM!

TO KEEP MULCH IN PLACE, COVER WITH EVERGREEN BOUGHS OR WIRE NETTING.

AFTER FREEZING WEATHER COVER WITH 6" OF STRAW OR LEAVES

COVER WITH SOIL TO THE 4th BUD.

WINTER PROTECTION FOR NORTHERN STATES.

It used to be the firm rule that plants should be set two to two and one-half feet apart, but most gardeners get excellent results with twelve to fifteen inches for tea and monthly roses, and have a better-looking bed. Hybrid perpetuals and larger bushes, of course, need more room.

Pruning. The purpose of pruning is to produce strong roots and shoots. New shoots must come from the base to take care of exhausted branches. Pruning opens the plant

tion. A good preventive is manganese-arsenate, which is both a fungicide and an insecticide. A home-made dust can be made of nine parts of dusting sulphur by bulk with one part of arsenate of lead (massey dust) to which tobacco dust may be added for aphides. Many other excellent dust powders can be obtained readily from your dealer.

The dust should be applied not only to the top of the leaves but to the underside as well. A thorough dusting requires the purchase of

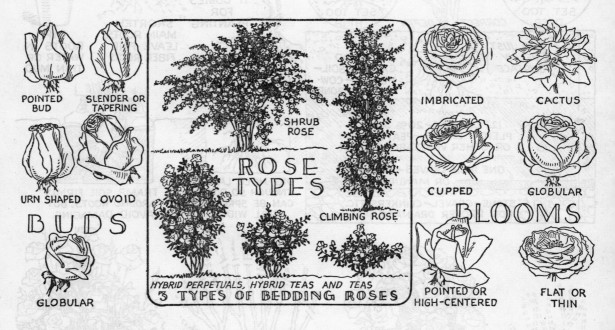

POINTED BUD SLENDER OR TAPERING

URN SHAPED OVOID

BUDS

GLOBULAR

ROSE TYPES

SHRUB ROSE

CLIMBING ROSE

HYBRID PERPETUALS, HYBRID TEAS AND TEAS
3 TYPES OF BEDDING ROSES

IMBRICATED CACTUS

CUPPED GLOBULAR

BLOOMS

POINTED OR HIGH-CENTERED FLAT OR THIN

to the sun and air by taking away the dense middle growth. It cuts away diseased and exhausted wood, prevents legginess and restricts the plant to the proper dimensions. The number of shoots must be limited, in order to encourage blooms. For general purposes, it is best to prune the weaker plant severely and to allow the stronger plant more freedom. During March to the middle of April, prune just above a bud that points outward from the plant so that the next branch will grow away from the center, leaving the center open to the sun and the air. Leave from three to five buds on the plant. Cut in a slanting direction so that the moisture from the plant and the water will drain off the wound. If you wish perfection, dress the cut ends with pine tar, which can be obtained in cans at most drug stores.

Disease. One of the most important steps in the summer care of roses is disease protec-

a dust gun but it soon pays for itself. Dusting should be done once a week, as should cultivation.

Mulching. A light working of the topsoil makes the plant food available and preserves the moisture. If you water in dry weather soak the ground; never sprinkle. Many rose growers prefer to mulch their plants about July 1 with peat moss or a domestic humus. In this case it is good to mix the mulch with about ten per cent of tobacco dust or stem-meal. If the mulch is used, be sure to dust the mulch as well as the plant. Cultivation must be stopped in September, to discourage late growth, but the plants must be soaked with water late in October before hilling up for the winter.

Hybrid teas and perpetuals need no coddling. Shelter from the cold winds and hill up the soil to eight inches, covering the six lowest buds.

If you wish to mulch with leaves, use only hardwood leaves and surround the bed with closely set stakes or wire netting to hold the leaves in place. A little brush may be laid upon the top but do not pack down the leaves, because a damp mulch is injurious. In the spring, remove the mulch piecemeal so that the plants will harden out gradually.

Climbers. The conditions applying to the bush type also apply to some extent to climbers. Planting in shade under the drip of trees will result in mildew. Since they must have drainage, raising their planting ground above the surrounding level sometimes avoids loss.

There are two distinct types of climbers whose pruning needs are often misunderstood. The rambler type bears its best blooms on new canes which spring from the base of the plant. Therefore remove all old canes, which are not needed, as soon as the flowering is over. This usually reduces the plant close to its supporting trellis and has the advantage of removing old wood to prevent disease spread. Train the new branches to replace the old. The idea is to renew the plant above ground each year as far as is practical.

Any pruning, of course, should be tempered to fit the needs of the plant. If a large cover or tall plant is desired, cut back the side growth in the spring, close to the main stems, to stimulate, removing a part of the oldest canes each summer.

For the many larger-flowered roses, which bloom abundantly on old canes, only light spring pruning is necessary. Prune to remove dead or diseased canes and to thin rank growth. The rest of the vine is pruned only to shape it.

ROSE TYPES AND RELIABLE VARIETIES

GROUND COVER

Rose wichuraiana
Rose Max Graf*

CLIMBERS

American Pillar—Crimson-pink
Blaze*—Scarlet
Chaplin's Pink Climber*—Pink
Christine Wright—Rose-pink
Dorothy Perkins—Blush-pink
Dr. W. Van Fleet—Pink
Evangeline—Carmine-pink
Excelsa—Scarlet-crimson
Gardenia—Yellow
Hiawatha—Crimson
Mary Wallace—Pink

New Dawn*—Pink
Paul's Scarlet Climber—Scarlet
Silver Moon—White
Tausendschon—Rose

POLYANTHUS

Eblouissant—Dark red
Echo—Soft pink
Erna Teschendorff—Deep crimson
Gloria mundi*—Orange
Golden Salmon—Golden salmon
Ideal—Dark scarlet
LaMarne—Salmon-rose
Miss Edith Cavell—Brilliant scarlet
Mrs. R. M. Finch*—Rose-pink
Triomphe Orleanais—Cerise-red

HYBRID TEAS

Betty Uprichard—Salmon-pink
Countess Vandall—Carmine pink, buff, and gold
Dame Edith Helen—Pink
Duchess of Wellington—Golden orange
Etoile de Hollande—Red
Everest*—White
General McArthur—Red
Gruss an Teplitz—Crimson
Joanna Hill—Salmon-yellow
Kaiserin Augusta Victoria—White
Lady Alice Stanley—Deep rose
Lady Ashtown—Pink
Lady Margaret Stewart—Golden yellow
Laurent Carle—Crimson
Mary Hart*—Red
Mme. Butterfly—Pink suffused gold
Mrs. Caroline Testout—Pink
Radiance—Light pink
Talisman—Scarlet-orange

HYBRID PERPETUALS

Anna de Diesbach—Rose carmine
Avrillago*—Pink
Frau Karl Druschki—White
George Arends—Light pink
J. B. Clark—Light red
Magna charta—Light pink
Margaret Dickson—White
Mrs. John Laing—Light pink
Paul Neyron—Rose-pink
Ulrich Brunner—Red

LANDSCAPE ROSES

Rosa blanda—Light pink
Rosa canina—Light pink
Rosa carolina—Rose pink
Rosa hugonis—Yellow
Rosa lucida—Bright pink
Rosa multiflora—White
Rosa nitida—Deep pink
Rosa palustris—Rose pink
Rosa rubiginosa—Bright pink
Rosa rubrifolia—Pink
Rosa rugosa—Pink
Rosa setigera—Bright pink
Rosa spinosissima—White
Rosa xanthina—Yellow

---

* Signifies new or uncommon varieties.

CHAPTER X

Bulbs, Corms, Tubers, and Roots

*The little brown bulbs went to sleep in the
  ground,*
In their little nighties they slept very sound,
And Winter he raged and he roared overhead,
But never a bulb turned over in bed.

But when Spring came tiptoeing over the lea,
Her finger on lip, just as still as could be,
The little brown bulbs at the very first tread
*All split up their nighties and jumped out of
  bed.*

— (Author unknown)

SPRING-FLOWERING BULBS

SPRING-FLOWERING bulbs bloom so
early in the season that they do not have
time to develop their root structure first.
Therefore, plant according to varieties in late
September or October—or even as late as November—so that roots will have time to fully
develop before winter. Narcissus, crocus,
bulb iris, snowdrops, snowflakes, and winter
aconite should be planted in September. Tulips, hyacinths, and scillas may go in later.

The soil must be reduced to good physical
condition about two feet deep, the bottom
foot being made to drain freely and, in case
of water-bearing soil or damp locations, a
three-inch layer of cinders must be placed in
the very bottom. The bulbs will rot if they
are not freely drained. The topsoil should
be mixed with peat lightly dusted with lime.
(Remember: Use no lime for lilies.) Use
the domestic peat humus or imported peat
moss.

More failures are caused by the use of fresh
manure than by any other condition. Fresh
manure is an excellent material, properly
rotted and composted, but its touch means
death to many bulbs. Mix it with the soil in
spring, fork it over several times during the
summer, and then sift it through a coarse
screen in the fall. This is the ideal planting
material.

Use one large handful of coarse raw bone
meal, one of steamed bone, and two of wood
ashes to each square yard of planting surface.
Mix deeply and thoroughly with the soil.
The potash in wood ashes develops new firm
bulbs.

Firm the soil beneath the bulbs, and press
the bulbs firmly upon it. Air pockets underneath may allow the bulb to rot before its
roots reach the moist soil. It is important to
plant with a trowel when naturalizing under
trees or in the grass, in order to be sure that
the bulb (no matter how small) sits firmly on
the subsoil.

In naturalizing, put a thin layer of sand
around the bulb and dust the bottom well
with bone meal.

The general rule is to cover the top of the
bulb with soil to three times its greatest diameter. A thorough watering just after planting will start root growth at once.

After the ground has frozen, cover the
plants with four to six inches of leaves and

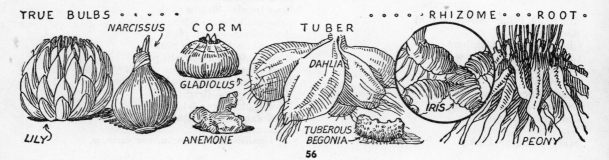

TRUE BULBS · · · · ·   NARCISSUS   C O R M   T U B E R   · · · · · RHIZOME · · ROOT ·
LILY   GLADIOLUS   ANEMONE   DAHLIA   TUBEROUS BEGONIA   IRIS   PEONY

surround them with stakes to keep the wind from blowing them away. Wire netting is also good for this purpose.

In the spring examine the mulch to see that it is light and dry, but leave it in place until danger of late frost is over. This will keep the bulbs from premature growth and injury by late frost. Take the mulch off carefully to avoid injury to young sprouts.

Crocus. This is a good, cheap bulb. Cover it three inches deep, or two to three inches apart for mass effect. It grows best in sandy or well-drained soil; avoid very damp situations. Use bone meal and leave it for several years. Plant in sun or partial shade in September. Naturalize it in grass or shrubbery. It will disappear if the top is mowed too soon.

Glory of snow. Plant in sun or light shade.

Application of liquid manure (two weak dressings) just as the buds are forming will increase flower size. Nitrate of soda, or chemical plant food, as a substitute for liquid manure, may be given in weak solution—one tablespoon to a gallon of water. Wet the ground well, and then wash the solution into the soil by a good watering. This solution is more successful on tulips than on other bulbs.

The varieties of spring-flowering types are so well known and are so well described in good plant catalogs that no descriptions will be given here. Cultural directions for the more popular bulbs follow.

Cover three inches deep and three inches apart in September or October. Keep soil moist but not wet while it is growing. Leave it undisturbed to seed.

Snowdrop. These are about the first to bloom in early March. Plant them in mass by dozens or hundreds. Cover two to three inches and the same distance apart. Snowdrops thrive in moist semishade.

Spring snowflake. These are white and three to four inches high. Cover them three inches in groups. Use moist, rich soil, and plant in shaded corner or semishaded rock garden. The spring snowflake blooms early.

The summer snowflake blooms in April, May, or early June, with the same culture.

Grape hyacinth. This prefers rich sandy or gritty soil, but is not particular. Cover two or three inches, three inches apart. It will thrive if left undisturbed and leaves fully ripened.

Squills siberica. This has a blue flower to combine with snowdrops for early spring bloom. Use sandy soil and top dress manure. It will grow under evergreens.

Scilla hispanica. The campanulata, best of scillas, blooms in May and June, and goes with some Darwin tulips. Place in edging beds or in borders. There are several colors. Cover them three inches, and four inches apart.

Scilla bifolia. This is the earliest squill. It is blue, and three to six inches high. It grows in rock gardens or indoors.

Winter aconite. This is a member of the buttercup family, not showy. It blooms early, in March or April, and is three to eight inches high. Cover it two to three inches in a semishady location, and keep moist while growing. Plant as early as possible. It is good among trees or shrubbery.

Star of Bethlehem. Avoid it. It is not very showy and soon becomes a weed pest.

Narcissus (daffodil jonquil). All narcissi are not jonquils, but the name of daffodil is usually applied to all narcissi. A yearly top dressing of bone, one pound to each 20 square feet, is excellent. Work in carefully. They delight in moist soil and drainage. They will stand some shade. They are best left undisturbed for several years, but when the clumps get to be twenty to thirty bulbs they should be dug and replanted.

Tulip. Tulips, favorite flowers for centuries, are the last planted of all fall bulbs. From October 15 until the ground freezes is the best time; they seem to suffer from too early planting.

In formal beds it is considered best to lift them each year and, as soon as their foliage ripens (see previous instructions), store them in a cool cellar to dry. Wood ashes (best), dry sand, or dry soil is good for storage.

Use only the large ones, planting small ones in a nursery bed where they will require two to three years to reach blooming size. Tulips need especially good drainage, adequate moisture, and a sunny location, although parrot types will stand some shade.

The procession of bloom starts in April with single and double early (ten to eighteen inches high); then cottage (16 to 30 inches high); parrot (22 to 36 inches high); and— in late May—Darwins (24 to 36 inches high), breeders (24 to 32 inches high), and Mandel, each class having a wide range of color. Remove blooms as they fade to save strength of the bulb, but save the foliage when cutting flowers for indoors.

Hyacinth. These plants prefer very light sandy soils. They root deeply and must be cultivated and fertilized two feet deep. Clay must be broken up with wood ashes or sand.

Well-rotted cow manure is permitted. Apply bone meal and other fertilizers together with humus materials as previously directed, using more lime than on the other bulbs.

Plant six inches apart and four to six inches deep (three times their greatest diameter) in a sunny location. Although they can stand sun for a part of the day, protect them from the strong wind which will blight their blooms and make them lopsided. Best results are obtained from early planting. September or early October produces good roots.

It is not necessary to buy the largest bulbs. Good two to two-and-a-quarter inch bulbs are satisfactory. It is best to lift them each year after foliage ripens and store them in a cool, dry place until they are ready to plant again.

SUMMER-FLOWERING BULBS

Autumn crocus or meadow saffron (colchicum). These plants are not particularly adapted to garden use, but are so interesting that they merit cultivation. Planted in early fall, two inches deep, the leaves appear in the spring to die and be followed in the fall by white lavender flowers rising directly from the ground. Planted in late summer, they will bloom in fall. Leaves will follow in spring.

Plant them in gardens close to the house where their flowers will be protected from the hot sun. In the house the plant is a novelty. Placed in sun in midwinter it will bloom without water or soil, having lavender flowers. Away from direct light its bloom is white.

Cluster amaryllis (Amaryllis halli; Lycoris squamigera). This is an interesting plant similar in blooming to the autumn crocus. The bulbs planted in early fall or early spring are perfectly hardy and should be set four inches deep and six to eight inches apart, in groups of three or more.

Plant them in perennial border or in very slight shade. The foliage dies down in early summer, followed by fragrant rose-lilac flowers, two feet high, in August, rising directly from the ground. It will multiply and must be divided after three or four years.

Calla. These are yellow, white, and spotted. Plant the dormant bulbs in April or May in rich heavy soil in a sunny spot with ample drainage. They bloom beautifully in August or September, just when the garden slumps. Protect them during the rest period.

Canna. These plants require the same culture as dahlias. They grow well in any drained soil, away from strong winds, where moisture is readily obtainable. They are vigorous growers but sensitive to frost. Do not plant them outdoors until the weather becomes warm.

Easy of culture, they may be started indoors in pots or in the open in soil top-dressed with well-rotted manure. Divide last year's roots into fairly large sections with several buds on each, and plant them two inches below the surface, and one to three feet apart. Lift them after frost kills the tops and store them in a cool place in dry, sandy soil or peat moss to avoid shriveling.

Dahlia. Strange to say, in spite of the large popularity of the dahlia, its simple cultural requirements are many times misunderstood. Its chief needs are drainage and moisture rather than fertility. The ideal soil is one-half sand and one-half loam.

A fair standard of fertility is required but excessive richness is to be avoided. An excess of nitrogen will make the plant run to stem and leaves at the expense of flowers. Heavy soil should be prepared in the fall with a good application of manure and bone meal. Superphosphate and manure may be used in spring on light or sandy soil.

The plants should be kept well and deeply cultivated until blooming commences. After that ordinary tillage is sufficient. This treatment is better than any amount of water, as it produces normal rather than sappy growth. Mulch in August with two inches of humus, peat, or well-rotted manure to cool the ground and conserve the moisture. Remember that careful culture produces good flowers and good roots for next year.

All need four to five hours sunshine and must be kept free from foraging roots of trees, shrubbery, or other plants, which deprive them of food and moisture. As soon as tops are killed by frost in the fall, roots should be dug from the ground and the tops cut off to eight inches above the crown. After a few hours' drying in the air, store them in a box of peat moss in a cool cellar protected from freezing.

In spring do not be in too big a hurry to plant. Dahlias are very susceptible to injury from cold. Lift them from the box and divide as shown in the illustration. Handle them with care to avoid bruising, which will produce decay.

To plant, dig a hole 14 inches deep, in heavy or clay soil—16 inches in sandy soil. Now condition the soil as previously instructed and replace eight inches or more of it in the bottom, firming it well. Drive stakes before planting in order that no damage be done to new roots and that the young plant may have its support in early development. Plant the tuber flat as illustrated with sprout nearest to stake, first covering the crown two inches deep. As soon as hardy growth has risen above the soil, fill in another and repeat until level is reached. This method keeps the tuber deep in the ground where it is cool and moist during the hot weather.

The practice of disbudding varies somewhat. On the dahlia shoot the top of the terminal flower bud is the first to develop. If all the conditions of growth and weather are perfect it makes the finest flower. The other flowers are produced on side shoots from the axils of the leaves, which are paired. Very good flowers can be raised when the three pairs of flower buds below each terminal bud are removed, but further disbudding will concentrate more strength in the terminal flower and give longer stems for cutting.

Elephant's-ear (caladium). Plant this late in May, two or three inches deep. Give it well-spaded soil, plenty of water, and 4:12:4 fertilizer and it will grow six feet high with immense leaves. It is too large for the average garden. Lift it after frost.

Gladiolus. Gladiolus is deservedly popular for its wide variety of color and uses, its ease of culture, and its general adaptability. It will grow anywhere in the United States and with a little preparation in almost any kind of soil that is well drained and sunny.

The preference of the plant seems to be for

a sandy loam, well pulverized, mellow, and deeply cultivated. In clay soil, sand should be added to make it drain well; in lighter soils, an extra amount of decayed vegetable matter is necessary.

Cultivating the soil 18 inches deep cannot be too highly recommended. If the soil is

Planting may be commenced in the spring as soon as the ground is in a condition to work.

The approved distance for planting is six inches apart. Good bulbs pay. Large old bulbs, which are usually flat and slightly hollowed on the bottom, are not as good as

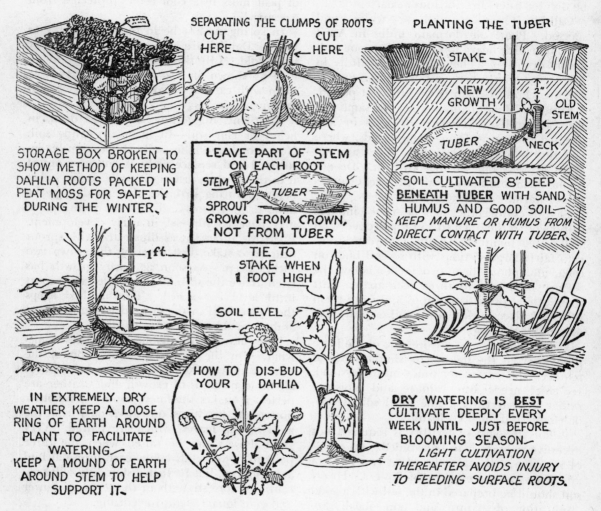

STORAGE BOX BROKEN TO SHOW METHOD OF KEEPING DAHLIA ROOTS PACKED IN PEAT MOSS FOR SAFETY DURING THE WINTER.

SEPARATING THE CLUMPS OF ROOTS — CUT HERE — CUT HERE

PLANTING THE TUBER

STAKE — NEW GROWTH — OLD STEM — TUBER — NECK

SOIL CULTIVATED 8" DEEP BENEATH TUBER WITH SAND, HUMUS AND GOOD SOIL — KEEP MANURE OR HUMUS FROM DIRECT CONTACT WITH TUBER.

LEAVE PART OF STEM ON EACH ROOT — STEM — TUBER — SPROUT GROWS FROM CROWN, NOT FROM TUBER

TIE TO STAKE WHEN 1 FOOT HIGH

SOIL LEVEL

1 ft.

IN EXTREMELY DRY WEATHER KEEP A LOOSE RING OF EARTH AROUND PLANT TO FACILITATE WATERING — KEEP A MOUND OF EARTH AROUND STEM TO HELP SUPPORT IT.

HOW TO DIS-BUD YOUR DAHLIA

DRY WATERING IS BEST CULTIVATE DEEPLY EVERY WEEK UNTIL JUST BEFORE BLOOMING SEASON — LIGHT CULTIVATION THEREAFTER AVOIDS INJURY TO FEEDING SURFACE ROOTS.

double spitted, well-decayed manure may be used if the bed is dug in the fall (a good practice) and allowed to lie rough all winter, but it should not be used on beds about to be planted. Get the manure as deep as possible so that the roots may go deep into the ground in search of moisture and cool temperature. The gladiolus corm is planted three to four inches deep and its roots will go considerably farther to feed. The black sedge humus sold commercially is ideal for use if the bed is made at planting time. Peat moss may be used but keep it away from the corm.

smaller, high-crowned young bulbs.

Depth of planting depends on the size of the bulb and the condition of the soil. Small bulbs should be planted as shallow as two inches in heavy soil, and large ones as deep as four inches in light soil. Deep planting requires less watering and less staking, as it gives more support to the plant.

For wire worms in the soil, sprinkle the planting soil with a weak solution of permanganate of potash and fumigate with sulphur at planting time. Burn any rotted corms to prevent spread of disease.

First cultivations may be fairly deep (three inches). As plants advance cultivation should be done with a rake. Merely keep the topsoil loosened to keep weeds from starting and to form a dust mulch. If done often the rake is sufficient and will save the labor of breaking up the ground after it has packed. Keep the ground fairly level. Hilling is doubtful practice. Never water lightly; if watering becomes necessary, soak six inches deep.

Cutting the spike as soon as the first flower opens allows the plant strength to go into the corm. Fine flowers come from fertilizing. Dress the plant with equal parts of fine steamed bone and dried blood (about one level teaspoon to each plant) when they are six to eight inches high and give liquid manure just as the plants are ready to bloom.

The best time to lift corms is when the tips of the leaves begin to turn brown. Store them in bunches for about eight weeks in open-slatted trays in a cool cellar. Never remove stalks as long as any green shows. If they must be stored in a furnace-heated cellar, they may be placed in dry sand or dry peat moss. Avoid dampness.

Cormels or bulblets may be planted in shallow trenches in mellow soil either in the open or in cigar boxes or trays inside in early spring. They will grow into flowering bulbs in about two seasons. Store for the winter in very slightly moistened peat moss.

Summer hyacinth. Summer hyacinths have slender stalks one to four feet high, and are good for the back of a perennial border. White, drooping, bell-shaped flowers come in midsummer. Plant in early spring six inches deep and six inches apart in clumps of several bulbs. Lift them in the fall and store until spring. For best results buy new bulbs each year.

Bearded iris. Of the several kinds of iris, all of which are worth cultivating, tall, bearded (German) varieties lead all the rest in well-deserved popularity. They need little attention but, being strong growers, they must be divided every two to five years, according to variety. The time to divide is soon after they have finished blooming in order that they may become established for results the following spring.

After transplanting, the leaves should be cut back to relieve the strain of the weakened root structure but this is the only case in which leaf-trimming is justified. Many gardeners do it each year for appearance but it affects the energy of the plants which is accumulating for the following season.

The planting of the rhizomes is simple. They do not necessarily need rich soil but drainage is necessary for complete health and success. They originally grew as hillside plants and thrive best in slightly raised beds or upon banks. Do not confuse them with flags, which grow in water, or the Japanese iris, which likes dampness. They will give reasonable results in semishade, but full sun is best. They will grow well in clay soil if sand is added for drainage. It has been said that any soil which will grow corn will grow iris. As they are very shallow rooted it is a waste to add fertilizer to any depth greater than five inches. In the clay the soil below this depth should be about one-third sand and thoroughly mixed, but no plant food need be added.

In making the original bed, work deeply some well-rotted manure and lime. The manure must be sufficiently well rotted to have lost all its former appearance. If peat humus or leaf mould is used for this purpose, give it a generous dressing of hydrated lime or ground limestone. Lime in small quantities proves very beneficial to these plants.

The iris borer is a night-flying moth which lays its eggs in the leaves; the eggs hatch after flowering time. The larva then eats its way down through the leaf and when fully grown enters the rhizome (root) near the flowering stem. The borer often destroys the lateral bud, which produces the bloom for the following year.

If you find a slimy trail of eaten leaves, remove them, mash the intruder, and destroy the chewed leaves. The borer usually leaves behind where it enters the root a little patch of plant material resembling sawdust. If the borer has entered the rhizome, destroy it with a sharp knife and you may save the roots. If not destroyed it will eat through the root and enter the soil for pupation and damage the succeeding year. Examine new purchases carefully for both rot and borer.

In spring the eggs are just below the dead leaves and may be easily destroyed by fire. Raise the leaves with a rake and allow the sun to dry them thoroughly. When they are dry sprinkle them lightly with gasoline. Have someone near-by to help prevent any possible

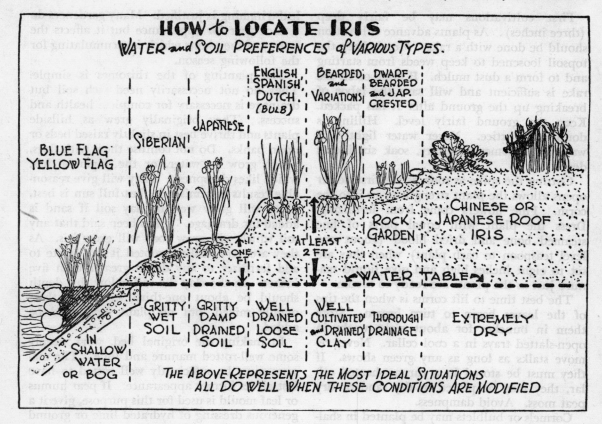

HOW to LOCATE IRIS
WATER and SOIL PREFERENCES of VARIOUS TYPES.

BLUE FLAG YELLOW FLAG | SIBERIAN | JAPANESE | ENGLISH SPANISH DUTCH (BULB) | BEARDED and VARIATIONS | DWARF, BEARDED and JAP. CRESTED | ROCK GARDEN | CHINESE OR JAPANESE ROOF IRIS

AT LEAST 2 FT.   ONE FT.

← WATER TABLE →

IN SHALLOW WATER OR BOG | GRITTY WET SOIL | GRITTY DAMP DRAINED SOIL | WELL DRAINED LOOSE SOIL | WELL CULTIVATED and DRAINED CLAY | THOROUGH DRAINAGE | EXTREMELY DRY

THE ABOVE REPRESENTS THE MOST IDEAL SITUATIONS ALL DO WELL WHEN THESE CONDITIONS ARE MODIFIED

spread of the fire and then burn the leaves. This is best done on a windy day, when the leaves may be fanned into a quick, hot blaze. Do not allow a prolonged fire to injure the roots. Careful burning is good practice upon any type of iris planting.

Oriental iris. This iris (Siberian, Japanese, etc.) does not properly belong in a chapter on bulbs. Oriental irises are fibrous-rooted. Care must be taken to see that these roots are spread when planting, just as is done with any perennial. They are lime-haters. The Siberian iris is the most hardy.

In regions of heavy clay soil oriental irises have the reputation of being temperamental. This need not be the case if they are given loose soil (the Japanese iris, especially), in which they delight. Mix sand with the clay and put in a large amount of rotted manure, peats, leaf mould, etc., until there is always a supply of moisture held for them. The ground should be very damp but not swampy. They bloom in June and July abundantly but daintily. The Siberian are the easiest of culture, the Japanese more exacting.

Plant oriental irises late in August or September, in extra well-drained soil, placing the crowns two inches below the soil and two inches apart for mass effect. Light shade seems to help. Mulch with leaf mould, peat, or well-decayed manure. The first year's plantings of all beardless iris should have a protective mulch during the winter.

Water iris. This type is also fibrous-rooted and consists for the main part of two sections, *iris versi color,* the common blue flag of the American prairies, and *iris pseudacorus,* the European yellow flag. Both are true water plants, growing best in boggy situations where the water does not stand over their crowns.

The yellow flag will grow freely in both sun and shade in fairly dry moist locations, and is excellent for wild plantings. It comes in several varieties of color. If grown in gardens, remove the seeds, as they become weedlike after a few years.

The blue variety is not so rampant-growing and is useful mostly for edges of ponds and bog situations.

Lily. The beauty, ease of culture, and low cost of garden lilies should make them one of our most prized plants. There seems to be an old notion that they are difficult to handle. Nothing could be farther from the truth.

Some of the reasons for lack of success are: (1) Planting too shallow. All lilies except the Madonna Lily need deep planting. (2) Lack of proper drainage. This is one thing all authorities agree upon. (3) Lack of food or the use of manure. It is better for the amateur to avoid manure in lily culture. (4) Planting certain varieties in lime or alkaline soil. (5) Failure to provide moisture in hot dry summer days. (6) Too frequent transplanting. They should be transplanted only about every three to five years, according to variety.

Use care in planting. Remember that if properly planted, they give results for years with no further attention. Select a proper site. As these plants are rarely planted in beds by themselves, it is necessary to dig holes separately for each group. These groups should consist of three to six bulbs. All but the madonna lily may be planted among perennials between peonies, shrubbery, evergreens, etc. They thrive in partial shade, especially about their roots.

Surface-rooted trees and shrubbery, such as elms, maples, etc., are not good for them and heavy-feeding, deep-rooted perennials should be kept at a distance. They will grow in full sun but most of them do well shaded for a part of the day. Do not plant them in complete shade. Of course it is understood that, once planted, the bulbs should remain in place three to five years, according to crowding.

Drainage and proper depth are more important than fertility. One thing they cannot tolerate is an excess of water. The meadow lily (canadense) and the American turk's-cap lily (superbum) like marshes and wet places; all others need perfect drainage. For the base-rooting varieties, dig a hole at least 16 inches deep and more than 12 inches square. If the ground is clay, fork into the bottom of this hole about four inches of sand, cinders, or fine gravel and one inch of thoroughly rotted leaf mould or peat humus, working it thoroughly and deeply. If the soil is sandy, use more humus. Now tramp this down firmly and water to settle it. Next place in the hole enough good, rich soil (mixed with four handfuls of wood ashes and two of coarse raw bone) to fill it to within six inches of the surface when well tramped. It is important that this soil be thoroughly settled so that the bulb remains at proper depth.

The bulb is then planted in a layer of clean, sharp sand, thick enough to leave three-quarters of an inch of sand above and below the plant. Some authorities recommend a pad of finely shredded peat moss just below the bulb and the sand. This is to give the roots their first start. The soil above the sand need not be fertilized and should not be firmed, but should be settled by watering.

For the stem-rooting varieties, dig the hole 20 inches deep, work in the gravel and peat humus, and fill with soil prepared as above described to 12 inches from the surface. The bulb is then placed in a layer of clean sand above and below and the hole filled with soil and settled by watering. In this instance the topsoil should be fertilized the same as the bottom soil for base-rooting lilies.

It is important that stakes (bamboo canes, 30 inches or more long) be set for each bulb as it is planted. This avoids root injury later.

If the foliage or buds show signs of blight (turn brownish), spray them three or four times a week with bordeaux mixture until the brown disappears. If the bulbs are properly planted in well-drained soil, danger of disease is small.

In cutting the blooms from the plant, be sure to cut reasonably near to the flower, leaving as much as possible of the long green stem. If this is cut off short the plant may die.

Lilies may be planted in spring but may not grow the first year. In this case, protect the spot from cultivation. They will probably come out with renewed life the second season.

Regardless of hardiness, always mulch lilies. All wild plants are mulched naturally each year. Try to imitate natural conditions. To fool the mice, wait until the ground is thoroughly frozen, then cover with one inch of straw or three inches of leaves, held loosely in place. Leave a small part of it in place in spring until all danger of frost is past. Early sprouts must be protected.

The madonna lily. The candidum or madonna lily is the most popular of all lilies but differs from other base-rooting varieties. It thrives best when planted shallow; and it needs a sandy loam, whereas other lilies require clay loam.

It should be planted in August if possible. It has, however, been successfully planted as late as October. The evergreen leaves are carried over the winter and must be protected along with the bulb by mulching after the ground is frozen with several inches of straw or leaves held in place by boughs or wire netting. This mulch is left until all danger of freezing is past. The plant requires full sun and will tolerate a certain amount of lime in the soil, although it does better without it.

Other popular lilies. Some of the most popular lilies are listed below, with a few of their identifying characteristics.

L. auratum (golden-banded Japan lily). Stem-rooting. Ivory spotted and striped. Three to four inches tall. Blooms July, August.

L. canadense (Canadian lily). Medium-sized, orange-yellow flowers, spotted brown. June to August. Two feet tall.

L. batemanniae (Turk's-cap lily). Large pale-orange, red, or apricot. Three to four feet tall. July, August.

L. henryi (yellow show lily). Apricot and yellow. Few spots, stem-rooting. Three to five feet tall. Blooms August.

L. regale platyphyllum (regal lily). Stem-rooting. White, yellow spots. Five to six feet. Blooms July, August.

L. specosium album (white show lily). Stem-rooting. White, greenish stripe. Blooms August and September.

L. specosium rubrum (show lily). Stem-rooting. White-tinted, rose-pink, crimson lots. Blooms August and September.

L. specosium magnificum. Stem-rooting. Large flowers, rosy, crimson. Blooms August and September.

L. tigrinum splendi (tiger lily). Stem-rooting. Bright orange, black spots. Four to five feet high.

L. candidum (madonna). Base-rooting. Fragrant white blooms. Blooms June and July. Three to four feet high. Plant in August if possible.

L. superbum (swamp lily). Base-rooting. Brilliant orange, scarlet-spotted. Five to six feet tall. Blooms July to September.

Montbretia (tritonia) and **tiger flower (tigridia).** These require well-drained soil and a protected location. They should receive much the same culture as gladioli, although they may be wintered with a heavy mulching. They do best in colder locations if they are lifted and stored. They produce flower spikes two to four feet high, orange and yellow in color. Plant them in early May, two to three inches deep and three to six inches apart in large clumps or masses. Plant when the trees are coming out in leaf.

Mariposa (calochortus). These are known as globe tulips, star tulips, mariposa tulips, etc. Mariposa means "butterfly" in Spanish. They have white, red, yellow, pink, lilac, and purple flowers. They grow one to two feet high.

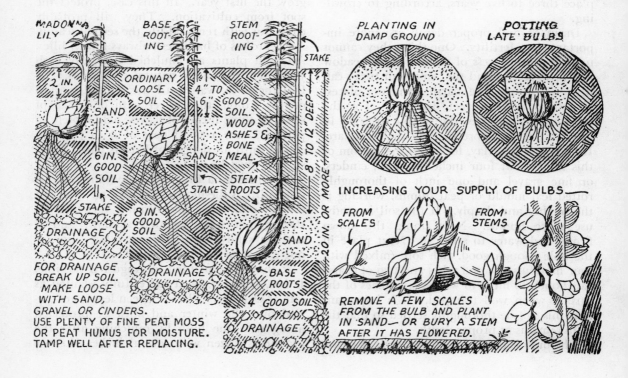

MADONNA LILY — BASE ROOTING — STEM ROOTING — STAKE

2 IN. — SAND — ORDINARY LOOSE SOIL — 4" TO 6" GOOD SOIL. WOOD ASHES & BONE MEAL. — 8" TO 12" DEEP — 20 IN. OR MORE

6 IN. GOOD SOIL — SAND — STEM ROOTS — STAKE ROOTS

STAKE — 8 IN. GOOD SOIL — SAND — BASE ROOTS — 4" GOOD SOIL — DRAINAGE

DRAINAGE — DRAINAGE

FOR DRAINAGE BREAK UP SOIL. MAKE LOOSE WITH SAND, GRAVEL OR CINDERS. USE PLENTY OF FINE PEAT MOSS OR PEAT HUMUS FOR MOISTURE. TAMP WELL AFTER REPLACING.

PLANTING IN DAMP GROUND — POTTING LATE BULBS

INCREASING YOUR SUPPLY OF BULBS

FROM SCALES — FROM STEMS

REMOVE A FEW SCALES FROM THE BULB AND PLANT IN SAND — OR BURY A STEM AFTER IT HAS FLOWERED.

Plant them in well-drained soil in October or November and cover well in early December. Plant two to three inches deep in groups of six to 12, and two to three inches apart. They may be dug and stored after blooming if the bed is to be heavily watered.

Peonies. After blooming, peonies rest somewhat and perfect their foliage. This period is completed in August when a season of intense root activity commences. Fertilize and cultivate monthly. Do not over fertilize. In working around the roots use care not to injure them. A light, double-pointed weeding hoe is good.

Peonies are remarkably free from disease. Many growers have them for years without any disease being manifest. However, there are a few foliage and stem diseases, which may cause bud blight. Many respond to sprays of bordeaux mixture, but botrytis blight sometimes needs a slightly different handling. Botrytis blight does not always show on the foliage, unless in an advanced stage. Dark-colored areas at the base of stems and below the soil level are early indications. If it does not respond to bordeaux mixture, dust it with copper-lime.

Watering in dry weather in early spring or summer may be necessary. Care should be used to keep the water off the foliage and flowers. In extreme dry weather mulching with peat moss or humus is good, but care must be used to keep the peat moss or humus several inches away from the stems. In the fall, plants should be treated with two handfuls of wood ashes and one of steamed bone meal worked into cultivated soil area. Use care to keep fertilizer away from roots. Cut off foliage as soon as frost kills it and burn to avoid spread of disease.

Peonies survive and bloom without all this care, but they do much better with it. Reasons listed for lack of bloom in peonies are as follows:

1. Too deep planting. Look after this in September.
2. Excessive shade. They grow well in partial shade.
3. Poor drainage. They do not like wet feet.
4. Late freezing in spring. Protect temporarily with crates covered with carpet, straw, etc.
5. Root disease.

6. Too small a division in transplanting.
7. Lack of fertility.
8. Lack of moisture at flowering time or at root-building time in late August and September.
9. Loss of moisture by proximity to trees and shrubbery roots.
10. Lack of division and transplanting. Divide every four or five years.

The uses for peonies in landscape design are numerous. In beds or rows by themselves they do very well and they may be mixed with shrubbery or used as a background for the perennial border.

An odd corner may be brightened by using peonies four feet apart each way. The space between should be planted in the fall with early spring-flowering bulbs (snowdrops, croci, scillas, chronodoxas, and early tulips). These are followed by gladioli, hardy lilies, etc. If necessary, a little cutting of the peony foliage will do no harm.

A few don'ts. Don't allow plants to go without transplanting over four or almost five years. They will stop blooming or bloom unsatisfactorily.

Don't try to divide roots in less than three years. At least four eyes to each new root is necessary for quick growth. A smaller amount takes time and the plant may not bloom for years.

Don't bruise or injure roots in transplanting.

Don't buy old clumps. Get new, active roots.

Don't plant in the same place twice if it can be conveniently avoided. New locations help prevent root diseases.

Don't leave earth on clumps to be planted. Wash clean and avoid possible root infection from old peony soil.

Don't plant in a small hole; use one 30 inches wide and two feet deep.

Don't use fresh manure. Better, use no manure unless it is black and decomposed.

Don't let any fertilizer come in contact with roots in any appreciable quantity. Mix it with soil.

Don't transplant all your peonies at once. They are liable to not bloom the following year. Alternate transplanting.

Don't plant in soil too light or too stiff. Make clay friable with sand and humus and haul garden loam in too sandy locations. A

SPRING CARE

HOOP AND STAKE SUPPORT

WELDED WIRE SUPPORT

PLANTS 3' TO 4' APART

30"

EACH SPRING GIVE SPROUTING PLANT A DRESSING OF 1 LARGE TROWEL OF SHEEP MANURE MIXED WITH 1 TABLE SPOON OF CHEMICAL FERTILIZER. WORK INTO CULTIVTED AREA KEEP AWAY FROM ROOTS, STEMS AND LEAVES. AVOID INJURING ROOTS—CULTIVATE 3" TO 4" EACH WEEK.

PROPER SUPPORT

BAD

GOOD

PROPER SUPPORT MAKES SIGHTLY PLANTS AND TAKES LESS ROOM

DISBUDDING

CUT MAIN BUD FOR LATE BLOOM

CUT SIDE BUDS FOR EARLY BLOOM

CUTTING OFF ALL BUT ONE BUD GIVES LARGER AND BETTER FLOWERS. CUT OFF SIDE BUDS FOR EARLIER BLOOM AND THE TOP BUD IF LATER BLOOM IS DESIRED

WATERING

WATERING IS NECESSARY IN DRY WEATHER— ESPECIALLY IN MAY, AUGUST AND SEPTEMBER—DO NOT GET WATER ON LEAVES OR FLOWERS. IF WATER DOES NOT RUN INTO SOIL QUICKLY, MAKE HOLES WITH IRON PIPE OR BAR—BE CAREFUL NOT TO INJURE ROOTS.

SUMMER CARE

WOOD ASHES

FINE STEAMED BONE

AFTER BLOOMING SEASON WORK IN 2 HANDFULS OF WOOD ASHES AND ONE OF FINE STEAMED BONE DUST TO EACH PLANT—CULTIVATE MONTHLY.

SANITATION

REMOVE AND BURN ALL DISCOLORED FOLIAGE

FALL CARE

AVOID POSSIBLE SPREAD OF DISEASE BY CUTTING AWAY AND BURNING FOLIAGE AS SOON AS WILTED BY FROST—DRESS CULTIVATED AREA WITH 1 HANDFULL OF STEAMED BONE AND 2 OF WOOD ASHES

rather heavy clay soil produces the best blooms.

Don't plant too close to trees or shrubbery where robber roots will take away moisture and food.

Don't leave parts of old roots in peony beds when transplanting. They may sprout and cause confusion as to variety after new plants have been arranged.

Planting peonies. Prepare the holes for planting peonies in advance and if possible in a new location. The lower 12 inches of the hole should be filled with friable soil well mixed with perfectly rotted manure and coarse ground raw bone. This slow-acting material is for the future growth of the plant when its new roots shall have reached into it. Tramp this layer of soil well and soak it several days before planting.

Now prepare the topsoil with several handfuls of wood ashes, one of finely ground steamed bone, and a bucket or two of commercial humus. Sprinkle well with hydrated lime or a few handfuls of ground limestone. If possible two people should dig against each other in removing the old plant. Watch this operation in a nursery where trees and shrubbery are dug with a ball. Remove as large a ball of earth as possible. Stay away from the stem 15 to 18 inches. Use forks, not spades. Go as deep as possible. When dug, the roots will be brittle. Allow the ball to be exposed to sun and wind a few hours until the tops wilt, and the roots are more pliable. Wash off the earth with a hose spray until thoroughly clean. Remove the tops to two inches.

Examine roots for diseases; if they have any, they will be knotted or rotted. They are usually discovered in advance by the sickly color of the foliage, thin stalks, and curled leaves. In this case smaller roots should be removed to a large extent and the plant carefully washed of all old soil. Immerse in hot

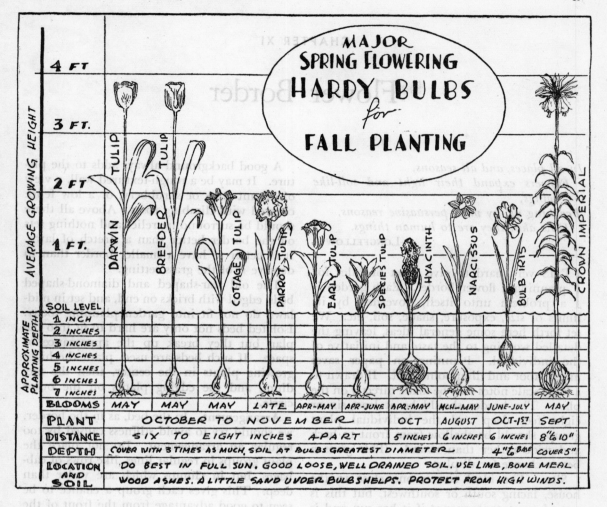

MAJOR SPRING FLOWERING HARDY BULBS for FALL PLANTING

	DARWIN TULIP	BREEDER TULIP	COTTAGE TULIP	PARROT TULIP	EARLY TULIP	SPECIES TULIP	HYACINTH	NARCISSUS	BULB IRIS	CROWN IMPERIAL
BLOOMS	MAY	MAY	MAY	LATE	APR-MAY	APR-JUNE	APR-MAY	MCH-MAY	JUNE-JULY	MAY
PLANT	OCTOBER TO NOVEMBER						OCT	AUGUST	OCT-1ST	SEPT
DISTANCE	SIX TO EIGHT INCHES APART						5 INCHES	6 INCHES	6 INCHES	8" to 10"
DEPTH	COVER WITH 3 TIMES AS MUCH SOIL AT BULBS GREATEST DIAMETER								4" to BARE	COVER 5"
LOCATION AND SOIL	DO BEST IN FULL SUN. GOOD LOOSE, WELL DRAINED SOIL. USE LIME, BONE MEAL WOOD ASHES. A LITTLE SAND UNDER BULBS HELPS. PROTECT FROM HIGH WINDS.									

water (120° F.) for thirty minutes, then plant in a new location. This trouble is from a soil parasite. New location gives it a new chance.

Bend the large clump carefully to find its weakest part and divide there. Cut with a strong, sharp knife. Then subdivide these clumps into strong roots having four or five eyes. Rub the cuts with powdered charcoal. Roots without eyes are worthless.

As the crown of the plant must remain at exactly two inches from the surface, it is essential that all soil be firmed with the fingers, fists, and trowel handle to avoid settling. Water as planting proceeds to settle earth. Use a yardstick to keep depth exact. A root planted too deeply may not bloom the following year, and one too shallow may suffer winter injury. Plant the more delicate colors in somewhat shaded places; give the plants protection from the wind in exposed spots. In selecting roots secure early and late blooming varieties to prolong the blooming season. For vines growing from bulbs see Chapter VIII.

CHAPTER XI

Flower Border

In all places, and all seasons,
  Flowers expand their light and soil-like
    wings,
Teaching us, by most persuasive reasons,
  How akin they are to human things.
                    —LONGFELLOW

IT IS very hard to give a set of rules for planning a flower border. Each garden is a problem unto itself, governed by its limits of size, exposure, shade, soil, etc. We set forth here some general ideas, leaving the detailed working to the taste and initiative of the individual. Planning on paper saves much labor and disappointment. If drawn to a large scale notes may be made directly on the plan. The border should be at least six or eight feet deep and the individual plant groups should be shallow from front to back and wide rather than round. This gives a better chance for display.

Site. The ideal site is one close to the house, facing south or southwest, but this is not of great consequence if it has sun and is away from the robbing roots of trees or shrubbery. No border can be successful if the plants are constantly robbed of food and moisture.

The illustration shows a method of keeping less rampant roots away from the bed. A wall, one brick wide and two feet deep, is placed in the ground between the plants and the flower border. This, of course, is best laid in mortar but loose brick will do if no crevices or openings are left. A wall of tight boards will also last for many years. If boards are used, fill the excavation with cinders to prevent rotting and help keep away roots.

These barricades will do no good against poplars and willows, which have no place in the small garden. Their robber roots will run 20 to 50 feet to stop a drain or desiccate a flower bed. Even with the separating wall, keep the border away from any hedge at least two to three feet.

A good background always adds to the picture. It may be a rough-textured wall, a view of distant trees or shrubbery, or a low fence covered with climbing roses. Above all there should be surrounding relief and nothing sets off the border better than a stretch of lawn. It is better to have a smaller border than to deprive it of the grass setting.

The old star-shaped and diamond-shaped beds, edged with bricks on end, and set in midlawn do not fit into garden planning today. Isolated beds not only are hard to fit into the plan but they break up the appearance of space. If such beds are used, plant the high-growing plants in the center, then the medium, and the edging plants on the outer circle.

Arrangement. In the bed, as in the border, we should try to avoid stiffness caused by too regular an arrangement. Do not place the plant groups in regular lines, like rows of cabbages, but in clumps which are wider than deep. This gives each group a chance to be seen to good advantage from the front of the border.

Of course taller plants (tied to stakes early) should be at the rear, then those of medium height, and the dwarfs in the front. This does not mean that some of the taller plants should not come out into middle ground or that the medium ones cannot be placed toward the front. For the charm of irregularity, break up height lines as well as planting lines. Try to imitate the irregular way in which nature grows her plants and yet place them in order for display, within the limits of your space. Strive for proportion; if the border is very narrow, tall plants should be avoided except for occasional accent. The border will appear topheavy if it is too tall and narrow. Groups should be of sufficient size for display but large masses of single plants in a border are seldom successful. Borders which are more than eight feet wide should have a two-foot grass service path behind them.

We hear a great deal about the gardens of our ancestors which outlasted the stones of the doorstep. This is purely a myth. With few exceptions, perennials must be divided every three or four years. The plant starts from the original clump and grows in all directions. After a while the center exhausts the food within reach and dies, leaving a ring of live growth with a dead center. The best portions of this ring must be lifted and divided. Cut away all dead roots and stalk and start a number of new plants. Make the holes wide enough to spread out the roots. If your bed has been properly prepared they need not be deep. In case of deep-rooted varieties, such as lupin, the holes must be as deep as the root, which should be dug without breaking.

The border must also be done over to correct the encroachments of rampant-growing plants which try to smother their less hardy

20 FEET

ANNUAL HOLLYHOCKS

AFRICAN MARIGOLD

DOUBLE CORNFLOWER

CALENDULA

ANNUAL CHRYSANTHEMUM

PHLOX SUBLATA

DWARF ZINNIA

CALIFORNIA POPPY

ANNUAL LARKSPUR

CANDY TUFT

PINKS

PETUNIA

CALLIOPSIS

VERBENA

SCABIOSA

DWARF PHLOX

DWARF MARIGOLD

ANCHUSA (DWARF)

SWEET ALYSSUM (COLOR)

AGERATUM

TEN WEEKS STOCKS

DWARF LOBELIA

SWEET ALYSSUM (WHITE)

DWARF NASTURTIUMS

GAILLARDIA

SINGLE NASTURTIUM

DWARF BROWALLIA

ZINNIA

ANCHUSA TALL

ASTERS

DELPHINIUM CHINENSE

GIANT SWEET SULTAN

SNAPDRAGON VARIOUS

COSMOS (ALL COLORS)

ARTEMISIA

DOUBLE SUNFLOWER

FOR WIDE BORDERS USE A GRASS WALK ALONG THE REAR

neighbors, and to replace the wayward seedlings which have a habit of growing in the wrong place. The seedlings can usually be turned to good account in regrouping but it is best to discard seedling phlox as it never runs true to original color and invariably disappoints.

Time. Some authorities recommend spring as the time to make over the border. Many things seem in favor of autumn. The weather is more stable in the fall. Any desired changes are fresher in the mind just at the close of the season. When we add to these reasons the freedom from the rush of spring tasks, the more easy identification of plant groups and their limits, and the chance that winter freezing has to pulverize the newly turned soil, it seems that the best time is September or October. This time allows the plants to get a new root start before becoming dormant at freezing time. Be sure to give them water.

Of course some perennials transplant better in the spring. Plants such as chrysanthemums do not divide well so soon after their blooming period. We should move these with as large a clump of earth and as little root disturbance as possible. If division is desired this may be done in the spring when they are more nearly dormant.

The general rule is to try to get well away from their blooming period. Divide spring and early summer perennials in the fall, and late summer bloomers in the spring. Remember this is a general rule and general rules must be used carefully. Phlox and oriental poppies, for instance, must be transplanted shortly after their flowering period to avoid loss of bloom the following season.

Directions for raising plants from seed are given elsewhere in this volume. Some perennial seeds are planted in spring and bloom the first year. Some are planted in fall just before frost in a sheltered spot under shrubbery, convenient for winter inspection. They seem to need freezing to germinate. The majority, however, do best sown in summer. Be sure to get good fresh seed.

Divisions of perennials or propagation by cuttings are the sure methods of having plants come true to color and shade.

Preparation of the bed. The digging and preparation of a bed is very important. There are few border perennials which are not better for drainage and friable soil, but few amateur gardens have properly prepared subsoil. The bottom soil need not be as well tilled as the top but once prepared it will last for many years, making it necessary to renew only the fertility of the topsoil from time to time.

If the bottom soil is heavy, incorporate in it some sand, cinders, or ashes to break it up. Lime is one of the best soil looseners and will compact sandy soil. Use it generously in the bottom spit. Work into it also a lot of partially decayed leaves, grass clippings, manure, peat moss, or humus. If the soil is sandy you may add clay or a large amount of vegetable matter. Do not firm it down but let it settle naturally.

The top should be made into fine loam by the addition of sand, if heavy, and well-rotted manure, humus, peat moss, or finely sifted leaf mould. Bone meal is very useful and should be used generously. Keep plant roots away from immediate contact with manure, for it is likely to burn them no matter how well rotted it appears. Wood ashes in the spring are excellent. Lime may be used in the topsoil for loosening. Most perennials grow well in limed soil. Lilies and acid plants, however, will need special ground treatment to overcome alkalinity.

After the bed has been double dug it will be higher than before but will soon settle. In planting, however, care must be used to firm the earth around the roots. Air pockets in the soil adjoining the roots may cause loss of plants.

It is a good plan to divide the bed into three or four sections, doing over one section each year. In this way the entire job is done over completely every three or four years without so much effort at any one time. During the spring rush, weeding must sometimes be entrusted to unskilled labor. The use of these divisions makes it possible to point out plant and weed vegetation in any one area and in the summer, too, it spots quickly the encroachments of more rapid growers.

The pegs, which should be light and about 15 inches long, should be driven 12 to 13 inches into the ground. The wire should be stretched loosely along the ground so that it will not pull upon the pegs if trampled. It will soon weather into invisibility.

Selection of plants. Selection of plants for the flower border is a weighty problem. All amateurs must expect to learn by experience the trial-and-error method. This means plant-

DIGGING

1 ST. SPIT

2 FT.

2 ND. SPIT

(MANURE HUMUS) GOOD GARDEN LOAM

FOR CLAY SOIL, MIX WITH SAND, LEAVES, HUMUS OR MANURE. FOR SANDY SOIL, USE MORE HUMUS, MANURE, ETC.

SHAPING

CIRCULAR

ELLIPTICAL

RECTANGULAR

USE A GARDEN HOSE TO SEE HOW THE IRREGULAR BED WILL LOOK

SEPARATING

USING A STRONG WIRE AND PEGS TO MARK THE BOUNDERIES OF PLANT AREAS MAKES SPRING WEEDING EASIER —

SHADE OR ACID PLANTS

A BRICK WALL WILL KEEP ROOTS FROM PERENNIAL BEDS —

4 IN. COURSE

BRICK 2 FT. HIGH

2 IN. GRAVEL OR COARSE CINDERS   1 IN HOLES

PLANT SHADE LOVING PLANTS IN TUBS TO PROTECT THEM FROM TREE ROOTS — ALSO ACID PLANTS, TO PROTECT THEM FROM SURROUNDING ALKALINE SOIL

DIVIDING

DIVIDE CLUMPS OF PERENNIALS, USING LIVEST PART OF THE OUTER RING OF PLANTS

FALL SOWING

SHADE

SOME SEEDS RESPOND BEST TO LATE FALL SOWING IN SPECIALLY PREPARED BEDS.

ing and testing after carefully studying your plant lists, looking up in several good catalogues the description of such plants as are not familiar. Use plant encyclopedias, such as Bailey's *Encyclopedia of Horticulture*, Bailey's *Manual of Cultivated Plants,* and other books in your public library, as well as the many free bulletins published by the United States Department of Agriculture and by your own state college and experiment stations.

Read and consult such works as *Home Flower Growing* (E. C. Volz), *One Thousand and One Garden Questions Answered* (Hottes), and the many others which are available at libraries.

Below is a list of points to be considered in acquiring the knowledge necessary to perfect plant selection. It is taken from *Home Flower Growing,* mentioned above.

"1. Length of life of the plant. Is it annual, biennial, or perennial?

2. Height under different soil and moisture conditions.

3. Lateral spread or breadth.

4. Growing habit, prostrate, erect or climbing.

5. Time and length of flowering period.

6. Color of flowers.

7. Color of foliage.

8. Persistence of foliage and decorative effect.

9. Moisture requirements.

10. Soil and plant food requirements.

11. Sun or shade loving.

12. Hardiness in a given region.

13. Does the plant spread freely?

14. Best methods of propagation."

We cannot hope to get this knowledge without observation, study, and trial over several seasons. We must know how long they last, when and how long they bloom, their color, their height, their texture of foliage, and their freedom of growth before we can consider them for placing. We can gain much of this information from plant lists.

Then we must add to this a knowledge of their soil and location requirements, their insect and disease enemies, and their hardiness under our weather conditions.

Many questions are asked concerning the disappearance of various plants and their reverting to other colors. Of course plants die for various reasons, but many times the amateur confuses a biennial (a plant lasting only two years) with a perennial which, under proper conditions, reproduces indefinitely. Many annuals are also confusing because they are self-sowing and come up each spring from seed.

Apparent change of color is due to the fact that the parent plant has perished from disease or lack of division or other care, and that its place has been taken by seedlings which do not run true.

Knowledge of height and freedom of growth is necessary for display in the border. Dwarf plants behind tall ones or plants hidden by the more spreading ones do us no good. We must remember that spread and height will be governed by the soil, water, and food which we supply, and by the shade and chemical condition of our soil.

Color. We see many lists of flowers for the blue garden, flowers for the white garden, etc. Few amateurs have space for such distinct features. The charm of the perennial border is change and we should strive for succession of bloom rather than for many everblooming flowers.

Color combination is much easier in the border planting than in preparing a bouquet or matching the colors of a costume. The amateur must not strive for too much close harmony. Even the best or colorists fail sometimes and to plan too cleverly is to open the door to disappointment.

Do not be afraid to mix colors. They are usually separated by green foliage. White or shades of cream or gray are always safe separation. They are the canvas on which we paint our color picture. Of course too much white will give an impression of coldness. Such dominating strong-colored plants as oriental poppy should be separated from their more delicately shaded neighbors by a space of white-blooming selections or plants of good foliage which bloom at other times. Some of our favorites of strong color spoil pastel beauty if too near. Omit massing such plants as bright red salvia; they clash with almost everything. Plant them separately or among greens. Red is the hardest color in the border. Softer colors are safer and need no great care of separation.

The following are a few color combinations which will mix well:

Blue (pale) with rose pink; blue with other shades of pink must shade together

Blue (deep) with pastel yellow; avoid deep yellow

Blue with orange, if red is kept away

Orange with bronze

Yellow with orange

Yellow with purple

Yellow with blue (equal shades)

Yellow with pink (equal pastel shades) except lavender pink

First in selection should be our accent plants, and those which are to be the backbone of planting: iris, peony, larkspur, columbine, veronica, Canterbury bells, chrysanthemum, hollyhock, phlox, asters, pinks, lupin, lily, anemone, etc. The red foliage of Japanese maple forms a pleasing foliage contrast and pyramidal evergreens are used as occasional accent or to break up height lines. Any border which is dependent upon too large a massing of one species is likely to become uninteresting as the season advances and the blooming period of these varieties expires. Change from week to week adds interest and there is also the safety of numbers. The failure of one planting does not spoil the season. Continuous bloom—an uninterrupted show of colors, from spring to fall—is feasible by selection. The garden need not go dead in August.

Annuals. Annuals are the answer to the vacant-space problem. The little effort needed to raise them, coupled with their low cost and easy maintenance, makes them very popular. They make the finest of cut flowers and used in a border of their own or among the dominating perennials they have many places of value. In rented property or for a short season at a summer home they have no equal.

Sown with bulbs they cover the space before or after the bulbs bloom and make it unnecessary to lift them before they ripen. Also they easily cover the bare spots left by early maturing or failure of perennials.

A secluded bed from which annuals and such showy plants as gladioli may be borrowed does much to fill out the summer deficiencies of the border. Many annuals may be easily transplanted, when small, to pots to mature until needed in the border. Gladioli are planted directly in good-sized pots from which they are easily set into the vacant spaces to be filled.

Care of the border. The chief requisites for success with annuals are good soil, proper location, and first-class, fresh seeds.

Seeds purchased from reliable companies are grown by experts in soil selected for their needs. Home-grown seed is usually unreliable, and mixed seeds rarely give satisfaction. Both annuals and perennials may be stimulated with chemical plant food but care must be used to avoid an excess of nitrogen or the plant will go to leaves at the expense of bloom. Plant tablets used one to the plant once a month are the best form of balanced ration. Chemical fertilizers add nothing to the soil. They are a short-time stimulant.

Just prior to and during the blooming season, liquid manure will give wonderful results in increasing size and quality of bloom. Get ahead of insects and disease. Spray with bordeaux mixture the crowns of plants that are subject to mildew (peonies, phlox, delphiniums, and hollyhocks) and spray often, dusting the soil with sulphur. Use arsenate of lead for holes in leaves and nicotine sulphate or pyrethrum for plant lice. When hollyhock, peonies, etc., wilt or break off easily, look for the stem borer. Pierce the holes with a wire or cut open the stem and kill.

Cut and remove hollyhock, foxglove, phlox, and delphinium stalks as fast as they fade. Burn them to keep down mildew and black spot. Plants subject to ground pests, such as asters, should have powdered tobacco mixed generously with the immediate topsoil when planted and again just before bloom. Sulphur and tobacco are usually safe things to mix in the soil around the plant.

Especially remember each fall to remove and burn all dead stalks, leaves, and branches of dormant perennials or dead annuals. This is destroying just so many spores or eggs against next year's crop of insects and fungus. Mulching material will do double work if five per cent tobacco dust is incorporated in it.

Cultivate often until July 1 and then if you wish to avoid labor and watering try mulching with one inch peat humus or peat moss, keeping this material slightly away from the stem. This can be raked off in the fall or left to be cultivated into the soil in the spring. Cultivation is necessary for the entrance of moisture and air. Bacteria cannot exist without air in the soil, and plants cannot grow without bacteria. Break up the ground as soon as it dries sufficiently in spring and repeat after each rain until July 1.

Pinch back tops for compact plants. In dry spells water thoroughly, rather than often. Stake such tall plants as delphinium at once. Tie raffia strip to the stake first and then to the plant. Remove all blossoms as soon as they fade to induce a prolonged flowering season. A second flowering can be secured from such plants as Canterbury bells by this method. Cut delphinium stalks to the ground after flowering to get new bloom stalks. Pansies bloom indefinitely if not allowed to seed.

Winter protection. Winter protection is something that is generally misunderstood. We do not use a mulch to keep plants warm but to keep them cold. Sudden changes in temperature causes the ground to heave and to break tiny roots. Warm days followed by cold nights do much damage, and most winter killing is from this cause rather than from extreme cold.

Therefore, as one writer puts it, we use the mulch as a parasol, not as a blanket. If we place a layer of hardwood leaves, which take a long time to decay, over the bed, it lies loose during the whole season if lightly held in place with brush or wire. It must be light and airy and stay dry. If we use ordinary leaves they soon pack into a heavy wet mass, which excludes air, smothers the plants, and induces decay. In the spring this type of leaf

WINTER PROTECTION

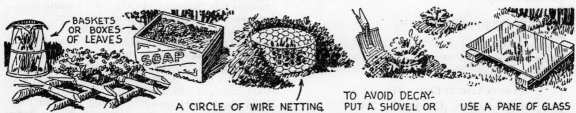

AFTER A GOOD FREEZE A NETWORK OF CORN STALKS OR BRUSH WILL KEEP LEAF MULCH FROM SMOTHERING THE PLANTS

A CIRCLE OF WIRE NETTING, 6 IN. HIGH, WILL KEEP COVERS AWAY FROM PLANTS HAVING WINTER FOLIAGE AND KEEP MULCH ON SURROUNDING GROUND

TO AVOID DECAY— PUT A SHOVEL OR TWO OF COAL ASHES AROUND DELPHINIUMS AFTER THE COLD WEATHER STARTS.

USE A PANE OF GLASS FOR THE MANY ALPINES AND OTHER PLANTS THAT NEED PROTECTION AGAINST MOISTURE ferments and produces heat which helps the dormant plants to awaken too soon and defeats the very purpose for which it was placed over them.

All protection should be applied only when the ground is well frozen. Remember it is to keep the bed cold. Do not cover too early. Let the mice find a winter home first. If they nest in your mulch they may feed upon your roots and bulbs.

Do not cover the plants which carry leaves over the winter. Use a row of stakes or poultry netting to keep mulch away.

Sometimes it is necessary to further protect plants which come to us from warmer climates (tritonias, etc.). Use boxes of leaves or baskets loosely filled with leaves and protected from moisture by roughly formed sheet-metal roofs. Fuzzy-leaf alpines and rock plants often winter better if protected from moisture by panes of glass.

If we start our borders with simple plants, hardy in our localities, they will need no coddling. We may then add to them, one by one, those plants whose needs we master from time to time.

Many of the following items are taken from Ohio Bulletin 525, also from "Annual Flowers" by Victor Reis.

Some Perennials Whose Leaves and Roots Should Not Be Covered

Alyssum (perennial)
Candytuft (Iberis sempervirens)
Campanula medium
Coral Bells
Coreopsis
Delphinium
English Daisy
Flax (perennial)
Forget-me-not
Foxgloves
Germander
Grass Pink (Dianthus plumarius)
Hollyhocks
Hardy bulbs
Iris (Bearded Dutch, etc.)
Madonna Lily
Pansy
Perennial Poppy (Oriental, etc.)
Rock Cress
Sedums (various)
Sweet William
Violas

Plants Which Easily Winter Kill

Campanula medium (Canterbury Bells)
Digitalis purpurea (Foxglove)
Early-flowered Chrysanthemums
Salvia patens (Gentian Sage)
Shasta Daisy

If you have been disappointed with these plants, try removing them to the cold frame for the winter. Heavy outside mulching results in crown rot. Cover with leaves (consult list number one and cover roots only), straw or evergreen boughs and keep dry by covering frame with boards.

Seeds Which Should Be Sown in the Fall

Actaea (Baneberry)
xAconitum (Monkshood)
xAdonis (Adonis)
Anthericum (St. Bernard Lily)
*xBaptisia (Wild Indigo)
Bellis (English Daisy)
Bocconia (Plume Poppy)
Cassia (Senna)
Catananche (Everlasting)
Cimicifuga (Bugbane)
*Clematis
*Delphinium (Larkspur)
Dicentra (Bleeding Heart)
*xDictamnus (Gasplant)
Echinops (Globe Thistle)
*Funkia (Plantain Lily)
Gunnera (Prickly Rhubarb)
xHelleborus (Christmas Rose)
Hypericum (St. John's Wort)
Liatris (Gayfeather)
Lobelia
Oenothera (Evening Primrose)
Pardanthus (Blackberry Lily)
xPhlox decussata (Hardy Phlox)
xPrimula polyantha (Cluster Primrose)
Romneya coulteri (California Tree Poppy)
Sidalcea (Prairie Mallow)
Silene (Catch Fly)
xSpiraea and Trollius (Globe Flower)

Plants to Be Handled as Biennials (Renew Every Other Year)

Althaea rosea (Hollyhock)
Anchusa azurea (Alkanet)
Campanula medium (Canterbury Bells)
Campanula pyramidalis (Chimney Bellflower)
Dianthus barbatus (Sweet William)
Digitalis purpurea (Foxglove)
Hesperis matronalis (Sweet Rocket)
Lunaria biennis (Honesty, Money plant)

Perennials Enduring Shady Conditions

Aconitum Fischeri (Azure Monkshood)
Ajuga genevensis (Geneva Bugle)
Amsonia tabernaemontana (Willow Amsonia)
Anemonella thalictroides (Rue Anemone)
Convallaria majalis (Lily-of-the-valley)
Cornus canadensis (Bunchberry)
Dicentra eximia (Fringed Bleedingheart)
Dodecatheon meadia (Shooting Star)
Helleborus niger (Christmas Rose)
Hosta caerulea (Blue Plantain Lily)
Hosta plantaginea grandiflora (Big Plantain Lily)

x—Do not bloom for several years after germination.
*—Seeds which lose their vitality quickly and must be sown as soon as they ripen.

Lobelia cardinalis (Cardinal Flower)
Mertensia virginica (Virginia Blue Bells)
Myosotis palustris semperflorens (Dwarf Perpetual
   Forget-me-not)
Polygonatum biflorum (Small Solomon Seal)
Thalictrum adiantifolium (Low Meadowrue)
Trillium grandiflorum (Snow Trillium)

PERENNIALS ENDURING SEMISHADY CONDITIONS

Anchusa italica (Dropmore Bugloss)
Anemone japonica (Japanese Anemone)
Aquilegia hybrids (Columbine)
Asperula odorata (Woodruff)
Belamcanda chinensis (Blackberry Lily)
Campanula rotundifolia (Hare Bell)
Chelone Lyoni (Pink Turtlehead)
Cimicifuga racemosa (Cohosh Bugbane)
Digitalis purpurea (Common Foxglove)
Doronicum plantagineum (Leopardbane)
Heracleum villosum (Cow Parsnip)
Heuchera sanguinea (Coral Bells)
Monarda didyma (Bee Balm)
Primula veris (Cowslip Primrose)
Pulmonaria saccharata (Bethlehem Lungwort)
Silene pennsylvanica (Peat Pink)
Trollius europaeus (Globe Flower)

PERENNIALS REQUIRING WELL-DRAINED SITUATIONS

Arabis alpina (Alpine Rock Cress)
Asclepias tuberosa (Butterflyweed)
Aubrietia deltoidea (Purple Rock Cress)
Coreopsis grandiflora (Tickseed)
Delphinium hybrids (Delphinium)
Dianthus barbatus (Sweet William)
Digitalis purpurea (Common Foxglove)
Echinops ritro (Steel Globe Thistle)
Eryngium maritimum (Seaholly)
Gaillardia aristata (Blanket Flower)
Globularia trichosantha (Globe Daisy)
Helianthus Maximiliani (Maximilian Sunflower)
Iris germanica (German Iris)
Liatris pycnostachya (Cattail Gayfeather)
Papaver nudicaule (Iceland Poppy)

PERENNIALS FOR DRY, SANDY SOILS

Achillea ptarmica (Sneezewort)
Ajuga reptans (Geneva Bugle)
Anthemis tinctoria (Yellow Camomile)
Asclepias tuberosa (Butterflyweed)
Aster novae-angliae (New England Aster)
Callirhoe involucrata (Poppymallow)
Cassia marilandica (Wild Senna)
Coreopsis grandiflora (Tickseed)
Dianthus plumarius (Grass Pink)
Echinops ritro (Steel Globe Thistle)
Euphorbia corollata (Flowering Spurge)
Helianthus (various) (Sunflower)
Limonium latifolium (Statice) (Bigleaf Statice)
Lychnis chalcedonica (Maltese Cross)
Papaver nudicaule (Iceland Poppy)
Rudbeckia laciniata (Goldenglow)
Yucca filamentosa (Common Yucca)

PERENNIALS FOR WET SITUATIONS

Arundo donax* (Giant Reed)
Asclepias incarnata (Swamp Milkweed)

Boltonia asteroides (White Boltonia)
Caltha palustris* (Marsh Marigold)
Eupatorium purpureum (Joe-pye-weed)
Helenium autumnale (Sneezeweed)
Hibiscus moscheutos (Rosemallow)
Iris pseudacorus* (Yellow Flag)
Iris versicolor* (Blueflag)
Lobelia cardinalis (Cardinalflower)
Lysimachia clethroides (Clethra Loosestrife)
Lythrum salicaria (Loosestrife)
Miscanthus sinensis (Eulalia)
Monarda didyma (Bee Balm)
Myosotis palustris (True Forget-me-not)
Onoclea sensibilis (Sensitive Fern)
Osmunda cinnamonea (Cinnamon Fern)
Osmunda regalis* (Royal Fern)
Sarracenia purpurea (Pitcherplant)

PERENNIALS FOR BORDERS OF PONDS AND STREAMS

(Well-drained soil)

SUNNY LOCATIONS

Anchusa myosotidiflora (Siberian Bugloss)
Chrysanthemum uliginosum (Giant Daisy)
Cimicifuga racemosa (Cohosh Bugbane)
Grasses (Ornamental grasses)
Hemerocallis (various) (Day Lily)
Iris (various) (Iris)
Lythrum salicaria (Loosestrife)
Myosotis palustris semperflorens (Dwarf Perpetual
   Forget-me-not)
Tradescantia virginiana (Spiderwort)
Trollius europaeus (Globe Flower)

SEMISHADY LOCATIONS

Anemone japonica (Japanese Anemone)
Cimicifuga racemosa (Cohosh Bugbane)
Epimedium macranthum (Longspur Epimedium)
Eupatorium purpureum (Joe-pye-weed)
Ferns (Ferns)
Iris cristata (Crested Iris)
Lythrum salicaria (Loosestrife)
Tradescantia virginiana (Spiderwort)

PERENNIALS FOR NATURALIZING

Asclepias tuberosa (Butterflyweed)
Aster (various) (Aster)
Cimicifuga racemosa (Cohosh Bugbane)
Convallaria majalis (Lily-of-the-valley)
Coreopsis grandiflora (Tickseed)
Geranium maculatum (Spotted Geranium)
Helianthus (various) (Sunflower)
Hemerocallis (various) (Roundlobe Hepatica)
Lythrum salicaria (Loosestrife)
Mertensia virginica (Virginia Bluebells)
Monarda didyma (Bee Balm)
Physostegia virginica (False Dragonhead)
Polemonium reptans (Creeping Polemonium)
Rudbeckia subtomentose (Sweet Coneflower)
Sanguinaria canadensis (Bloodroot)
Smilacina racemosa (False Solomonseal)
Solidago canadensis (Canada Goldenrod)

---

* May be grown in water.

PERENNIALS FOR GROUND COVER

SUNNY LOCATIONS

Cerastium tomentosum (Snow-in-summer)
Ceratostigma plumbaginoides (Larpente Plumbago)
Coronilla varia (Crownvetch)
Dianthus plumarius (Grass Pink)
Helianthemum mutabile (Fickle Sunrose)
Iberis sempervirens (Evergreen Candytuft)
Nepeta Mussini (Mussini Mint)
Phlox subulata (Moss Phlox)
Sedum sarmentosum (Stringy Stonecrop)
Sedum spurium (Running Stonecrop)
Thymus serphyllum (Mother-of-thyme)
Veronica teucrium (rupestris) (Rock Speedwell)
Vinca minor (Periwinkle)

SHADY LOCATIONS

Aegopodium podograria (Goutweed)
Ajuga reptans (Geneva Bugle)
Asperula odorata (Woodruff)
Convallaria majalis (Lily-of-the-valley)
Hedera helix (English Ivy)
Mitchella repens (Partridgeberry)
Nepeta Mussini (Mussini Mint)
Pachysandra terminalis (Japanese Pachysandra)
Sedum ternatum (Mountain Stonecrop)
Vinca minor (Periwinkle)

PERENNIALS FOR COVERING BANKS AND TERRACES

Ajuga reptans (Geneva Bugle)
Alyssum saxtile (Goldentuft)
Arabis alpina (Alpine Rockcress)
Cerastium tomentosum (Snow-in-summer)
Coronilla varia (Crownvetch)
Dianthus deltoides (Maiden Pink)
Hedera helix (English Ivy)
Nepeta Mussini (Nepeta)
Pachysandra terminalis (shade) (Japanese Pachysandra)
Phlox subulata (Moss Phlox)
Saponaria ocymoides (Rock Soapwort)
Sedum sarmentosum (Stringy Stonecrop)
Veronica teucrium (rupestris) (Rock Speedwell)
Vinca minor (Periwinkle)

PERENNIALS FOR EDGING

Aegopodium podograria (Goutweed)
Ajuga reptans (Geneva Bugle)
Alyssum saxatile compactum (Dwarf Goldentuft)
Arabis alpina (Alpine Rockcress)
Bellis perennis (English Daisy)
Campanula carpatica (Carpathian Bellflower)
Cerastium tomentosum (Snow-in-summer)
Ceratostigma plumbaginoides (Larpente Plumbago)

Dianthus plumarius (Grass Pink)
Festuca plauca (Blue Fescue)
Heuchera sanguinea (Coralbells)
Iberis sempervirens (Evergreen Candytuft)
Papaver nudicaule (Iceland Poppy)
Primula veris (Cowslip Primrose)
Sedum album (White Stonecrop)
Sedum reflexum (Jenny Stonecrop)
Statice armeria (Thrift)
Tunica saxifraga (Tunicflower)
Veronica teucrium (rupestris) (Rock Speedwell)
Viola cornuta (Tufted Pansy)

PERENNIALS FOR BACKGROUND PLANTING

Althea rosea (Hollyhock)
Aster novae-angliae (New England Aster)
Aster tataricus (Tartarian Aster)
Bocconia cordata (Plume Poppy)
Boltonia asteroides (White Boltonia)
Campanula pyramidalis (Chimney Bellflower)
Cimicifuga racemosa (Cohosh Bugbane)
Delphinium hybrids (Delphinium)
Helenium autumnale (Sneezeweed)
Helianthus Maximiliani (Maximilian Sunflower)
Hibiscus grandiflorus (Great Rosemallow)
Rudbeckia laciniata (Goldenglow)
Solidago altissima (Tall Goldenrod)
Valeriana officinalis (Common Valerian)
Yucca filamentosa (Common Yucca)

PERENNIALS SUITABLE FOR CUT FLOWERS

Achillea millefolium rosea (Pink Yarrow)
Anemone japonica (Japanese Anemone)
Aster (various) (Aster)
Chrysanthemum maximum (Shasta Daisy)
Coreopsis grandiflora (Tickseed)
Delphinium hybrids (Delphinium)
Dianthus barbatus (Sweet William)
Gaillardia aristata (Blanket Flower)
Gypsophila paniculata (Babysbreath)
Helenium autumnale (Sneezeweed)
Iris (various) (Iris)
Paeonia (various) (Peony)
Pyrethrum roseum (Painted Lady)
Rudbeckia (various) (Cone Flower)
Salvia azurea grandiflora (Azure Sage)
Veronica longifolia subsessilis (Clump Speedwell)

FRAGRANT PERENNIALS

Centranthus ruber (Jupiter's Beard)
Convallaria majalis (Lily-of-the-valley)
Dianthus plumarius (Grass Pink)
Hemerocallis flava (Lemon Daylily)
Hosta plantaginea grandiflora (Big Plantain Lily)
Lathyrus grandiflorus (Perennial Pea)
Valeriana officinalis (Common Valerian)
Viola cornuta (Tufted Pansy)

EASILY GROWN, HARDY PERENNIALS

The Varieties Marked R are Particularly Suited for the Rock Garden

	COLOR	BLOOMING SEASON	HEIGHT	LOCATION
Achillea (Milfoil) Boule de Neige	White	July–Oct.	2 ft.	Dry, sunny
Achillea Perry's White	White	July–Oct.	1–2 ft.	Dry, sunny
Acorus Calamus (Sweet Flag)	Yellow	June–Aug.	2 ft.	Marshy
Agrostemma coronaria (Rose Campion)	Deep crimson	July–Aug.	2½ ft.	Dry, sunny
R Alyssum saxatile compactum (Gold Dust)	Yellow	April–May	6 ins.	Dry, stony
R Aquilegia (Columbine) alpina	Blue	May–June	1–2 ft.	
R Aquilegia cœrulea	Blue and white	May–June	1½–2½ ft.	Sunny or semi-shade
Aquilegia chrysantha alba	White	May–June	2–3 ft.	
Aquilegia Pink Shades	Pink	May–June	2–3 ft.	Moist loam soil
Aquilegia nivea grandiflora	White	May–July	2–3 ft.	
R Armeria formosa (Sea Pink)	Pink	May–Aug.	12 ins.	Sandy
R Armeria formosa alba	White	May–Aug.	12 ins.	Sandy
R Armeria Laucheana	Bright rose	May–July	3–6 ins.	Sunny
Aster Belgian Queen	Bluish lilac	Sept.–Oct.	3–4 ft.	Average garden
Aster Emilie Thoury	Light blue	Sept.–Oct.	3–4 ft.	soil, sunny
R Aster Mauve Cushion	Light mauve	Oct.–Nov.	9 ins.	partial shade
Baptisia australis (False Indigo)	Dark blue	May–July	2–3 ft.	Sunny, rich soil
Centaurea Montana	Blue	June–Sept.	15 ins.	Sunny border
R Cerastium tomentosum	White	May–July	6 ins.	Sunny border
Chelone Lyoni (Shell Flower)	Rosy purple	July–Sept.	3–4 ft.	Sunny or shade
R Dianthus deltoides (Maiden Pink)	Pink	June–July	9 ins.	Sunny, dry
R Dianthus plumarius (Cyclop)	White and crimson	May	6–8 ins.	Sunny, dry
Euphorbia corollata (Spurge)	White	June–Aug.	18 ins.	Sunny, dry
Heliopsis pitcheriana (Hardy Zinnia)	Orange	July–Sept.	3 ft.	Sunny
Heliopsis scabra zinniæflora	Yellow	July–Aug.	2–3 ft.	Sunny
Hemerocallis aurantiaca (Day Lily)	Orange-yellow	June–Sept.	3 ft.	Moist, semishade
Hemerocallis minor (Dwarf Day Lily)	Bright yellow	June	1 ft.	Moist, semishade
Hesperis matronalis (Sweet Rocket)	Purple	June–July	2–3 ft.	Moist, sunny
Hesperis matronalis alba	White	June–July	2–3 ft.	Moist, sunny
R Linum perenne (Blue Perennial Flax)	Blue	June–Aug.	2 ft.	Sunny
R Linum perenne (White)	White	June–Aug.	2 ft.	Sunny
Lobelia cardinalis (Cardinal Flower)	Rich red	Aug.–Oct.	2–2½ ft.	Moist, rich soil
Lobelia syphilitica (Great Blue Lobelia)	Blue and white	July–Sept.	2½–3 ft.	Moist, rich soil
Monarda, Cambridge Scarlet (Bergamot)	Scarlet	June–July	3 ft.	Sun or semishade
R Myosotis palustris semperflorens	Blue	June–Oct.	1 ft.	Moist, shady
Pentstemon barbatus Torreyi	Scarlet	June–Sept.	2–3½ ft.	Rich, sunny
R Phlox amoena	Rose-pink	April–June	6 ins.	Sunny and dry
Physalis Franchetti (Chinese Lantern)	Scarlet seed pods	Sept.–Oct.	2 ft.	Sun or semishade
Polemonium cœruleum (Jacob's Ladder)	Sky-blue	April–Sept.	1–1½ ft.	Semishade, well-drained
Polemonium album	White	April–Sept.	1–1½ ft.	Semishade, well-drained
R Potentilla formosa (Cinquefoil)	Cherry-rose	June–Sept.	2 ft.	Sunny, bright soil
R Potentilla rupestris	White	June	1 ft.	Sunny, bright soil
Ranunculus acris fl. pl. (Buttercup)	Yellow	April–Aug.	2 ft.	Moist, sunny
R Ranunculus repens fl. pl.	Golden-yellow	May–June	3–4 ins.	Moist, sunny
Rudbeckia Newmani (Cone Flower)	Gold, black center	Aug.–Sept.	2–3 ft.	Sun or shade
R Ruta Patavina (Paduan Rue)	Yellow	June	1 ft.	Shady
Salvia azurea	Light blue	June–Aug.	2–3 ft.	Sunny border
R Sedum acre (Wall Pepper)	Yellow	June–Aug.	3 ins.	Sunny, dry, or semishade
R Sedum album	White	June–July	3 ins.	Sunny, dry, or semishade
R Sedum ibericum (Spurium)	Pink	August	6 ins.	Sunny, dry, or semishade
R Sedum kamtschaticum (Evergreen)	Yellow	June–July	6 ins.	Sunny, dry, or semishade
Sedum spectabile, Brilliant	Deep red	Aug.–Sept.	16 ins.	Sun or shade
Spiraea ulmaria fl. pl. (Meadow Sweet)	Creamy white	July–Aug.	5 ft.	Sun or shade
Veronica amethystina (Speedwell)	Deep blue	May–July	2 ft.	Good garden soil
R Viola Blue Perfection	Deep blue	May–Oct.		Semishade or sun, rich soil
R Viola G. Wermig	Violet-blue	May–Oct.		Semishade or sun, rich soil
R Viola G. Wermig alba	White	May–Oct.	6 ins.	Semishade or sun, rich soil
R Viola lutea splendens	Golden-yellow	April–Sept.		Semishade or sun, rich soil
R Viola papilio (Butterfly Violet)	Violet and dark blue	April–Sept.		Semishade or sun, rich soil

ANNUAL FLOWERS

Accepted scientific name is in italics, unaccepted name in parentheses.

Symbols: H.—Height of plant. P.D.—Planting distance.

Ageratum. *A. houstonianum* (mexicanum) H.—6 to 24″ P.D.—8 to 12″

A charming, constant bloomer, essential in every garden. The dwarf and compact forms are generally preferred to the tall ones. The blue-violet color combines with practically any other garden color, but the white varieties are not as decorative. Start seed early indoors. It will sometimes self-sow.

Amaranthus. *Amaranthus.* H.—3 to 5′ P.D. —2′

A coarse group of plants, related to cockscomb and pigweed, some with colored foliage, others with long red spikes of flowers. They should be used sparingly, if at all, and then only with the coarser annuals and shrubs. They will stand the hottest and driest locations.

Arctotis. *Arctotis grandis.* Blue Eyed African Daisy. H.—24″ P.D.—8 to 12″

A day-time bloomer, closing at night, white flowers, lilac blue outside, effective gray-green foliage. Easily grown in the borders. Good for cutting.

Balsam. *Impatiens balsamina.* H.—18″ P.D. —12″

An old-fashioned favorite but with flowers too much hidden by the leaves to be really effective. Rather formal, compact form of growth; sensitive to frost, will usually be grown more through association than desire for the flowers. It will often self-sow.

Bartonia. *Mentzelia aurea.* (Bartonia) H. —12″ P.D.—8 to 12″

An interesting but little grown plant with grayish foliage and gorgeous golden flowers. Sow the seed where it is to bloom.

Blistercress. *Erysimum perofskianum.* (Annual Wallflower). H.—12 to 15″ P.D.—8″

A really delightful flower resembling an orange wallflower. Although blooming best in cool weather it is worthy of trial. It will often self-sow and even naturalize.

Browallia. *Browallia.* H.—12″ P.D.—12″

Effective and free blooming, it makes an excellent filler among tulips, where if winter mulched it will often self-sow. The flowers are good for cutting as well as garden effect.

Both *B. speciosa* and *B. demissa* (*alata*) should be grown. Potted up in fall they will bloom during winter.

Butterflyflower. *Schizanthus pinnatus.* H.— 2 to 3′ P.D.—15 to 18″

Although commonly grown as a greenhouse plant, it is worthy of garden culture. It will appreciate just a little shade from the intense sun and several pinchings back to make it more bushy. Foliage attractive, flowers interesting.

Cape bugloss. *Anchusa capensis.* H.—12″ P.D.—6 to 8″

It is surprising that this gorgeous blue flower is not grown more extensively. A constant bloomer under all conditions, it supplies the clear blue given only by the forget-me-not and Chinese forget-me-not. It will often self-sow.

California poppy. *Eschscholtzia californica.* H.—8″ P.D.—8 to 12″

This favorite hardly needs introduction, with its colors of brilliant yellow, white, pink, and red, with the intricate pattern of its grayish-green foliage, and its constant bloom from June until frost. Difficult to transplant; should be sown in place. It can always be relied upon.

Calendula. *Calendula officinalis.* H.—12″ P.D.—6 to 8″

No garden is complete without calendulas. Hardy, free blooming, and decorative; best used in solid colors. Although the Orange King is excellent, the Yellow Ball and Orange Ball are better. Calendulas make excellent combinations with blues and lavenders. For profuse midsummer bloom, plant a few in partial shade.

Calliopsis. *Coreopsis.* H.—16 to 36″ P.D.— 8 to 12″

The calliopsis in its several forms is an asset to any garden. Its one handicap is its profuse blooming and abundance of seed; unless the old flowers are removed it will soon spend its energy and cease blooming. This is especially true during hot weather.

Reds, crimsons, browns, rich yellows, are the colors found in the many varieties of annual coreopsis.

The dwarf forms are useful for borders and mass effects, whereas the taller forms are better for cutting as well as garden effect.

Goldenwave (*C. drummondi*) has large yellow flowers with mahogany around center. H.—18 to 24″

Crown Coreopsis (*C. coronata*) has pure yellow flowers. H.—24"

The several dwarf forms (including *C. radiata*) Quill coreopsis are delightful. H.—4 to 8"

Candytuft. *Iberis.* H.—6 to 12" P.D.—8"

An old favorite, worthy of greater recognition today. *Iberis umbellata,* with its rather flat heads of flowers, comes in beautiful colors, but *I. amara,* the rocket and hyacinth flowered candytuft, with its long spikes of flowers, is more showy. They are all fragrant and profuse blooming. Several sowings should be made for later bloom.

Cape marigold. *Dimorphotheca aurantiaca.* H.—8 to 12" P.D.—8"

Often listed as African Daisy. Although coming in colors from white to salmon, the orange is most interesting. Excellent for cutting and garden effects. Several sowings should be made.

Castor bean. *Ricinus communis.* H.—4 to 8' P.D.—3 to 5'

This is the most vigorous of all annuals which one will be likely to grow, giving a coarse, luxuriant, even rank growth, which soon crowds out all other flowers. It is best used as a shrub. Caution is necessary in regard to the seeds, since they contain a very active poison. It is claimed that a few contain a fatal dose.

China aster. *Callistephus chinensis.* H.—12 to 36" P.D.—8 to 12"

At one time the china aster was one of our most important annual flowers. Today the aster yellows and the aster blight often make it difficult and sometimes impossible to grow it successfully.

The aster blight (wilt) is controlled only by growing the plants on new soil and selecting seed from disease resistant plants. The aster yellows may be controlled by regular applications of Bordeaux mixture to repel the leaf hopper which transfers the disease from perennial weeds. The tarnished-plant-bug and blister-beetle may be controlled by spraying with one of the pyrethrum extract sprays. All badly diseased plants should be burned.

Asters will do best in good rich soil, where they may be given liberal cultivation and plenty of space to grow. In many cases a partial shade may be beneficial.

The China aster has been developed into many interesting types, among which are early

flowering, such as Queen of the Market and the Royal; and later flowering, such as Comet, King, Late Branching and Crego.

Aster seeds should be sown in the early spring and kept growing.

Chinese forget-me-not. *Cynoglossum amabile.* H.—2' P.D.—15"

A glorified blue forget-me-not which should be in every garden. Keep the old flowers removed or production of seed will stop blooming. Even then the plants may be cut back and will produce a crop of flowers in September. Plants will self-seed although seeds are a nuisance on the plants, being of a stick-tight type.

Clarkia. *Clarkia elegans* and *C. pulchella.* H.—2' P.D.—8"

An old-fashioned annual which is worthy of the attention it receives. The colors run from white through the pinks to deep rose, in single and double flowers. It is free blooming and makes an excellent cut flower. The seed may be sown in the fall or spring.

Cockscomb. *Celosia.*

One of the gaudiest of all annuals. The common cockscomb (*Celosia cristata*) is rather coarse and of doubtful beauty.

Feather cockscomb (*C. plumosa*) is rather decorative with its pink, yellow, and red flower masses. But even this variety should be used sparingly. Flowers may be dried for winter bouquets. It will sometimes self-sow.

Collinsia. *Collinsia.* H.—6 to 8" P.D.—6"

A native western plant, preferring cool weather and a well-drained soil. It will generally require special care to last through our hot, dry summers but it is charming when well grown.

Coneflower. (Pinewoods Coneflower) *Rudbeckia bicolor.* H.—2' P.D.—12"

Resembling our wild black-eyed susan except that it often has mahogany in with the orange color; it is surprising that it is not grown more often. A constant bloomer, an excellent cut flower, and an interesting garden subject.

Cornflower. *Centaurea cyanus.* H.—18 to 24" P.D.—6 to 8"

This flower is available in a variety of colors from white to lavender through to purple and blue and pink; the pink and the blue, however, usually are preferred. Easily grown, absolutely hardy, always self-sowing, it produces a wealth of flowers which are enjoyed by our selves as well as by the goldfinches. Add another attraction in color effect. There is a dwarf form available but seldom grown. Always fall-sow a few for early bloom.

Cosmos. *Cosmos bipinnatus.* H.—4 to 6′ P.D.—2′

Many disappointments with cosmos are due to the use of the late blooming type rather than the early types. Only the early blooming can be depended upon to give any amount of bloom before frost. In addition to the standard single form the double or crested type is worth growing. In most parts of Ohio, late types are valuable for foliage effects alone. Cosmos prefers plenty of room to grow. It may be planted in among the shrubs or even in back of the lower ones. As a cut flower it is unexcelled.

Cow soapwort. *Saponaria vaccaria.*

Another short season bloomer used for cutting or general border planting. Sow at intervals for succession. It is used mainly as a filler.

Chrysanthemum. H.—2 to 3′ P.D.—18″

The Crowndaisy (*Chrysanthemum coronarium*), and annual Chrysanthemum (*Chrysanthemum carinatum*), are surprisingly little grown when one considers their value. Interesting divided foliage, large daisy-like flowers, in yellow or white, often with darker rings in the center, they may be used either for cut flowers or for general garden effect. Given a good soil and plenty of room they seldom fail to give results.

Cupflower. *Nierembergia rivularis.* H.—6″ P.D.—6″

A compact plant covered with a mass of lavender tinted white flowers. Useful as rock plant or in the front of borders.

Datura. *Datura.*

Sometimes called the trumpet flower. It is a rather coarse plant with large flowers; coming in white (*Datura fastuosa*), the white often overcasts with purple, and yellow (*D. chlorantha*) they are grown more as a curiosity than for any actual beauty. It is related to the jimpson weed.

Evening primrose. *Oenothera.* H.—12 to 36″ P.D.—18″

Resembling some of our common weeds, it is doubtful if this group will ever be very popular. The plants are rather coarse, but their brilliant flowers of yellow, rose or white attract some. Difficult to transplant, they should be sown in place in the early spring. They are of little value as cut flowers.

Everlasting. *Helipterum.* H.—12″ P.D.—6″

Although this name is often applied to any type of flower which may be dried, it is properly applied to helipterum, which is usually catalogued under the name of *Acrolinium roseum* and *Rhodanthe manglesi.* Rather small, delicate plants, they are really grown more for their dried flowers than for their garden effect. The best place for them is in rows in the vegetable garden, where they may be cut when in bud and hung up to dry.

Many people consider it best to strip the leaves off all forms of everlastings and strawflowers before drying. Others prefer to leave them on for their decorative effect.

Flax. *Linum grandiflorum coccineum.* H.—12″ P.D.—6″

Although the commercial flax with its blue flowers, *Linum usitatissimum,* is sometimes grown, far superior is *L. grandiflorum coccineum,* the scarlet flax, with its brilliant red flowers. It blooms day after day throughout the summer. Several sowings may be made for late summer.

Feverfew-camomile. *Matricaria parthenoides (capensis).* H.—2 to 3′ P.D.—18″

A sturdy, dependable plant bearing a profusion of white flowers. Not especially beautiful but always reliable. It will often live over in protected situations. There is also a dwarf form, with yellow or white flowers.

Four o'clocks. *Mirabilis jalapa.* H.—24″ P.D.—15″

Although most of us know the four o'clocks as annual hedge plants, they may be used in other ways. Not mixing well with flowers, due to their colors, they should be grown by themselves or as a group in front of the shrubs. The plants self-sow or the heavy roots may be dug in the fall and stored in the cellar over winter.

Forget-me-not. *Myosotis.* H.—6″ P.D.—6″

The annual varieties are as fine as the perennial. If not allowed to seed, the plants will bloom all summer. Partial shade will help during hot, dry weather. Grow in masses. Forget-me-nots will often self-sow.

Gaillardia. *Gaillardia.* H.—12 to 24″ P.D.—15″

One of the old standbys necessary to every garden. Easily grown, vigorous and free blooming, it is highly desirable for cutting or garden effect. *G. amblyodon* has single maroon flowers—interesting but not as showy as *G. pulchella,* with its globular heads of yellow, pink, and red.

Gilia. *Gilia.*

G. capitata with its dainty blue flowers is good for relieving the "heavy" effect of such plants as petunias, gaillardias. H.—12″ P.D. —8″

G. coronopifolia, a newcomer to most American gardens, gives sturdy accents of red, yellow and pink. H.—36″ P.D.—12″

Godetia. *Godetia grandiflora.* H.—12″ P.D. —12″

A relative of the evening primrose; the commoner form, *G. grandiflora,* forms a dwarf, compact plant bearing a mass of large flowers. Adapted to poor and sandy soil. An all season bloomer. Sow early if possible.

Goldencup. *Hunnemannia fumariaefolia.* H. —18 to 24″ P.D.—12″

A relative of the poppy, sometimes called Bush Eschscholtzia. It forms a mass of golden yellow blooms. The plants prefer full sun and will withstand drought. If flowers are cut in the bud they will keep very well.

Gomphrena. *Gomphrena globosa.* H.—18″ P.D.—12″

Another of our everlastings of easy culture, with white, rose, purple and salmon flowers. It is decorative as a garden plant.

Gypsophila. *Gypsophila elegans.* H.—12″ P.D.—6″

The annual babysbreath is useful as a cut flower and temporary garden effect. Its short blooming period of three weeks necessitates resowing every three weeks, but it will bloom six weeks from sowing. *G. muralis* is daintier and blooms all summer.

Hollyhock. *Althea rosea.* H.—5 to 6′ P.D. —2′

Similar to the well-known perennial form, this stately flower blooms the first year, during late summer. Combined with its perennial sister it will give us hollyhocks all summer long.

Honesty. *Lunaria biennis.* H.—2 to 3′ P.D. —15″

Although uninteresting as a garden subject, it is useful for its seed pods which may have the outer layer removed after they are dried, leaving a thin transparent disk for decorative

use in winter bouquets. **Seed, unless sown** early, will not produce **seed pods** until the second year.

Immortelle. *Xeranthemum annuum.* H.— 3′ P.D.—12″

A good garden plant and a source of flowers for winter bouquets. Foliage silver-gray, flowers in clusters, purple, lavender, pink and white. Sow seed in April.

Laceflower. *Trachymene (Didiscus).* H.— 24″ P.D.—12″

An interesting cut flower, but usually difficult to grow. It is not particularly ornamental as a garden plant but excellent as a cut flower. Difficult to transplant. Sow in pots or where it is to bloom, in early spring.

Larkspur. *Delphinium.* H.—24 to 36″ P.D. —12″

One of the most widely grown annuals. The rocket or hyacinth flowered type, *D. ajacis,* has long compact flowers. The candelabrum type, *D. consolida,* has open, branched flower masses. It may be fall sown; will often self-sow.

Leptosyne. *Coreopsis stillmani.* H.—12″ P.D.—8″

Coreopsis maritima. H.—2′ P.D.—12″

Interesting variations, with yellow flowers, closely resembling calliopsis.

Lobelia. *Lobelia erinus.* H.—6″ P.D.—6″

A low compact plant with brilliant blue flowers. Unfortunately it is often associated only with straight line flower bed edging, whereas it is really charming in mass plantings. The trailing varieties are fine for porch boxes or hanging baskets. Sow seed early.

Love-in-a-mist. *Nigella damascena.* H.—8 to 12″ P.D.—8″

A delightful hardy annual flower with finely cut leaves and lacy blue and white flowers. It blooms when very small. May be fall or spring sown or even early summer sown. It is often used to add grace to the flower garden.

Lupine. *Lupinus luteus, L. hirsutus, L. hartwegi.* H.—24 to 36″ P.D.—12″

Interesting as border plants, exquisite as cut flowers. Sow in pots or where they are to bloom. Partial shade will give better results. There are several species, of different colors. Removal of old flowers will increase bloom.

Madagascar periwinkle. *Vinca rosea.* H.— 18″ P.D.—12″

One of the best annuals for blooming **under**

trying conditions. They are bushy, compact plants, the seed of which must be sown very early indoors or the plants purchased from a florist. Flowers pink or white.

Marigolds. *Tagetes.*

Marigolds in their common forms need no introduction. For tall plants use African Marigold (H.—3′; P.D.—18″), which has large, heavy flowers and is rather stiff and formal. More graceful are the French Marigolds (H.—12 to 18″; P.D.—15″), of compact, free-flowering habit. There are many fine varieties of this latter group.

For a dainty plant, use the Mexican Marigolds, *Tagetes signata pumila* (H.—15″; P.D. —12″), with small, starry, orange flowers. Hardy, free blooming, easily grown, there are few other annuals so universally satisfying.

Mignonette. *Reseda odorata.* H.—12″ P.D. —8 to 12″

Everyone knows and enjoys the fragrance of this old-fashioned flower. Although blooming best during cool weather about May, sowings in partial shade will give midsummer bloom. Difficult to transplant, seed should be sown in pots or where it is to bloom. Liberal fertilization will increase size of flowers.

Monkeyflower. *Mimulus lutens, M. moscha-tus.* H.—12″ P.D.—12″

Brilliant, curiously shaped flowers preferring partial shade and plenty of moisture. Started indoors or in a cold frame they should be set out after weather warms up. Sometimes used for porch boxes or hanging baskets.

Morning-glory, dwarf. *Ipomea.* H.—12″ P.D.—12″

A very low, compact, free-blooming plant, inclined to trail a little. Prefers full sun. Does *not* transplant easily; should be sown in early spring, where it is to bloom.

Nasturtium, dwarf. *Tropaeolum.* H.—12″ P.D.—12″

Nasturtiums may be sown where they are to bloom as early as ground can be worked. The plants are sometimes bothered with lice, which can be controlled by spraying (see chap. XXI).

Nemesia. *Nemesia strumosa, N. versicolor.* H.—12″ P.D.—8″

A worthy plant, all too little known. The "saucy little faces" of the various colored flowers are borne in profusion from June until frost. Sow seed in April. The large flowered hybrids are most showy.

Nemophila. *Nemophila.* H.—8 to 12″ P.D. —6 to 8″

Small dainty flowers, preferring partial shade and fairly moist soil. Profuse bloomers throughout the summer. May be used in rock gardens or on shady side of house. Best adapted to cooler climates, and consequently need attention to produce results.

Nicotiana. *Nicotiana.* H.—2 to 4′ P.D.—8 to 12″

The fragrant, evening blooming white flowered *Nicotiana affinis* is by far the commonest flowering tobacco, due possibly to its ability to self-sow. Even more decorative, however, is *N. sanderai* with pink, red, and lavender flowers. *N. Sylvestris* is a day blooming, white flowered variety.

The nicotianas are desirable for use among the coarser flowers, such as zinnias or even cannas, to give a more airy effect.

Oenothera. Evening Primrose. *Oenothera.*

   O. America—large white flowers. H.—3 to 4′ P.D.—18″

   O. rosea—pink flowers. H.—2′ P.D.— 15″

   O. drummondi—yellow flowers. H.—12 to 24″ P.D.—12″

Large flowered rather coarse plants, demanding full sun. They are showy in the garden but useless for cutting. Do not transplant easily, so seed should be sown early, in open ground.

Painted spurge. (Mexican Fire Plant) *Euphorbia heterophylla.* H.—24 to 36″ P.D.—18″

An interesting foliage plant; the margins of leaves and sometimes the entire leaves turn scarlet, especially in September. It prefers heat and full sun but will stand rather poor soil. Sow after danger of frost is past.

Pansy. *Viola tricolor.* H.—6″ P.D.—6″

Although every one knows the pansy, few grow it in sufficient quantity. Seed best sown in August and wintered with a light mulch of straw, in a shaded cold frame sash. Seed may also be sown in early spring for summer bloom. Buy only the very best fresh seed, even though it seems expensive; old pansy seed is unsatisfactory. Many of the best colors are slowest to germinate and develop. Partial shade and sufficient moisture will give best results, especially for summer bloom. Many people prefer to buy their pansy plants each year rather than to grow their own.

Perilla, purple. *Perilla frutescens nankinensis.* H.—18" P.D.—12"

An old fashioned plant with dark purple leaves resembling the coleus. Used only as a foliage plant, either with flowers such as pink balcony petunias or with gray foliage such as Dusty Miller. Usually self-sows in Ohio, coming up year after year.

Petunia. *Petunia hybrida.* H.—12 to 24" P.D.—8 to 12"

Another of our old faithful friends. Always satisfactory. Seed should be sown early indoors or in a cold frame. The smallest and slowest growing seedlings are often the best colors. The best seed, although costing considerably more, will give the finest flowers.

Small, single flowered forms are the hardiest and most vigorous, but larger flowers are usually preferred. Borders, banks, rock walls, porch boxes, and hanging baskets are some of the possible places to use petunias.

Phacelia. *Phacelia campanularis.* H.—9" P.D.—6 to 8"

Another blue flower, giving a full season of bloom. It prefers full sunlight and a light soil. Pinch when small to produce bushy plants. Useful for border effects.

Phlox. *Phlox drummondi.* H.—6 to 12" P.D.—8 to 12"

A continuous bloomer, producing a brilliant mosaic of color when planted in mixtures. Both the dwarf and tall forms are very fine for garden effects and cut flowers. Sow in cold frame, or in open ground in April.

If planted in full sun, and the seedpods removed, the annual phlox will seldom disappoint the gardener.

Pinks. *Dianthus chinensis.* H.—8 to 12" P.D.—6 to 8"

As desirable as its perennial sisters, the several forms of annual pinks come in single and double forms. Constant bloomers, they desire rich soil and sunlight. Plants will live over if mulched and give early bloom, but cannot always be depended upon the second year.

Poppy. *Papaver.*

Gorgeous flowers in a variety of colors and forms. The Shirley Poppy, *P. rhoeas* (H.—24 to 36"; P.D.—12"), with long, slender, hairy stems and single or double flowers, is more dainty and graceful than the Opium poppy, *P. somniferum* (H.—18 to 24"; P.D.—8"), with heavy leafy stems and larger flowers.

Forms of this are known as the tulip, peony, and carnation flowered poppies.

The very fine seed of poppies should be sown where the plants are to bloom, either fall, spring, or summer. To keep up a supply of bloom do not allow seed pods to develop.

Poppies are excellent cut flowers if cut in the bud stage.

Portulaca. *Portulaca grandiflora.* H.—6" P.D.—6"

Possessing an ability to grow in hot, dry, almost impossible places, we must respect this brilliant gaudy flower, even if we hesitate to grow it in our borders. Try it in hot, dry spots where nothing else will grow.

Pricklepoppy. *Argemone mexicana.* H.—3' P.D.—18"

Interesting as a foliage plant, with its spiny white-veined leaves; also as a flowering plant. It is a vigorous, hardy plant with yellow flowers, often self-sowing. It is a good filler in any border. Difficult to transplant, it should be sown in its permanent bed.

Princesplume. *Polygonum orientale.* H.—5 to 6' P.D.—2'

Also called "kiss-me-over-the-garden-gate." A tall, graceful plant with pendulous terminal panicles of pink flowers. May be used as a background for other flowers or as spots of color in the shrub border. Sown early out of doors, it will bloom until frost.

Rose-of-heaven. *Lychnis coelirosa* (*Agrostemma*). H.—12" P.D.—6"

A dainty flower which must have several sowings made for succession of bloom. Apt to seed too freely in some gardens.

Salpiglossis. *Salpiglossis sinuata.* H.—2 to 3' P.D.—12"

Highly decorative in the garden or as cut flower. Resembles a refined petunia but with more delicate effects, and more intricate color patterns. Sow seed early, preferably indoors. Pinch seedlings back to produce bushy plants. It will grow in the sun or in partial shade and prefers a sandy soil. Charming flower arrangements may be made with the cut flowers.

Salvia. *Salvia.* H.—2 to 3' P.D.—18"

Commonest of all is the scarlet sage, *Salvia splendens,* although unfortunately so often misused and overused in our yards and gardens. When grown it should be used with other foliage as a background and in relatively small masses. Sow seed early indoors or in cold frame and plant out after last frost.

Mealycup Sage, S. farinacea, also usually listed as a perennial, is a free blooming, attractive plant worthy of wider use. Its blue flowers and gray stems make it useful as a cut flower or as garden subject. Often self-sows profusely and never fails to give satisfaction.

Blue Sage, Salvia patens, a brilliant blue, which will be welcomed to most gardens. Not as showy as the Scarlet Sage, it is far more suitable for garden use.

Sanvitalia. *Sanvitalia procumbens.* H.—6″ P.D.—8 to 12″

A very satisfactory ground cover and edging plant, it is surprising that it is not grown more extensively. The golden yellow flowers with dark centers resemble small zinnias, and are borne in profusion until frost. Sow seed in early spring. Try a few in the rock garden.

Scabiosa. *Scabiosa atropurpurea.* H.—24″ P.D.—12″

One of our best annual cut flowers. The wide range of colors—white, pink, rose, scarlet, yellow, blue, and maroon—may either be grown as single colors or in mixture. Sow seed indoors or out, give sufficient room and fertilizer and they will bloom until frost if we but keep the old flowers picked.

Snapdragon. *Antirrhinum majus.* H.—12 to 36″ P.D.—8 to 12″

The variety of colors, the differences in height of dwarf, medium, and tall, and the long season of bloom, make these charming flowers beloved by all. Use either as border plants, or in rows for cutting.

The very small seed is best sown early but may be sown outdoors in May for later bloom. Snapdragon rust may be a serious handicap in some sections. Destroy any snapdragon plants which have lived over winter and allow no old leaves or stems to remain. This sanitary precaution, together with a sulphur dust, will help to check the rust.

Sensitive plant. *Mimosa pudica.* H.—8 to 12″ P.D.—12″

An odd plant, grown not for its beauty but for its sensitive leaves which slowly fold together when disturbed. Sow seed indoors and set out in hot, dry place after all danger of frost is past.

Snow-on-the-mountain. *Euphorbia marginata.* H.—3′ P.D.—12″

An old-fashioned flower which has escaped and become a pest in some gardens. The upper leaves, margined with white, make a showy effect. A few in the border give an interesting effect. May easily be naturalized and will hold its own.

Spiderflower. *Cleome spinosa.* H.—3 to 4′ P.D.—12″

A vigorous, rather coarse plant, well adapted to poor soil, and useful as an accent among the shrubs or a filler in an odd corner of the yard. Plants have a peculiar odor—objectionable near windows or porches.

Flowers are lavender, pink, or white. In a small garden a few plants will suffice. Sow seed in early spring. You may find it will self-sow.

Stocks. *Mathiola incana.* H.—12 to 18″ P.D.—12″

Although stocks prefer a cool, moist climate with a rich soil, they often do well in Ohio gardens. Sow some seed early and some later for continuous garden effect.

Stocks come in several forms, dwarf and tall, and a variety of colors. Some strains seem to bloom better than others in our warm dry summers.

Straw flowers. *Helichrysum bracteatum.* H.—3′ P.D.—12″

This name is properly applied only to the *Helichrysum,* although often loosely to any flower which may be successfully dried. The *Helichrysum* is the largest and most showy of the everlastings. Start the plants early indoors or in the cold frame if possible, and give them plenty of space to grow.

Remember to cut the flowers before they are open—since small buds will open when dried. Tie in bunches and hang up until dry.

Summer cypress. *Kochia tricophylla.* H.—24″ P.D.—18 to 24″

Whether we like it or not, the summer cypress demands admiration for its ability to grow under most trying conditions, produce its formal light green bushes, turn brilliant red in the fall and then self-sow most profusely. Once you grow it you will always have it.

Summer fir. *Artemesia sacrorum viridis.* H.—3′ P.D.—18 to 24″

An interesting foliage plant for background effects or temporary hedges. Leaves finely cut, delicate green. It will sometimes self-sow.

Sunflower. *Helianthus.* H.—3 to 7' P.D.— 2 to 3'

The annual sunflowers are an interesting group of plants giving a variety of flowers both in size, form, and color. The red flowered forms seem to appeal to many gardeners.

The larger forms are rather coarse, but the lower-growing varieties with small flowers harmonize with zinnias and cosmos. Useful as a background for other annuals or as color accents among shrubs. If started early indoors many will go to seed and die before frost. The seed makes excellent bird food.

Swan-river-daisy. *Brachycome iberidifolia.* H.—6 to 12" P.D.—6 to 8"

A dainty dwarf plant with blue, white, or mauve daisy-like flowers. Often used in rock gardens. It prefers full sun but unless liberally watered does better in partial shade during hot weather.

Sweet alyssum. *Alyssum maritimum.* H.— 8" P.D.—12"

Everyone knows and grows this sweet-scented flower, but all too many seem to feel it must be grown in straight rows along the edge of beds. It is really more effective in masses in informal beds.

Hardy, it may be sown very early and will bloom in six weeks from sowing. There are many varieties, some slightly colored, some compact, others trailing. They all bloom early from summer until they freeze up in October.

Sweet sultan. *Centaurea moschata.* H.—2' P.D.—12"

Showy flowers and decorative plants preferring non-acid soil. Flowers will last well if cut when in bud. It will bloom from June till frost.

There is also the Royal Sweet Sultan, *Centaurea imperialis,* H.—2'; P.D.—12"; the flowers are sweet-scented, lasting well as cut flowers. It is an enlarged form of the Sweet Sultan, and preferred by many.

Sweet peas. *Lathyrus odoratus.* H.—5 to 8' P.D.—3'

Preferring a cool deep soil, the ground should be thoroughly prepared in the autumn by digging a trench two feet deep. Place several layers of manure in the bottom and fill in with the best soil or compost available. Mound well to take care of settling.

Sowing seed: If soil is well drained, seed (especially of dark seeded varieties) may be sown in late November, but otherwise during early spring. The old rule of Good Friday is not as far off as most of the old garden myths, for it insures early sowing.

It is not necessary to sow the seed in a trench and fill it in, as some people aver, as sweet peas need little attention, if the soil has been properly prepared.

Supports: A support of string or wire should be ready for the seedlings as soon as they start to climb. It is neater than brush.

Summer blooming will be obtained in most sections only by liberal weekly watering, together with a mulch of straw, leaves, or peat moss. Monthly applications of a complete chemical fertilizer, 2 pounds to 100 square feet of soil, should be added.

Keep all old flowers picked. To control the red spider which so often ruins the vines, spray daily with a garden hose or dust with sulphur every two weeks.

Tasselflower. *Emilia (Cacalia) flammea.*

The tasselflower, although dainty and far from showy, always attracts attention. Its feathery tufts of orange or yellow give a charming and unique effect. Combined with *ageratum* or *bowallia* it is stunning. It may be used in the rock garden, the border, or as a cut flower.

Thrift. (Statice) *Limonium.*

Although always catalogued as Statice, this should be called Thrift; the scientific name is *Limonium,* instead of Statice. It is considered by many as the choicest of the everlastings. *Limonium sinuata* with its open airy sprays of flowers, comes in white, pink, and lavender. *L. bonduelli* resembles *L. sinuata* except that the flowers are yellow. *L. suorowi* produces gorgeous pink spikes. All of these flowers are equally effective in the garden, as freshly cut flowers, or as dried winter bouquets.

Seed is best sown early, and if pot-grown will start blooming surprisingly soon. Staking may be necessary unless the plants are protected from the wind. They prefer sandy soil.

Tidytips. *Layia elegans.* H.—18" P.D.— 12"

Resembling a *Gaillardia,* these flowers are seldom seen although relatively easy to obtain. Grow in full sun and pinch when small to produce branching. They will amply reward us for their care.

Torch lily. *Kniphofia.* (*Tritoma*). H.—2′ P.D.—12″

Although we all enjoy the perennial Torch Lily, but few try the annual form; it is not as showy but is worth trying. Sow seed early indoors, even though they do not bloom until August.

Torenia. *Torenia fournieri.*

A low, compact plant producing a constant mass of flowers until frost. The lavender flowers with intricate markings of white and yellow are interesting in themselves. It is suitable for use in the border or as a pot plant.

Sow seed indoors or in cold frame in March. Do not set plants out until weather is warm.

Treemallow. *Lavatera trimestris.* H.—2 to 3′ P.D.—12″

Resembling a hollyhock, these rather coarse annuals are effective. May be used for accent in the border, for color among the shrubs, or as a bold mass of color by themselves.

Seed best sown where they are to bloom, but well thinned and spaced 18 inches to 24 inches apart. Abundant moisture and plenty of sun are their preference.

Verbena. *Verbena.* H.—8 to 12″ P.D.—12″

We all know and enjoy the common type of verbena with its brilliant flowers, especially in the newer, large-flowered types. These are fine for border effects or cutting.

The moss verbena (*V. erinoides*) although not as showy, has excellent foliage and fern-like leaves. Ideal for a ground cover.

The tuber verbena (*V. venosa*) is coarser and more compact, but equally fine for foliage effect. Its lavender flowers add to its decorative value.

Virginia stock. *Malcomia maritima.* H.—6 to 8″ P.D.—8″

Not as showy as the common stock, but more delicate in appearance. Often used for rock gardens as well as borders. Seed may be fall or spring sown. In fact, it will often self-sow.

Winged everlasting. *Ammobium alatum.* H.—18″ P.D.—8″

A satisfactory everlasting having white flowers with yellow centers. More interesting as a cut flower than as a garden subject. Prefers a sandy soil.

Woodruff. *Asperula orientale azurea.* H.—12″ P.D.—6″

Although many know the perennial sweet woodruff, few grow the oriental woodruff (*Asperula orientalis azurea*). A splendid airy effect is obtained with its blue flowers, which tend to relieve the heaviness of coarser flowers.

Zinnia. (Youth and Old Age) *Zinnia.*

At least no one need be ashamed to profess a liking for zinnias. There are a number of forms and varieties some of which are neglected, such as:

Z. mexicana (H.—12 to 18″; P.D.—12″), a dwarf, small-flowered type, with both single and double flowers. Its smaller size enables us to use it where other varieties might prove too coarse.

Z. pumila (H.—18″; P.D.—12″), with its compact growth, is more or less a miniature of the giant ones. It is more suitable for cut flowers for small bowls and baskets.

The giant Zinnias (H.—3 to 4′; P.D.—2′), Dahlia, California Giant, and Colossal Flowered types, are all glorious forms. There are also Quilled and Picottee types.

To secure the best results with Zinnias, the very best strains of seed are recommended. The cheaper strains, although producing good flowers, will not give the large size or wide range of unusual colors as will the more expensive seed.

WHAT TO PLANT FOR GARDEN COLOR

The best in hardy perennials arranged by size and season

SEASON	WHITE AND SHADES	YELLOW—ORANGE	PINK	RED	BLUE—PURPLE
SPRING Bulbs in great variety are also valuable spring flowers. Most things in this group are best if planted in the fall.	DWARF Arabis Dianthus Hepatica Iberis Iris pumila Papaver nudicaule Phlox subulata Sedum Viola MEDIUM Aquilegia Campanula TALL Gypsophila Peony (tree)	DWARF Alyssum Caltha Erythronium Iris pumila Papaver nudicaule Primula Sedum Viola MEDIUM Aquilegia Doronicum Hemerocallis Trollius TALL Hemerocallis Peony (tree)	DWARF Aubrietia Gypsophila Lychnis Papaver nudicaule Phlox subulata Primula Sedum Viola MEDIUM Aquilegia Campanula Dicentra Megasea TALL Peony (tree)	DWARF Lychnis Papaver nudicaule Phlox subulata Primula MEDIUM Papaver orientale TALL Peony (tree)	DWARF Anemone pulsatilla Aster alpinus Aubrietia Gentiana Hepatica Iris pumila Nepeta Phlox divaricata Trillium Veronica Viola MEDIUM Anchusa Aquilegia Campanula
EARLY SUMMER In most gardens this is the height of the color display. Many in this season group are also found in the next two because of their continued blooming. Bulbs such as Lilies, Montbretias, Tigridias, Gladiolus and others add to the display during the summer months. Early summer is the time to plan and plant for fall color.	DWARF Achillea Arenaria Cerastium Dianthus Gypsophila Helianthemum Heuchera Saxifraga Sedum Silene Thymus Viola MEDIUM Achillea Aquilegia Astilbe Campanula Gypsophila Hesperis Iris Linum Lychnis Papaver orientale Phlox Platycodon Pyrethrum Scabiosa Thalictrum Veronica TALL Aconitum Althaea rosea Delphinium Dictamnus Digitalis Iris Lupinus Monarda Peony Yucca	DWARF Alyssum Helianthemum Potentilla Primula Sedum Thalictrum Viola MEDIUM Aquilegia Coreopsis Doronicum Gaillardia Geum Helenium Hemerocallis Iris Oenothera Potentilla Thalictrum Trollius TALL Althaea rosea Digitalis Iris Lupinus Thalictrum Thermopsis	DWARF Allium Dicentra Dodecatheon Erica Helianthemum Heuchera Potentilla Sedum Silene Thymus MEDIUM Achillea Agrostemma Aquilegia Armeria Astilbe Dianthus Hesperis Incarvillea Iris Lychnis Papaver orientale Pyrethrum TALL Althaea rosea Digitalis Iris Lupinus Monarda Peony Valeriana	DWARF Armeria Erica Helianthemum Heuchera Primula Thymus MEDIUM Agrostemma Astilbe Dianthus Gaillardia Geum Lychnis Papaver orientale Phlox ovata Potentilla Pyrethrum TALL Althaea rosea Dictamnus Iris Monarda Peony	DWARF Campanula Myosotis Nepeta Veronica Viola MEDIUM Agapanthus Anchusa Aquilegia Campanula Delphinium Geranium Iris Linum Mertensia Phlox Platycodon Scabiosa Thalictrum TALL Aconitum Anchusa Campanula Delphinium Iris Liatris Lupinus NOTE—These classifications as to color and height indicate in a general way the variations. Check all varieties carefully in one or more comprehensive catalogs where many additional kinds will be found. Color indications are approximate as so many varieties come in between the above groups.
LATE SUMMER This period is likely to be lacking in color unless special efforts are made both in planting and care. Annuals in masses should freely supplement the perennials. Shearing back and feeding help many varieties.	DWARF Arenaria Dianthus Sedum Silene Viola MEDIUM Campanula Erigeron Gypsophila Linum Phlox Physostegia Scabiosa Sidalcea Stokesia TALL Aster Boltonia Cimicifuga Delphinium Eupatorium Hibiscus Phlox Romneya coulteri	DWARF Achillea Allyssum Dianthus Hypericum Sedum Sempervivum Viola MEDIUM Centaurea Coreopsis Gaillardia Geum Oenothera Potentilla TALL Cassia Helenium Helianthus Heliopsis Rudbeckia Senecio Thalictrum Tritoma Verbascum	DWARF Dicentra Sedum Silene Tunica Viola MEDIUM Achillea Armeria Centaurea Erigeron Lythrum Phlox Physostegia Sedum Sidalcea TALL Aster Boltonia Hibiscus Phlox	DWARF Sempervivum MEDIUM Gaillardia Geum Pentstemon Phlox Potentilla TALL Helenium Hibiscus Lobelia Phlox Senecio Tritoma	DWARF Gentiana Myosotis Plumbago Veronica Viola MEDIUM Campanula Centaurea Erigeron Funkia Lavandula Linum Phlox Scabiosa Statice Stokesia Veronica TALL Aconitum Anchusa Aster Campanula Delphinium Liatris Lobelia Senecio Thalictrum
FALL The right varieties supply color even after early frosts.	DWARF Viola MEDIUM Anemone Stokesia TALL Aster Chrysanthemum Delphinium Pyrethrum uliginosum	DWARF Sempervivum Viola MEDIUM Coreopsis Gaillardia TALL Chrysanthemum Helenium Helianthus Senecio	DWARF Aster Viola MEDIUM Achillea Anemone TALL Aster Chrysanthemum	DWARF Sempervivum MEDIUM Gaillardia TALL Chrysanthemum Helenium	DWARF Viola MEDIUM Delphinium Stokesia TALL Aconitum Aster Delphinium Echinacea purpurea

Compiled for THE AMERICAN HOME   Copyright, 1933, by American Home-Country Life Corp.   by ROMAINE B. WARE

The greatest degree of success with flowers is acquired by knowing the likes and dislikes, the natural habits

Red	Pink	Orange	Yellow	Blue	Purple	White	Height in Inches	May	June	July	August	September	October	Variety Name	Sun	Shade	Partial Shade	Cutting	Flower Boxes	Cemetery	Rock Gardens	Borders	Bedding
	×						6	×	×					Abronia, Umbellata—Sand Verbena	×				×		×		
×	×		×				36–48			×	×	×	×	Abutilon—Flowering Maple	×								×
	×					×	24			×	×			Acroclinium—Everlasting	×							×	
×							12	×	×	×				Adonis—Pheasant's Eye	×		×					×	
				×			24–36			×	×	×		Agathea—Blue Daisy	×								×
				×		×	6–18			×	×	×	×	Ageratum—Floss Flower	×				×	×	×	×	×
×							18–20			×	×	×	×	Agrostis Nebulosa—Cloud Grass	×			×				×	
×							15–18			×	×	×	×	Alonsoa—Maskflower	×			×			×		
					×	×	2–6			×	×	×	×	Alyssum—Sweet Alyssum	×	×	×	×	×	×	×		×
×		×		×	×		6–8			×	×	×		Anagallis, Grandiflora	×				×		×		
					×		18–24			×	×	×		Anchusa, Annual	×		×					×	
×	×	×	×		×	×	8–24			×	×	×		Antirrhinum—Snapdragon	×		×	×	×			×	×
				×	×	×	24			×	×	×		Arctotis—Lavender Daisy	×		×					×	×
	×		×			×	24–36			×	×	×		Argemone—Prickly Poppy	×							×	×
×	×	×	×	×	×	×	12–18			×	×	×		Asters—China Asters	×		×	×				×	×
×	×	×		×	×	×	18–24				×	×		Balsam—Lady's Slipper	×		×					×	
			×				12–24			×	×	×		Bartonia—Blazing Star	×							×	
				×			9–12			×	×	×		Brachycome—Swan River Daisy	×				×		×	×	
				×		×	12–18	×	×	×	×	×		Browallia	×				×		×	×	
×		×					18			×	×	×		Cacalia—Devil's Paint Brush	×			×				×	
×	×						6–18			×	×	×		Calandrinia	×							×	
		×	×				12–18			×	×	×	×	Calendula—Pot Marigold	×		×					×	×
×	×	×	×		×		12–18	×	×	×	×	×		Calliopsis—Annual Coreopsis	×			×				×	
×						×	6–15	×	×	×	×	×		Candytuft—Iberis	×		×	×	×	×		×	
×	×	×	×		×		24–30			×	×	×		Celosia—Various	×							×	
×	×			×	×		18–24			×	×	×		Centaurea, Cyanus—Bachelor's Button	×		×	×				×	×
×	×		×		×	×	18–24			×	×	×		Centaurea—Sweet Sultans	×		×	×				×	
×	×		×			×	24–36			×	×	×		Chrysanthemums—Annual Painted Daisy	×			×				×	×
×	×	×					24			×	×	×	×	Clarkia	×		×	×	×			×	
	×						24–48			×	×			Cleome—Spiderflower	×							×	
×							9–12			×	×	×		Collomia, Coccinea	×						×		
					×		12			×	×	×		Convolvulus, Mauritanica	×				×		×		×
			×				24			×	×	×		Cosmidium, Burridgeanum	×							×	
×	×		×			×	48–72			×	×	×	×	Cosmos—Mexican Aster	×			×				×	
				×			12–24	×	×	×				Cynoglossum—Summer Forget-Me-Not	×		×			×		×	
			×		×	×	24–36			×	×	×	×	Datura—Horn of Plenty	×							×	
×	×	×			×	×	9–12	×	×	×	×	×		Dianthus—Carnations and Pinks	×			×		×	×	×	
	×						12			×	×	×		Diascia—Twinspur	×			×			×		
				×			12–24			×	×	×		Didiscus—Queen Anne's Blue Lace Flower			×	×				×	×
		×					8–12			×	×	×		Dimorphoteca—African Daisy	×							×	
		×					18–24				×	×	×	Erysimum—Fairy Wallflower	×					×	×	×	
		×					9–12	×	×	×				Eschscholtzia—California Poppy	×		×				×	×	×
×	×		×			×	24–30			×	×	×	×	Four O'Clocks—Marvel of Peru	×							×	
×			×				18	×	×	×	×	×	×	Gaillardia—Blanket Flower	×			×				×	×
		×	×				8–10			×	×	×		Gamolepis Tagetes	×						×	×	
×	×	×	×		×	×	24			×	×	×		Gerbera—Transvaal Daisy	×			×				×	
					×	×	12–24			×	×	×		Gilia—Thimble Flower	×						×	×	×
	×				×	×	12–18		×	×	×			Globe Amaranth—Gomphrena Everlasting	×							×	×
×	×	×				×	9–15	×	×	×	×	×	×	Godetia—Satin Flower			×	×				×	
×	×					×	12–24			×	×	×		Gypsophila—Annual Baby's Breath	×		×	×				×	×
×	×	×	×			×	24–36			×	×	×		Helichrysum—Strawflower	×							×	
				×	×		24	×	×	×	×			Heliotrope	×				×	×			×
			×				24					×	×	Hunnemannia—Golden Buttercup Poppy	×			×			×	×	

FLOWER CHART

and the best treatment of each individual variety. We hope this chart will help you to this knowledge.

Red	Pink	Orange	Yellow	Blue	Purple	White	Height in Inches	May	June	July	August	September	October	Variety Name	Sun	Shade	Partial Shade	Cutting	Flower Boxes	Cemetery	Rock Gardens	Borders	Bedding
X	X					X	18			X	X	X		Impatiens—Garden Balsam			X					X	
				X			3–4			X	X	X		Ionopsidium, Acaule—Diamondflower			X			X			
	X	X	X			X	10–12			X	X	X	X	Lantana	X								X
X	X	X	X	X	X		X	24–30			X	X	X		Larkspur, Annual	X		X	X				X	
	X						X	24–30			X	X	X		Lavatera—Annual Mallow	X		X	X				X	
		X	X	X	X		10			X	X	X		Leptosiphon	X						X		
			X				18			X	X	X		Leptosyne Stillmani—Stillman Coreopsis	X			X				X	
			X			X	6	X	X	X	X			Limnanthes Douglasi—Marshflower			X					X	
X	X	X					12–18			X	X			Linaria, Annual	X			X			X	X	X
X							12–18	X	X	X	X	X	X	Linum—Flowering Flax	X			X			X	X	X
			X				6–9			X	X	X	X	Lobelia, Annual			X		X		X	X	
	X			X		X	18–24			X	X			Lupines, Annual			X	X				X	X
X	X					X	24–30			X	X	X		Malope—Mallow Wort	X							X	
		X					6–18			X	X	X	X	Marigold—Tagetes	X			X					X
		X				X	9–36			X	X	X	X	Matricaria—Double Feverfew	X						X	X	X
					X		15–18		X	X	X	X	X	Matthiola—Evening Scented Stocks	X						X	X	
X					X	X	6			X	X	X		Mesembryanthemum Ice Plant	X				X		X		
X	X		X			X	12			X	X	X		Mignonette—Reseda	X			X	X	X	X		X
X	X	X	X				6–12	X	X	X	X	X		Nasturtium	X				X				X
X	X	X			X		X	9–12			X	X			Nemesia	X							X	X
				X		X	12			X	X	X		Nemophila—Baby Blue Eyes		X	X	X			X	X	
X				X		X	24–36	X	X	X	X	X	X	Nicotiana—Flowering Tobacco	X		X					X	
				X		X	15–18			X	X	X		Nigella—Love-in-a-Mist	X							X	
				X			6			X	X	X		Nolana	X				X		X		
					X	X	9			X	X			Nycterinia—Capensis	X						X		
			X				18–24			X	X	X		Oenothera—Evening Primrose	X		X					X	
X	X	X	X	X	X	X	4–6	X	X	X	X	X		Pansy—Heartsease	X		X	X	X				X
X	X			X	X	X	9–18			X	X	X	X	Petunia	X		X		X		X	X	X
				X			9–12			X	X	X		Phacelia—Harebell Phacelia	X						X	X	
X	X	X	X			X	6–18			X	X	X		Phlox, Annual	X			X	X	X	X	X	X
X	X	X	X	X	X		X	18–24			X	X			Poppy, Annual	X							X	X
X	X	X	X			X	2–6			X	X	X	X	Portulaca—Rose Moss—Sun Plant	X				X	X	X		
			X				24–30				X	X	X	Rudbeckia—Coneflower	X			X				X	
X	X	X	X	X	X	X	24–30			X	X	X		Salpiglossis—Velvet Flower	X		X	X				X	
X							24–36				X	X	X	Salvia—Scarlet Sage	X							X	X
			X				6	X	X	X	X	X	X	Sanvitalia	X				X	X	X	X	
	X					X	8–24			X	X	X		Saponaria—Bouncing Bet	X						X	X	
X	X	X	X			X	X	24–30			X	X	X	X	Scabiosa—Mourning Bride—Pincushion Flower	X			X				X	
	X	X			X	X	X	12–18			X	X	X		Schizanthus—Butterfly Flower			X		X			X	
			X				6–8				X	X		Sedum—Annual Stonecrop	X					X		X	
X					X	X	18			X	X			Senecio Elegans—Ragwort	X		X					X	
	X				X		18–24			X	X			Statice—Limonium	X			X			X	X	
						X	24			X	X	X		Stevia Serrata	X			X				X	
X			X				42–84				X	X	X	Sunflower—Helianthus	X							X	
X	X	X	X	X	X	X	X	12–30				X	X	X	Stocks—Gilliflower	X			X				X	X
X	X	X	X	X	X	X	X	12–48	X	X	X	X	X		Sweet Peas	X			X	X			X	X
			X		X		X	12	X	X	X	X			Ursinia Anethoides	X			X				X	
		X					24–36			X	X	X		Venidium Fastuosum	X			X				X	
X	X			X	X	X	6–12			X	X	X	X	Verbena	X		X	X	X	X	X	X	X
	X					X	18–24			X	X	X	X	Vinca—Periwinkle	X							X	
	X					X	8–12			X	X	X		Virginian Stocks—Malcomia	X					X	X		
X			X				12–18			X	X			Wallflower, Annual	X			X					X
X	X	X	X			X	X	12–24			X	X	X	X	Zinnia	X					X		X	X

Flower Chart by Permission of the Templin-Bradley Company, Cleveland, Ohio.

CHAPTER XII

Flower Arranging

IT IS impossible to give a complete guide to flower arrangement in the space which we can assign to it. It requires thought and practice in actual handling and the interested gardener will find many books upon the subject in libraries. We offer the following as only a few hints to help the gardener avoid the most common mistakes.

Selection. The first thing to consider before selecting the flowers is how you wish to use them. Some flowers have such an intimate appeal that they seem made to be looked into; others have a stately and dignified appeal—these are to be looked upon. Select your flowers to fit the use and location. Violets, lilies-of-the-valley, pansies, water lilies, and many roses show to better advantage when looked into or down upon. These are examples of the intimate flowers and do well upon tables and lower locations. Gladioli, hollyhocks, etc. are seen best slightly above the eye and against a background. This does not constitute a hard and fast rule, but is only a good general suggestion.

Color harmony also enters into selection. Colors must not clash with each other or with wall paper or furnishings. Flowers must suit the container in which they are displayed. Both vase and flowers may be beautiful but they do not belong together unless they complement one another.

Containers. Bright or gaudily colored vases or bowls make artistic arrangement difficult because they dominate the arrangement, making the flowers secondary. Highly ornamented glass is bad for the same reason. Plainer glass may be used for such intimate plants as roses, pansies, etc. Silver is not flattering to most flowers and should be used only with plants of good color and foliage, such as fine roses. Dark, heavy bronze or pottery is for bold material, while those pieces of finer glaze and more delicate coloring can be had for all types of flowers, approximating

them in quality. It is best for the amateur to stay away from modernistic effects.

Attractively proportioned containers are now to be had so cheaply that anyone can command a supply. Ideally, a home should contain the following containers: (1) One heavy large container for flowering shrubs, thick-stemmed flowers, or foliage. This may be copper, pewter, or pottery, but should be unglazed and dull in tone. (2) One tall vase about a foot high for long-stemmed flowers. (3) Several vases ranging in size from five to ten inches high in various materials and colors. (4) One large shallow bowl about 14 inches wide. (5) A few smaller bowls for dining tables, etc. (6) Where water lilies are available, a flat bowl of bronze or irridescent glass, three inches deep, about 14 inches wide, and having a basin of six inches with a four-inch, almost flat lip or edge.

Arrangement. Upon the apparent weight or bulk of the container depends the proper height and width of the arrangement. A metal or pottery bowl will allow for a much larger assembly than transparent glass of the same size, because the pottery seems heavier.

Try to get proportion and balance. An old Japanese rule is that the flowers shall be one and one-half times the height of a tall vase or the width of a flat one. Balance must be obtained without monotonous symmetrical effect. Use an uneven number of flowers with stems of uneven length. No flowers should be directly above each other and none should be upon exactly the same level.

In the mass or full arrangement, arrange large flowers at the base and hide the edge of your container by overhanging the leaves or blooms. Also in mass arrangements place the darker, heavier material at the base nearest the center. The most flagrant sin in mass arrangement (and in all others, too, for that matter) is overcrowding. Do not use too many varieties of flowers. There is dignity and restraint in an arrangement of one variety in its own foliage. In the use of several varieties and colors, do not scatter them through the composition but try to hold color together, allowing no two colors to be equal in amount but having one color dominate and the others act as complement to it.

Line arrangements are more interesting than the mass but much more difficult. A simple principle is to allow one gracefully curving stem or the tallest flower to become the center of the composition, being careful to keep the tip directly over its base. It may curve away from the base but must return at the tip. Upon either side of this (using but few flowers) are assembled the stems, rising in strong lines from a central source. None of these stems are of the same height and they must not cross or parallel. Curves must be strong and definite.

All nature has taught man to expect an appearance of stability at the base. A tree or shrub is heavier there and a flower arrangement must be also. Strong lines at the base give this effect in line composition. The use of heavier mass at the base gives it in other arrangements.

In combining mass and line, avoid confusion. Use a little of both types but do not complicate them with a tangle of ferns, baby's-breath, or sprays of weak growth. They blur the lines and clutter composition. Bold and vivid contrast, strong and graceful lines always win over a fussy attempt at prettiness. If these materials are used they should be a studied part of it and not an afterthought. Make the composition logical if not seasonal. Do not try to combine greenhouse or exotic plants with garden flowers.

Under-water or floating plants, while not good flower-show practice, sometimes make a charming table decoration. Roses and sweet peas will stand submerging and may be so displayed in a small crystal jar. A strip of sheet lead around the stem will hold them

½ IN. WIRE MESH HOLDERS CAN BE FORMED TO FIT ANY SIZE BOWL

½ INCH WIRE MESH

HEAVY LEAD STRIPS 1 TO 1½ IN WIDE MAY BE BENT INTO ANY SHAPE HOLDER

PERFORATED GLASS BLOCK

SUPPORTING WITH LEAD STRIPS.

VASE WALL SUPPORT FROM REAR EDGE OF VASE WITH LEAD STRIPS OR WIRE.

USING THE THIN WIRE

SIMPLICITY IS THE KEYNOTE FOR THE WATER LILY DISPLAY

AN EXAMPLE OF SUBMERGED DISPLAY

AN OPEN COMBINATION OF MASS AND LINE

A BLACK BASE BENEATH A TRANSPARENT VASE WILL ADD WEIGHT

A SIMPLE AND AN EFFECTIVE ARRANGEMENT

CUT FLOWERS
FROM SPRING-FLOWERING BULBS

Cut just as the bud is about to open. Don't cut off many leaves.

DEEP VASE   WRAP IN PAPER

Plunge in water up to blooms for an hour to stiffen stems.

Keep away from direct sun, drafts, heat registers or radiators.

CUT ON A SLANT

Lasting qualities are increased by daily renewal of water and trimming off a thin slice of stem.

which have no place in arrangement. A glass block with large holes is necessary for heavy-stemmed flowers but wire holders are more practical. These can be purchased in all sizes or made of one-half inch wire mesh, obtainable at hardware stores. A piece of this material fitted into a vase or bowl sometimes proves useful.

Strips of sheet lead have innumerable uses. The lighter weights wrap around stems to hold them in place and may be hooked over the rear rim of the vase to support some stem. Heavier weight may be used to form an easily changed flower base. Lead is obtainable from plumbers or supply houses and fine wire just the right size for support is sold by stationers for fastening shipping tags.

How to keep cut flowers. Scientific investigations in the laboratories of several colleges have proved the use of salt, aspirin, or other chemicals to make cut flowers last longer to be without basis in fact.

All plants reach their highest activity when distended by water. When the roots of growing plants fail to supply water faster than the leaves transpire, the plant wilts. The problem of keeping cut flowers is likewise to keep a supply of water coming up through their stems. All processes of cutting and care are to accomplish this end.

Plants are endowed by nature with the ability to start immediately to heal over (callus) a cut or wound to avoid loss of the vital juices. This happens in the cut-off portions when stems are exposed to the air. The callus, or tissue, retards the absorbing of water from the flower vase. Therefore, we cut off stems longer than needed and recut them to proper length with a sharp safety-razor blade under water to avoid exposure of the callus.

The original cutting is done with a sharp scissors or knife, using care to have sharp tools to avoid injury to the growing plant. A special pair of cutting scissors may be bought which holds the cut-off stem, allowing the removal to be a one handed operation. It is best to carry a small bucket of water to the garden, rather than the familiar cutting basket.

After the second (under-water) cutting the stems should be immediately plunged into cool water up to the blooms to avoid loss through the leaves and to absorb moisture through the stems. Keep them there for several hours or overnight. Flowers wilted by

upon the bottom. Water lilies will only float, so they are displayed with smaller specimens of their foliage in the flat bowl previously described. The smaller pads are arranged upon the flat sides, while a white and a colored flower floats in the basin, separated by two diminutive leaves of water hyacinth or a spray of primrose creeper. Night bloomers will stay open better indoors. A little paraffin (barely warm enough to melt) dropped into the center will help keep others open. Chewing gum applied to a very short section of the stem as soon as cut also prevents closing.

Many arrangements require some mechanical support. In flower blocks, avoid figures shipments, etc., can often be revived by this process.

Most plants should have a slanting cut to expose a larger absorbing surface and to avoid sealing them by resting upon the bottom of the vase. Woody stems (shrubs, peonies, etc.) should have the ends slit or a little bark peeled away. Chrysanthemum stems do best when slightly battered but the stems of plants which exude a sticky or milky sap after cutting (dahlias, oriental poppies, heliotropes, poinsettias) must be sealed by searing them with the flame of a match or by dipping the tips in boiling water. The tips of hollyhock cuttings may be dipped in a solution of one-tenth of one per cent nitric acid. Be careful to protect the blooms and foliage during searing or dipping. When this type of plant is placed in the cool water bath, the moisture is absorbed through the sides of the stems and loss of the vital sap is prevented by the sealed ends.

Another important step in long-lasting bouquets is the cutting at the proper stage of development. Most flowers fade immediately after pollination. It is best to cut them just as they begin to mature and where possible remove the stamens to prevent pollination. This is quite easy on many flowers, such as lilies, amaryllis, etc. Cut gladioli as the first bud opens; peonies as the outer petals develop; roses in the soft bud; dahlias in full bloom after the sun goes down; poppies the night before and allow them to open in the water. A few drops of gelatine on the ends of the stems of the orientals help. Immediately upon cutting the calla lilies, cover all leaves and stems overnight with cool water. A bathtub or any large, open receptacle will do. They seem to be unable to absorb enough water any other way. Wilted arrangements may be revived in the same manner. Wild flowers, except buttercups, daisies, and goldenrod, seldom ever keep as cut flowers. Iris, if going a distance, should be cut in the bud.

Plants are the most filled with sap in the morning. Therefore, cut at this time those which wilt most easily. Early morning or late evening is the best time to gather.

Flowers should never be crowded into a small-mouthed vase. Air should easily reach the water. Water must be clean, cool, and pure. In stale water, bacteria forms quickly upon the ends of the stems and chokes the passage of moisture. It is best to cut a thin slice from stem ends daily and supply fresh water.

In the case of special arrangements which will not stand disturbing, three drops of formalin and a teaspoonful of charcoal to the quart of water will keep it uncontaminated. Never allow leaves below the water, especially the leaves of chrysanthemums, dahlias, etc.

Straw flowers and other "everlastings" should be dried in loose, uncrowded bunches, head down, in cool shade. This will prevent the drooping of the blossoms before drying. Cut them in various stages of development for variety and always dry more than you need so that you may select the ones which "cure" best and reject the rest. Plant some of these easily grown annuals now for indoor color next winter. Arranged with evergreen creepers, etc. for living foliage, they give a very convincing effect all during the winter months.

Forcing flowering branches. When you begin to tire of winter it is time to brighten the home with flowering branches forced in water. The early-blossoming varieties force the easiest. These are from buds formed during the previous summer. Their blossoms are borne directly upon the old wood and, after a short dormant period, are ready to burst into bloom as soon as they receive light, warmth, and, most of all, sufficient water. The flower buds on such shrubs as forsythia and spicebush are sufficiently well formed to be really visible.

For the best results immerse the branches in tepid water, in a bathtub or laundry tray, for the better part of the day. Do not use hot water. Then place them in jars of water in a sunny window of a cool room for about a week. When the buds are about to burst, bring them into the warm room for display. If the branches do not seem to respond, repeat the soaking for an hour or so.

Since the branches will absorb considerable water, care must be taken to have the water changed often. Use only water at room temperature. A little charcoal in the containers will keep the water sweet. After they are in bloom, the cooler they are kept the longer the bloom will last.

Many common and easily procured plants produce brilliant results. We may use apple, pear, plum, cherry, peach, red maple, Japanese maple, dogwood, forsythia, early-flowering spireas (thunbergia and bridal wreath—prunifolia), flowering almond, witch hazel, lonicera, deutzia, flowering quince, azalea, and many others. Catkins from American and European alder make attractive displays and sometimes the common Carolina poplar gives good results.

The first important matter is the receptacle. Transparent bowls or light-colored porcelain do not fit. Dark, rather heavy pottery is best. The Japanese use brass jars. We illustrate a method of trimming branches. Figure 1 indicates primary or upright branches; Figures 2 and 3, side arrangement. The finished arrangement is shown below.

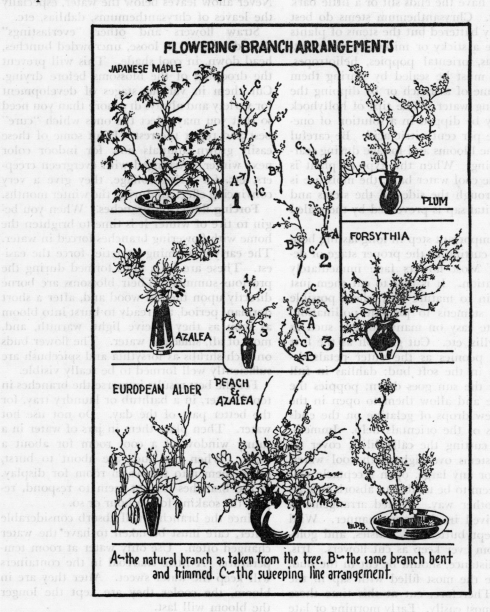

FLOWERING BRANCH ARRANGEMENTS

JAPANESE MAPLE

PLUM

FORSYTHIA

AZALEA

EUROPEAN ALDER

PEACH & AZALEA

M.P.B.

A—the natural branch as taken from the tree. B—the same branch bent and trimmed. C—the sweeping line arrangement.

CHAPTER XIII

The Rock Garden

Flower in the crannied wall,
I pluck you out of the crannies;
Hold you here, root and all, in my hand,
Little flower—but if I could understand
What you are, root and all, and all in all,
I should know what God and man is.
— TENNYSON

ROCKERIES are unique in the fact that they maintain our interest the year round. Some of the plants bloom as early as February and as late as December. Because it takes so little space and is readily adapted to any contour it is ideal for the amateur. Combined with water gardening in a small pool it is one of the most interesting of the garden features. While few of the plants may be used for cut flowers, a careful selection will insure a continuous bloom, and the foliage of many of them is as beautiful as the flowers themselves. In order to be at its best a rockery should be almost covered with plants. A mound with a few petunias is not a rockery; it is more likely to be an eyesore.

Site. The first essential to success is the careful selection of the site. This should be a sunny location. A few plants suitable for a rock garden thrive in shade. If no slope is available a low mound may be constructed against a wall in the corner or at the edge of the garden plan. Mounds used in the center of a lawn should be avoided. Drainage is absolutely necessary for success. The illustration shows how to treat a rock garden on a hill, which is composed of heavy clay soil. In this instance the topsoil should be stripped off, if it is worth saving, and composted with some good humus or well-rotted manure; work in some sand and have the soil perfectly light and friable before using.

Remember, you cannot reach under the rocks and condition the soil when it has once been placed. See that it contains plenty of vegetable matter before using. If necessary, bring in a load or at least a few barrels of rich soil with which to build the rockery. It is better to build one square yard with the proper soil than the larger one with the improper soil. Avoid excessive chemical fertilization. All stones must go through to drainage and they should be tilted up to an angle so that any rain falling on its surface is thrown back into the ground.

Stones. Place the stones irregularly with good-size pockets of soil between. Leave out a stone once in a while to make the larger pockets. Irregularity is essential. A rockery must not look like masonry wall, unless you are building a wall garden, and even then, broken courses add to the charm. Enough stone must be used to keep the ground from washing, but by using smaller pieces of stone between to block these washes a large amount of dirt can safely be exposed. The idea is to use as few stones as possible for the effect desired and to use this material so that it looks like a natural formation. For instance, a limestone rockery in connection with a pool and waterfall should look like the natural outcroppings of limestone in hills.

A wall garden is essentially artificial and need not be an imitation of any natural setting. However, an appearance of ruggedness and rustic effect is essential; it must not look like a brick wall. Decide what you want the rock work to look like; spend your efforts toward that end.

The material to be used will, of course, depend upon what is readily obtainable. Limestone or well-worn rock of any kind is very good. However, it should not be so soft that it will crumble away in a few years. Boulders properly handled make a good moraine garden, but they should not be used for ledge effect. Avoid absolutely broken concrete and building rubbish. Do not build a rockery if you have to use these materials. Better to raise the plants without the use of stone.

Soil. The next essential to drainage is firm soil. The soil between the crevices should be

ROCK GARDEN ON A HILL 2" TO 4" OF GOOD SOIL — NOTE ANGLE OF STONES — TO MAKE WATER RUN INTO THE BANK —

SOIL LEVEL

2" CINDERS OR GRAVEL FOR DRAINAGE

CLAY SOIL

HOW TO BUILD A WALL GARDEN

SLOPE FACE OF WALL INWARD

FILL WITH GOOD RICH SOIL

SLOPE OF BANK

FOUNDATION BELOW ORIGINAL LOWER LEVEL OF LOT

RAM DIRT IN WELL. ALL CREVICES MUST GO THROUGH TO DRAINAGE.

TREATMENT OF A SLOPING LOT

USE AN OCCASIONAL DEEP POCKET. IRREGULARITY IS ESSENTIAL TO CHARM. LARGE POCKETS FOR MASSES AND SMALL POCKETS FOR INDIVIDUAL PLANTS.

BEFORE AND AFTER PLANTING. IN PLACING STONES KEEP THE WORK REALISTIC. STUDY NATURAL OUTCROPINGS AND IMITATE THEM.

firmly compacted. Some plants have the tendency to work themselves out of the ground or to expose their roots. Small pieces of stone left from building of the rockery should be saved and placed around the roots of plants, both to conserve the moisture and to keep them in the ground. Additional soil must be added from time to time to protect root growth.

Plants. As to the selection of plants: Shade plants will bear sunshine, whereas sun-loving plants will not do well even in partial shade. It is therefore necessary that the major part of the rockery be in the open, and that a careful study be made to plant only shade-loving plants in the unexposed portions. Most plants do not like lime, and this should be avoided, although a mulching with limestone chips firmed into the top part of the exposed soil has a tendency to keep it from drying out and adds to the naturalizing of the plant. Some of the plants like moderately alkaline soil and others acid soil. Ordinary soil will do for the alkaline-loving, but the acid-loving plant should have soil composted with peat moss or treated with aluminum sulphate.

Visit places where plants grow or are offered for sale in bloom. Consult the grower as to whether the plant is rampant or slow in growth. Attempt to group them according to foliage and color of bloom, bearing in mind whether the rampant growers will crowd out the slow-growing plants. Trailing plants should have room to spread or hang down from projecting ledges. Do not be afraid to weed out the quick growers and keep them from strangling the others.

VIGOROUS PLANTS FOR THE BEGINNER'S ROCK GARDEN

Achillea tomentosa (Millifoil)
Alyssum saxatile (Goldentuft)
Anchusa myosotidiflora (Bugloss)

Aquilegia nivea (Columbine)
Arabis alpina (Rock Cress)
Asperula odorata (Woodruff)
Campanula carpatica (Bell-flower)
Cerastium tomentosum (Snow-in-summer)
Dianthus caesius (Cheddar Pink)
Dianthus deltoides (Maiden Pink)
Gypsophila repens (Creeping Gypsophila)
Helianthemum mutabile (Sunrose)
Heuchera sanguinea (Coralbells)
Iberis sempervirens (Candytuft)
Iris pumila
Myosotis palustris semperflorens (Forget-me-not)
Nepeta mussini (Catnip)
Phlox subulata (Moss Pink)
Primula polyantha (Primrose)
Polemonium reptans (Creeping Polemonium)
Saponaria ocymoides (Rock Soapwort)
Sedum album (White Stonecrop)
Sedum ellacombianum (Stonecrop)
Sedum reflexum (Stonecrop)
Sedum spurium coccineum (Stonecrop)
Sempervivum soboliferum (Hen and Chickens)
Sempervivum tectorum (Roof Houseleek)
Teucrium chamaedrys (Germander)
Thymus serpyllum (Thyme)
Tunica saxifraga (Coatflower)
Veronica incana (Speedwell)
Veronica teucrium (rupestris) (Speedwell)
Viola Jersey Gem (Violet)

Dwarf Shrubs for Rock Gardens

Abelia grandiflora
Berberis thunbergi minor (Barberry)
Cotoneaster horizontalis
Potentilla fruticosa (Cinquefoil)
Stephanandra flexuosa

Dwarf Evergreens for Rock Gardens

Chamaecyparis obtusa nana (Dwarf Hinoki Cypress)
Daphne cneorum (Garlandflower)
Euonymus radicans (Evergreen Wintercreeper)
Euonymus radicans minimus
Juniperus horizontalis (Creeping Juniper)
Pinus montana mughus (Swiss Mountain Pine)
Taxus cuspidata nana (Japanese Yew)

Ground Cover Plants for Rock Gardens

Ajuga reptans (Carpet Bugle)
Arabis alpina (Rock Cress)
Campanula carpatica (Bellflower)
Cerastium tomentosum (Snow-in-summer)

Steps and walks can be made a part of the garden itself by proper planting and construction.

Dianthus deltoides (Maidenpink)
Euonymus radicans minimus
Myosotis palustris semperflorens
Nepeta mussini (Catnip)
Phlox subulata (Moss Pink)
Saponaria ocymoides (Rock Soapwort)
Sedum album (Stonecrop)
Sedum spurium (Stonecrop)
Thymus serpyllum (Thyme)
Veronica filiformis (Speedwell)
Veronica pectinata (Speedwell)
Veronica teucrium (rupestris) (Speedwell)

CHAPTER XIV

Window Boxes

She lifted their heads with her tender hands,
And sustained them with rods and osier bands;
If the flowers had been her own infants she
Could never have nursed them more tenderly.
—SHELLEY

ALTHOUGH we hear much of interior decoration, few people realize the possibilities of improving the appearance of the exterior of the house by the use of vines and window boxes. They may be made to soften lines or to add gay colors to brighten somber shades. The box need not match the architecture of the house. In fact, this would sometimes be impossible. It should harmonize and not be painted a color which clashes. It sometimes adds to the appearance if an attempt is made to work window boxes in as an added architectural detail.

Size and material. Do not make them too small. They will appear to better advantage if they are many times as long as they are wide. If placed in a window allow them to extend past the opening four to six inches on either side rather than fit them into the sill. This will be found to add considerably to their appearance and they may be supported on brackets attached to the wall. On a porch rail it is better to have the larger portion outside the rail.

One of the chief objections to flower boxes has been that they are only an ornament in the summertime. They can be made attractive in winter as well by the use of small evergreens and vines, or they can be made removable to be stored away during the winter. Material for the box should be white pine or, still better, cypress. Ordinary clear yellow pine will last a long time if carefully painted. All joints should be thoroughly painted with at least two coats before the box is put together and brass screws should be used instead of nails.

Soil requirements. There should be plenty of drainage. About two inches of coarse gravel should be placed in the bottom. Over this should be placed enough sand to cover the gravel well. In this type of box, watering is required almost daily. If the ground is allowed to dry it will crack away from the boards and the plant will suffer.

Fertilizer. If the soil is carefully selected and reworked with some sheep manure each year, the box need not be refilled for several years. Liquid manure, applied as previously instructed, adds to the bloom. A little chemical plant food or, still better, plant tablets, may be given once a month but care should be used not to apply it until the plants are well established and then not to overdo it.

Plants. A wide variety of plants are available and the simple favorites are many times the best. Select the plants to fit conditions of sun or shade. Even partial shade affects them.

For sunny exposure use:

Upright—lantana, petunia, nasturtium, dwarf marigold, heliotrope, geranium, everblooming begonia, candytuft, sweet alyssum, ageratum, coleus, dusty-miller.

Trailing—trailing geranium, trailing lantana, asparagus plumosa, asparagus sprengeri, vinca, German ivy, English ivy, wandering Jew.

For the shady boxes use:

Upright—begonia, viola, fuchsia, forget-me-not, almost any fern or foliage plant.

Trailing—same as for sunny box.

WINTER   WINDOW   SUMMER
BOXES

INSIDE MEASUREMENTS 8 IN. WIDE BY 8 IN. DEEP

FOR ENGLISH OR SWISS TYPE HOUSE

FOR COLORED SHINGLE HOUSE

COLONIAL - DECORATIVE

COLONIAL - PLAIN

LATTICE DESIGN

2 SUB-IRRIGATING TYPES

2 IN. GRAVEL   SOIL   WATERING SPOUT

NOTCH

WATER HERE   SOIL

SAND OR GRAVEL.

12 IN.   8

7 IN.

2 IN

14 IN.

METAL PAN SHAPE OVER BOX

2" PEBBLES

BOX WITHOUT SUB IRRIGATION

MUST HAVE 2 IN PEBBLES IN BOTTOM & PLENTY OF DRAINAGE HOLES.

BEND OVER

AND FLATTEN.

PIONEER - RUSTIC

LOG CABIN - RUSTIC

STUCCO COVERED OR WOOD BOX WITH SILHOUETTE CUT-OUT DESIGN OF METAL.

MAKING A CONCRETE WINDOW BOX.

CUT DESIGN FROM CARDBOARD OR FIBRE. TACK ON TO INSIDE OF MOLD — OIL ENTIRE INTERIOR BEFORE POURING CEMENT.

USE TAPERED WOODEN BOX OR METAL CORE.

CAST BOX UPSIDE DOWN

WIRE BOX TIGHTLY.

BEND DOWN

TO RE-ENFORCE CONCRETE USE 1/2 IN. GALVANIZED IRON WIRE MESH

KEEP WIRE MESH IN CENTER OF CONCRETE. TAMP FIRMLY ON BOTH SIDES.

POUR 1/2 OF BOTTOM OVER CORE — LAP MESH OVER CONCRETE AND COMPLETE POURING

REMOVE FORMS & LIFT OUT CORES.

CHAPTER XV

House Plants

He has no yard behind his house,
No garden green to till,
And so he works the hothouse plan
Upon his window sill.

—OLD SONG

Light. Unless otherwise directed, it is safe to say that all blooming plants should be placed in the sun for at least a part of the day and turned often for even bloom. Ferns, vines, and foliage plants do well at north and east windows but flowers come from exposure to the south and west sun. Ivies and several other plants will thrive away from windows but all must have light.

Potting transplanting. The illustration shows pot sizes, both in inches and by name. A very common error is made in potting by the beginner. Ordinarily one would think that the larger the amount of soil the better for the plant. This is not the case. Contrary to previous belief, experiments have proven that glazed decorative pots are satisfactory receptacles. If watering is carefully done, some plants, such as succulents and moisture loving kinds, even do well in pots without bottom drainage holes. New pots seem to get an alkali in the process of manufacture which injures the plant roots.

It is best for the gardener who expects to do any great amount of gardening to have a potting table. The potting itself is simple. (See the illustration.)

When we talk of potting we mostly mean repotting or shifting from one container to another. Most repotting is to obtain proper rooting. Sometimes a pot becomes so rootbound that the pot must be broken to get it out. This is better than injuring the roots by cutting. Do not be in a hurry to repot.

After the spring renovating the plants should have a chance to renew their vitality in the fresh air. There should be open sun for the bloomers (slight protection for begonias); semishade for many foliage plants; and more dense shade for the ferns. Do not overlook summer watering and pest inspection and before taking the plants indoors examine the soil for worms.

Most plants should be plunged (still in their pots) outdoors during the summer. Bury them to the rim and place a concave piece of pot below the drainage hole to keep it open. When ready to bring the plant indoors, knock the soil from the pot and wash it inside and out so that it starts the winter clean.

Care of leaves. Never pour water over the foliage of the plant but apply a fine misty spray with a bulb-syringe sprinkler every ten days to flush off soot and dust. The smooth, strong-leaved ones should be washed with lukewarm water and mild soapsuds once a month, using a soft sponge. For ferns and palms and rubber plants mild soapsuds is used every ten days as a spray instead of just plain water. Protect plants from indirect sunlight while wet. Plants with hairy foliage (African violets, etc.) do not like water on their leaves at all.

All dead or yellowed foliage should be removed to its base and all flowers must be removed as soon as they have passed their usefulness as ornaments. Pinch out the top of geraniums and cut back such plants as begonias, which are inclined to become straggly, to make them bushy for better blooming.

Food. Plants with heavy roots require a heavier, more loamy soil; plants with fine, fibrous roots need a more open, sandy soil. For quick-growing plants a quart of sheep manure or dried cow manure may be incorporated in each bushel of soil. For slowgrowers a quart of bone meal is better. This figures from one to three tablespoons to each five-inch pot. The bone meal can be applied to any pot (except azaleas and other acid plants) as it is safe and beneficial.

The use of liquid manure must also be understood. A few handfuls of cow, horse, or sheep manure in a bucket of water makes a good top dressing for healthy plants about to bloom. Applied to a sickly or dormant plant, it serves as a rude shock rather than a benefit. First pot, water, and sun your plant until it starts active growth; then gradually feed it until it starts active growth; then gradually feed it until it flourishes. Dilute the liquid manure to the color of very weak tea and apply the same as other waterings. Quick-growing plants may have it every ten days; slow-growing plants once every thirty days.

A solution of chemical plant food, one tablespoon to three gallons of water, may be applied as a substitute for liquid manure. Plant tablets are excellent, especially on plants used for window boxes: geraniums, petunias, lantana, vinca vines, etc. Press the tablets down into the soil close to the stem and wet them thoroughly. Never use either liquid or dry plant food upon dry soil. Water first, then fertilize. Never permit the soil food to touch the leaves.

Loosen the soil carefully on the top of the

HOW TO POT PLANTS

13 IN. 6'S
15 IN. 4'S

4½ IN.
48'S
6 IN.
32'S
8½"
24'S
9 IN.
16'S
11½ IN.
12'S
12 IN.
8'S

3 IN. 60'S
2½ IN. THUMBS.
2 IN. THIMBLES.

POT
PAN.

POTS ARE USUALLY SAME DEPTH AS DIAMETER. SOMETIMES MENTIONED BY SIZE—OFTEN BY NAME

18 IN.
2'S

SCRUB OLD POTS INSIDE AND OUT

BOIL OR SOAK NEW POTS

HAVE A SHELF OVER POTTING TABLE

DRAINAGE & CROCKS IN BOTTOM

ADD A FEW LEAVES OVER DRAINAGE

SIFTED SOIL COMPOST

HUMUS   SAND   SOIL

½ GOOD GARDEN LOAM

¼ SAND

¼ PEATMOSS HUMUS OR PULVERIZED LEAF MOULD

BONE MEAL

4 TEASPOONS STEAMED BONE TO EACH 5 IN. POT OR 1 QT. TO A BUSHEL OF SOIL.

BONE MEAL

POTTING BENCH. 3 X 3 FEET.

PROPER ROOTING AND WHEN TO RE-POT

LOOSENING   NEEDS LARGER POT.   NEEDS SMALLER POT.

USE POTS AS SMALL AS POSSIBLE—MANY PLANTS BLOOM BEST WHEN SLIGHTLY POT BOUND

COMB OUT ROOTS LIGHTLY WITH A FORK BEFORE REPOTTING

WATERING AND WASHING

VERY DRY PLANTS CAN BE WATERED BY IMMERSION.

WASH OR SPRAY LEAVES FREE OF SOOT OR DUST. GET UNDER THE LEAVES.

ON FERNS, PALMS OR RUBBER PLANTS, USE SYRINGE OF MILD SOAP-SUDS, EVERY 10 DAYS.

WHEN AND HOW TO FERTILIZE.

TOO SMALL TO STIMULATE

TOP FERTILIZE ONLY WHEN PLANTS ARE WELL DEVELOPED.

A BUCKET OF WATER WITH A POUND OR SO OF SHEEP OR OTHER MANURE MAKES A GOOD DRESSING FOR PLANTS READY TO BLOOM—(APPLY THE COLOR OF WEAK TEA.)

THE SUN IS THE BEST FRIEND OF MOST BLOOMING PLANTS

HAVE PROPER WATERING DEVICE. USE WATER AT ROOM TEMPERATURE ONLY.

SOAK NEW POTS 1 WEEK. CLEAN OLD POTS THOROUGHLY.

BROKEN BITS OF POTS OVER DRAINAGE HOLE—ALWAYS KEEP OPEN.

PINCH OUT TOPS TO MAKE BUSHY.

REMOVE FADED LEAVES AND SPENT FLOWERS AT THEIR BASE.

LEAVE ½ TO 1 INCH AT TOP FOR WATER.

APPLY WATER GENTLY TO SOIL—DON'T FLOOD THE LEAVES.

GOOD COMPOST LOOSELY COMPACTED

DRAINAGE

WASH OFF INSECTS WITH A FINE, STRONG STREAM OF WATER

FOR APHIS, AND OTHER PLANT PESTS, USE A HAND SPRAY WITH NICOTINE SOLUTION.

INVERT SAUCER IN JARDINIERE

REMOVE STALE WATER OFTEN.

pot as frequently as possible. This admits air to sweeten the soil. Never use lime on house plants unless specifically directed to do so.

Pests. Surface spots on foliage indicate fungus troubles. A good fungus spray is a solution of one ounce of liver of sulphur (potassium sulphide) in three gallons of water. Get the underside of leaves, too. Dusting with this is a safe remedy for mildew. Separate the diseased plants and in severe cases destroy them.

Control aphids with a solution of nicotine sulphate as directed on the container. Mix with soapsuds. Washing strong-leaved plants with a hose spray and syringing others usually destroys red spider, scale, mealy bugs, etc. If it doesn't, a spray of miscible oil will do so.

Angle worms sometimes get into the pots, especially after summer plunging. A few matches stuck into the soil are said to kill them, but a better method is a piece of lime a little bigger than your fist in a gallon of water. Crush, stir, and wait until the mixture settles, then bottle for use at any time. An application or two will drive away the worm. If azaleas or hydrangeas are treated, it is better to apply a solution of one ounce of aluminum sulphate to a gallon of water to neutralize the alkalinity.

Watering. Watering may be divided into two distinct parts: moistening the soil and cleaning the leaves. These should not overlap. It is stated that more plants die from overwatering each year than from any other cause. General rules are misleading but the idea is to water well but not often. Get enough water on the plant to thoroughly moisten all the soil in the container. Excess water must be allowed to run off freely. Jardinieres are dangerous if the plant is allowed to stand in water or if stale water is allowed to remain to breed fungus growth. Change it often.

Humidity and temperature. Many flower-lovers have been disappointed with indoor blooms because of the hot, dry condition of the air in living rooms. When the temperature is comfortable for human beings, it is a deadly thing for the plants. A temperature of 70° F. is the top for plants indoors and the number which will stand this much is quite small. Bulb plants in bloom last much longer at 60° to 65° and tropical ferns and poinsettias do well at this rate. Most plants thrive at from 40° to 60°. How to attain this in our homes is a problem. Most people would feel decidedly chilly at this temperature.

It is generally thought that plants need an even temperature maintained at all times. Such is not the case. Cool rooms are better than those constantly warm but if the temperature is high in daytime and reduced at night it is a decided benefit and flowering is prolonged. The temperature must not, however, be less than 55°. Plants must not be allowed to freeze, and drafts and sudden changes must be kept away.

Another thing needed is humidity. In greenhouses and conservatories it is accomplished by spraying leaves, benches, floors and the plants themselves. Tests in well-managed greenhouses indicate that the humidity runs 75 to 85 per cent while in the average living room it runs 20 to 30 per cent.

Selection of plants. Below is a list of house plants taken from a bulletin of the Ohio State University, prepared by Irwin Klein, floriculture specialist.

FOLIAGE PLANTS

Cast-iron plant (*Aspidistra lurida*). This plant easily rates as the most tolerant house plant. It will live for months without direct sunlight; it doesn't object to too much or too little water, and it can withstand fluctuations of temperature. Because of its extreme tolerance the plant is put to many uses.

The leaves are large with long petioles arising from the rhizome. The drooping leaves give the plant a somewhat graceful appearance. Insects seldom attack this plant. An occasional bath will make it appear attractive at all times.

Wandering jew (*Tradescantia fluminensis*). This is a trailing vine of succulent growth with green leaves, often purplish beneath. Its requirements are few: plenty of moisture, a fair amount of sunlight, and approximately 60° temperature. Any type of soil will do; in fact, it will grow well in water. It is easily propagated by cuttings, placed in water, sand, or soil.

English ivy (*Hedera helix*). Another popular plant, perhaps because it does well in places receiving little sunlight and heat. It takes rapid growth under normal conditions and can be trained to supports for unusual effectiveness. If a bushy plant is desired, the ends of the branches should be pinched off.

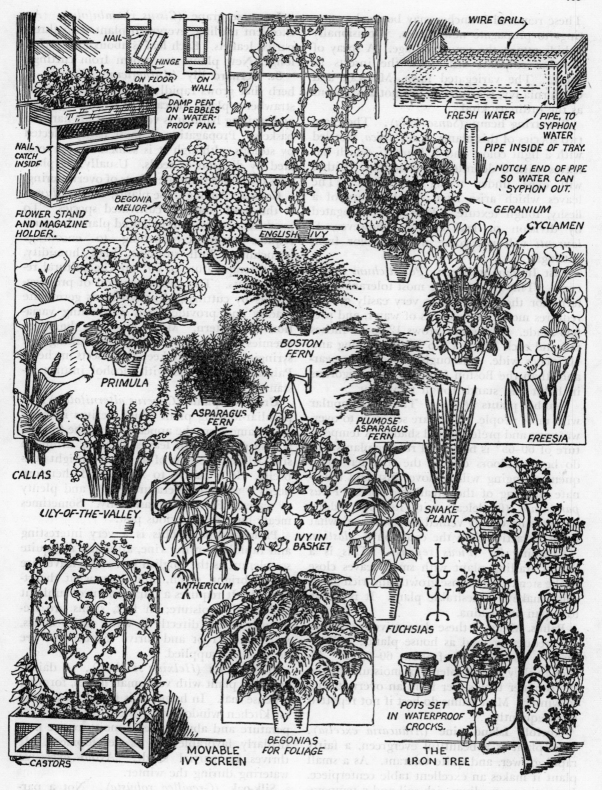

NAIL

HINGE

ON FLOOR

ON WALL

DAMP PEAT ON PEBBLES IN WATERPROOF PAN.

NAIL CATCH INSIDE

FLOWER STAND AND MAGAZINE HOLDER.

BEGONIA MELIOR

ENGLISH IVY

WIRE GRILL

6 IN.

FRESH WATER

PIPE, TO SYPHON WATER

PIPE INSIDE OF TRAY.

NOTCH END OF PIPE SO WATER CAN SYPHON OUT.

GERANIUM

CYCLAMEN

PRIMULA

BOSTON FERN

ASPARAGUS FERN

PLUMOSE ASPARAGUS FERN

FREESIA

CALLAS

LILY-OF-THE-VALLEY

IVY IN BASKET

SNAKE PLANT

ANTHERICUM

FUCHSIAS

BEGONIAS FOR FOLIAGE

POTS SET IN WATERPROOF CROCKS.

CASTORS

MOVABLE IVY SCREEN

THE IRON TREE

These removed branches may be used as cuttings to propagate new plants. Occasionally aphids attack the young foliage. A spray of nicotine sulphate will hold the insects in check. The variegated form, Mexican and California ivy, is attractive but not as vigorous as the ordinary kind.

Bowstring hemp (*Sansevieria*). There are two species of this plant: *S. zeylanica,* mottled with a light color; and *S. laurenti,* which has leaves with a definite white margin. Either will exist under trying conditions. The leaves which arise from the base are of a fleshy, tough texture. They are propagated by division or leaf cuttings; however, *S. laurenti* will not come true to color from cuttings.

East Indian hollyfern (*Polystichum aristatum*). This is one of the most tolerant of all ferns for the house. It is very easily grown, requires moderate amounts of water, and prefers shade. The plant grows 12 to 18 inches tall and each leaf is 12 to 24 inches long and 10 inches wide. Although coarser in appearance than the Boston fern, it is very vigorous in habit and stands rough treatment.

Rubber plants (*Ficus*). These are popular with most people. They are sensitive to overwatering and prefer partial shade. A temperature of 60–65° is best. All rubber plants will do best outdoors during the summer. Frequent sponging will remove dust and eliminate clogging of the breathing pores. *Ficus pandurata* (fiddleleaf) with its large, fiddle-shaped, and deeply veined leaves, is somewhat more attractive than the common *F. elastica*.

Creeping fig (*Ficus repens*). This is a dainty trailing plant with small leaves close to the stem. The dense growth and rich green color make it a desirable plant. It is native to Japan and China.

Palms. Many of these decorative evergreens are frequently used as house plants. All require a temperature of about 60–65° F. Although they require plenty of moisture during the summer they suffer from an overwatering in winter. Most palms do best if not repotted too frequently.

Norfolk Island pine (*Araucaria excelsa*). This plant is a beautiful evergreen, a fairly rapid grower, and quite tolerant. As a small plant it makes an excellent table centerpiece. It requires a medium rich soil and a temperature of 60°. During the summer it thrives in partial shade.

Japanese grape (*Cissus rhombifolia*). An excellent trailing, evergreen plant with three-parted leaflets. Each leaf is about four inches long. New plants are grown from cuttings.

St. Bernard lily (*Anthericum liliago*). A herb that grows rapidly from stolons like the strawberry plant. Because of its rapid growth and trailing habit it is very useful for hanging baskets. Propagation is most easily effected by stolons, although it is sometimes perpetuated by division or seeds. Usually the plant does not suffer from the effects of overwatering.

Coleus. Among these plants, *Coleus blumei* is the most common cultivated species. To produce a bushy, well-balanced plant the stems require frequent pinching to encourage branching. Full sunlight, high humidity, and a temperature of 60° are the cultural requirements. The easiest method of propagation is by cuttings, although seeds germinate readily and provide many interesting variations in pattern. Mealy bugs are the worst enemies of this plant. Frequent washing and syringing will help to keep the insects in check. Painting the insects with alcohol insures instant death.

Umbrella plant (*Cyperus alternifolius*). A peculiar-looking plant which derives its common name from the appearance of the foliage, a long petiole with leaves (blades) arranged similarly to the ribs of an open upright umbrella. It is native to Africa and therefore needs a warm temperature (65°) and plenty of water. Fertilize occasionally. Sometimes mealy bugs are a serious pest.

Philodendron. This is a very interesting and rapidly growing vine, although not quite so tolerant as the English Ivy. The leaves are large, bright green, and somewhat heart-shaped. It requires a fair amount of sunlight and much moisture; in fact, stems are frequently placed directly in water in ivy bowls, where they root and thrive if nutrients are occasionally supplied.

Baby's-tears (*Helxine soleiroli*). A dainty creeping plant with very small leaves, forming a dense mat. In homes it is found frequently on kitchen window sills where the high temperature and abundance of moisture are particularly favorable for its development. It thrives in partial shade. Avoid excessive watering during the winter.

Silk-oak (*Grevillea robusta*). Not a particularly showy plant, but a very rapid, vigorous grower. In its native land of Australia it becomes a tree 150 feet tall. As a pot plant it produces a slender stem with long horizontal branches and feathery fern-like leaves. The usual method of propagation is by seed.

Periwinkle (*Vinca minor*). An excellent vine for window boxes and wall vases. The variety with variegated foliage is most attractive.

Leopard plant (*Ligularia koempferi*). This plant is used chiefly for its spotted foliage of white, yellow, or pink. New plants are started by cuttings or division.

Boston fern (*Nephrolepis exaltata bostoniensis*). One of the most popular house plants, although many people find it difficult to grow properly. Ferns are sensitive and require a temperature between 65° and 70°; lower or higher temperatures may cause poor growth. Poor drainage, together with overwatering, will turn the leaves yellow. Oversized pots create excessive moisture in the soil. High humidity (air moisture) is essential; it may be provided by frequent washing of the leaves. A partial shade is preferred to direct sunlight. All ferns are propagated by runners or division. Be on the lookout for white flies, aphids, and scales.

Asparagus fern. This fern is a native of South Africa. The species *A. Sprengeri* and *A. plumosus* are the two most common types used as house plants. Both produce long fronds which occasionally bear red to black berries. Overwatering and a hot, dry atmosphere will cause the leaves to drop.

House hollyfern (*Cyrtomium falcatum*). This interesting plant has dark green, glossy, pinnate leaves. The fronds are long and graceful.

Dumb cane (*Dieffenbachia brasiliensis*). Grown as a potted plant because of its broad, five to seven-inch variegated leaves. It is propagated from short stem cuttings, planted horizontally in sand. The natives of Central and South America become temporarily paralyzed from chewing the canes, the juice of which has a spicy taste.

Chinese rubber plant (*Crassula arborescens*). A slow-growing plant with very fleshy, oval leaves, and a thick stem, growing well in partial shade with moderate amounts of water. Most Japanese gardens contain at least one of these plants which are propagated from the tip cuttings or the fleshy leaves. A warm temperature with moderate humidity is necessary.

Nandina (*Nandina domestica*). An evergreen shrub native in China and Japan. As a house plant it makes an excellent specimen with its thin branches, bright red berries, and delicately colored leaves. It thrives in shady or sunny positions. Seed is the usual method of propagation.

Copper-leaf (*Acalypha macafeana*). A colorful plant, with copper colored leaves. It is propagated by heel cuttings. A temperature of 65° is best.

Screwpine (*Pandamus*). The most common species of the screwpine is *P. Veitchi*. The leaves are long, variegated, sword-like, with sharp teeth on the margins. It objects to excessive moisture in the winter and insufficient sunlight. New plants are produced by offsets.

Dracenas (*Dracaena*). Beautiful plants, grown for their variegated foliage. The genus *Cardyline* is similar to *Dracaena*, differing only in the flower parts. *D. fragrans* (corn-plant) is most common, with its large cornlike leaves. *Cordyline australis* (*indivisa*) has long, drooping, narrow leaves. The leaves of *D. godseffiana* appear in whorls or opposite on the stem, three to four inches long, with numerous white spots; flowers are greenish-yellow. *C. terminalis* has large leaves (12 to 30 inches long by three to four inches wide) in many colors. *D. goldieana* is a fine foliage plant with its broad, rounded leaves (seven to eight inches long and four to five inches wide) of white and green bands. Sponging the leaves with water at frequent intervals will improve their growth. Moderately warm temperature is necessary. The leaves will brown at the tips if overwatered.

Bird's-nest fern (*Asplenium nidus-avis*). This interesting plant is sometimes grown as a house plant. The leaves are broad and of a delicate green color. The arrangement of the leaves suggests a nest for birds. Strong sunlight will spot the leaves, and too much moisture may cause a loss of color.

FLOWERING PLANTS

Most of the flowering house plants are best grown if purchased as small plants from the florists. Home germination of seed is not very satisfactory.

Lemon, orange, and grapefruit. These are the most common citrus plants used as house plants. Of all flowering plants these are the most tolerant. They thrive in the high temperature of the average home. Although tolerant to partial shade they grow better in full sunlight. Overwatering is objectionable only during the winter. They react favorably to additions of complete fertilizers at regular intervals. On mature plants scales are troublesome occasionally.

Garden balsam (*Impatiens balsamina*). An old-fashioned plant popular with most people. The stems and leaves are quite succulent and the flowers are of various colors borne close to the stems. Pinching the terminal growths keeps the plant bushy and shapely. It thrives in a fertile soil in direct sunlight when supplied with plenty of water. It can be perpetuated by seeds or cuttings.

Cigar-flower (*Cuphea platycentra*). A native of Mexico. The flowers resemble a cigar, with their bright red calyx and white mouth with a dark ring at the end. It is easily grown in the house and is propagated by seeds.

Geranium (*Pelargonium*). Includes many species, such as the Fish Geranium, one of the most common house plants. The Lady Washington Pelargoniums are smaller leafed, many flowered, white to red with black blotches on the two upper petals. Madame Sellori, a variety of the Fish Geranium, is characterized by its variegated leaves. All species prefer plenty of sunlight and an abundance of water, although overwatering during the winter may cause the leaves to drop. A temperature between 65° and 70° increases flower production. Applications of fertilizer in fall and spring will improve the quality of the foliage and flowers.

Roses (*Rosa*). Many species make good house plants if given proper attention. A temperature of 60° is most desirable. When the plants are in flower a lower temperature and less water is essential. In the spring they may be planted out into the garden. Red spider is the most serious insect to fight. Frequent washing and syringing with water will give satisfactory control when applied during bright, sunny days. Dust with sulphur to prevent the spread of mildew, a white, powdery growth which appears on the leaves.

Pocket-book plant (*Calceolaria hybrida*). A very attractive plant. The flowers are shaped like an open purse, and are of many brilliant colors. Good drainage is essential. A good fibrous loam soil will produce quality plants if grown at a temperature not above 50°.

Poinsettia (*Euphorbia pulcherrima*). This is the favorite Christmas flower. While the plant is in bloom, refrain from adding much water. During its growing season it requires a temperature of 65° and plenty of sunlight. Avoid sudden chills. The plant is propagated by cuttings taken in early summer from plants carried from the previous winter. If the flower is cut from the plant, dip the end of the stem into boiling water or sear with a flame to prevent bleeding.

Hydrangea (*Hydrangea*). This beautiful plant seldom makes a good house plant because it is impossible to satisfy its needs in the ordinary home. It requires a cool temperature, an abundance of water, and an acid soil. If hydrangeas are desired in the home it is best to secure the plants from a florist while they are in flower. In spring transplant to a place in the garden having an acid soil. Protected the first year with a mulch they overwinter well outdoors. To be used again as a house plant they require a light freezing before lifting. Keep the plants in a cool place until December and then force into growth.

Gloxinia (*Sinningea speciosa*). An interesting plant. The flowers are large and bell-shaped, in velvety colors of violet to red or even white. It requires a warm, humid atmosphere and partial shade. After blooming, the tubers should be stored in a cool place until February, when they may be started into growth. Be careful not to wet the foliage. Flowering plants can be produced from seeds or cuttings in about twelve months.

BULBS INDOORS

In the cultivation of house plants, indoor bulbs are the most easily raised and maintained as well as the surest of bloom.

Hyacinths in jars of water. Regular hyacinth jars are for sale at your seedsmen. Quart food jars do just as well. Examine the jars once in a while to add tepid water. Temperature should stay between 40° and 50°. In about 8 to 15 weeks roots will have reached the bottom of the glass and some of the best developed ones may be moved to a warmer place (55° to 60° is best), and covered with a paper cone until a sprout about five inches long has formed. The foliage will be sickly, but upon removal of the cone it will turn bright green. Then set in a sunny window to bloom and turn daily for even growth.

Good results can be had by merely bringing

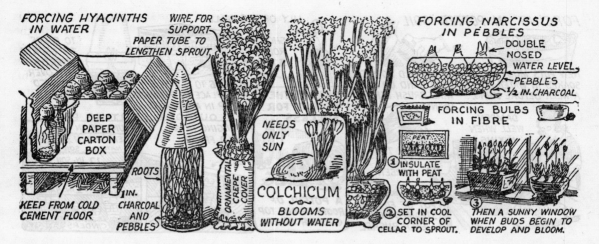

FORCING HYACINTHS IN WATER — WIRE, FOR SUPPORT PAPER TUBE TO LENGTHEN SPROUT — DEEP PAPER CARTON BOX — ROOTS — KEEP FROM COLD CEMENT FLOOR — 1 IN. CHARCOAL AND PEBBLES — ORNAMENTAL CREPE COVER — NEEDS ONLY SUN — COLCHICUM BLOOMS WITHOUT WATER — FORCING NARCISSUS IN PEBBLES — DOUBLE NOSED — WATER LEVEL — PEBBLES — 1/2 IN. CHARCOAL — FORCING BULBS IN FIBRE — ① INSULATE WITH PEAT — ② SET IN COOL CORNER OF CELLAR TO SPROUT. — ③ THEN A SUNNY WINDOW WHEN BUDS BEGIN TO DEVELOP AND BLOOM.

the jars as needed from the cool cellar into a dark corner of a slightly warmer one until top growth is started, and then placing them in a sunny window. Young hyacinth bulbs force easiest, Roman hyacinths easiest of all. Forcing in fiber or peat are excellent methods and just about as easy as in water.

Narcissus in water. Paper white narcissus bulbs and Chinese sacred lilies (which are really a variety of narcissus) can be forced in a bowl of pebbles easiest of all the bulbs. In fact they will give some degree of bloom if the bowls are merely placed in the light. They do best, however, if placed six or more in a glass bowl, which is set away in a dark spot in the cellar for three or four weeks. When brought into the open keep them away from direct sun for a few days until the tops turn bright green. It takes about five weeks from the time bulbs are started before they bloom. If water level is retained, cold drafts are kept away, and they are kept in a temperature of about 60°, the blooms will last at their best for two or three weeks. Paper-white bulbs bloom best if started about December 1. If you get them sooner expose them to the sun on a window sill for a week or two.

Growing in fiber. Prepared peat moss and prepared fiber are for sale at all seed stores. Using these is far superior to any other water method and can be successful on a much wider range of bulbs. It is not as good as forcing with soil but has the advantage of cleanliness in the house.

The fiber or peat is treated with plant food so that it holds the water for the bulbs and at the same time provides nourishment for roots and flower.

If the receptacle is watertight put a layer of charcoal in the bottom, press down firmly but not hard a layer of fiber, and place the bulbs in position. They should be about one-half their diameter apart and the peak of the bulb should be just below the top of the bowl. Now press the fiber gently but firmly into place so that it covers all but the tips of the bulbs, which should leave it one-half inch from the top of the vase. Add the water slowly until the fiber has reached full absorption and let it stand about one-half day. The same process of forming roots first is used with fiber as with other water methods.

Hyacinths, tulips, narcissi, croci, callas, freesias, muscari, scillas, snowdrops, spireas, and Easter lilies are particularly adapted for fiber growing.

Forcing bulbs in soil. Prepare soil by mixing two parts of good garden soil with one part commercial humus, peat moss (mix the two together if you have them), and enough sand (it will usually take one part sand to three parts soil mixture) so that you cannot pack the soil into a ball when squeezed wet. Sift it through a coarse riddle as you need it, first adding a five-inch pot of fine steamed bone flour to each bushel of soil.

Place a piece of broken pot over the drainhole and fill the pots lightly. The bulbs must be placed as the pots are filled, not screwed in afterwards. They should be just even with the top of the soil, which should be one-half inch from the pot rim. Do not pound soil into the pots, but fill them and tap once or twice to settle. The roots will strike down more easily in loose soil. They must have room to grow or they will force the bulb from the soil. After a thorough watering they are ready to take to the cool cellar.

FORCING IN POTTED SOIL

NEW POTS MUST BE SOAKED IN WATER FOR A WEEK BEFORE USING.

SCRUB OLD POTS CLEAN WITH SAND OR A FINE WIRE BRUSH BEFORE USING.

DAMPEN WELL WHEN MIXING

RUN THRU COARSE SCREEN

SAND

GOOD SOIL

PEAT OR LEAF MOULD

ADD 5 IN. POT OF FINE, STEAMED BONE TO EACH BUSHEL

HERE IS THE SECRET FOR SUCCESS

A POTFUL OF ROOTS BEFORE TOP GROWTH STARTS.

LILY OF THE VALLEY

SHORTEN ROOTS TO 3 INCHES

PLANT 6 TO 8 IN A 5 IN. POT.—PLACE IN PEATMOSS. KEEP IN A WARM PLACE.

TO FORCE TOP GROWTH, INVERT A POT OVER ROOTED BULBS.

OUTDOOR ROOTING PITS

PLUNGING IN A COLD FRAME.

SASH

PEATMOSS

SOIL

SOIL

CINDERS

SOIL

PLUNGING IN A PIT.

LEAF MULCH

NATURAL SOIL LEVEL

12 IN. SOIL

SOIL

2 IN. SAND

CINDERS

The easiest and best way to root them is out of doors. This is known as "plunging." The ease with which the peat can be removed for examination makes this arrangement attractive.

At the end of the time for rooting the pots must be uncovered and examined. They may be knocked loose by gently tapping the inverted pot. If the root is protruding from the drain-hole you will know it is fully developed. The best-developed roots should be brought indoors as needed and placed in a temperature of 50° for the development of top growth.

Lily of the valley. Valley lilies are not really bulbs. Their roots, called "pips," are excellent for indoor forcing. If you want to secure them from your own bed after freezing, discard the pointed crowns and select only the older, thicker crowns which end in a stubby blunt point. It is much better to purchase them from your seedsman as they are sure to bloom, while those dug from your garden are doubtful.

Place six or more in a five-inch flowerpot, with tips just above the surface. Soaking the pips in warm water (90° or 95°) for several hours will help foliage. Cut roots to about three inches and plant vertically.

CAPE BULBS

These plants get their name from their natural source, the Cape of Good Hope in South Africa. They include both bulbs and corms, such as freesias, ixias, and oxalis. Anemones and ranumculaceae are not cape bulbs but require the same culture, so we include them here.

Anemones and ranunculaceae. Plant them in deep pots, covering the roots two to three inches. Start potting in September and continue at monthly intervals until February for succession of bloom. Use rich soil—six or eight bulbs in a pan if you wish—and place in a cool, fairly light cellar. Keep them moist but not soggy until top growth begins. When brought to a sunny window give them more water and keep some standing in the saucer. The foliage of the anemone is fernlike and attractive and it flowers successively until through blooming. Allow the bulbs to ripen naturally and then keep them in sand or peat to prevent drying out until needed. Plant spent bulbs outdoors in fall or spring and use fresh bulbs for indoors each year.

Freesias. New colored hybrid varieties make this fragrant plant more attractive than ever. They will bloom from fall until spring under careful management. Large bulbs bloom sooner than small ones, which may take until April. A succession of bloom is obtained by pottings every three or four weeks from September 1 to October, but they may be potted as late as February provided cormels have not started to form on top of the old ones. They should bloom in 10 to 14 weeks. Bulbs are said to grow better if dried for two weeks in a sunny window. They may be planted all at one time and held back until needed in a cold frame or pit. They are tender and must never be put in freezing temperatures.

Plant six to a deep bulb pan two inches apart and cover tips not over one inch with soil made of garden loam, humus, and sand in equal parts. If peat moss is used it must be finely pulverized. Moisten the soil (not wet) as it is mixed and press the bulbs gently to proper depth. Place in a cool light spot (about 50°). When sprouts show bring them into room where temperature stays over 50° and under 70°.

As the buds show, give a little weak liquid manure at watering. Water frequently with water that is not cold after the sprouts start, avoiding water-soaked soil, and support blooms with thin stakes of wood or with heavy wire.

Oxalis. This is a dwarf trailing plant producing an array of dainty cup-shaped flowers, much used for hanging baskets and window boxes. Its leaf is similar to shamrock. It comes in pink, lavender, and white. Planted in spring outdoors, it is used for an edging flower to be dug before frost.

Put three or four bulbs in a four-inch pot covered one inch deep and place at once where it is to flower; there it will bloom in a few weeks and continue through the season. Water sparingly but keep soil moist. It has a rest period for a couple of months when the leaves die. Dry out by gradually withholding water and put in a warm place (which need not be dark) for a couple of months. In July or August pot the new bulbs which will be found at the end of the roots in the bottom of the pot.

Ixias and sparaxis. These are fairly hardy bulbs outside, but are good for inside also. The first is sometimes called African corn lily, and the second harlequin flower. It has beautiful flowers in many colors with attractive foliage growing 18 inches to two feet high. Plant outside in October or November and protect thoroughly, or plant in early spring, three inches deep and three to four inches apart.

MISCELLANEOUS BULBS FOR INDOORS

Alstroemeria (Chilean lily). Pot in August or as soon as possible, two inches deep, with sand about bulb. Root in cold frame or pit and bring directly to best sunlight. Water moderately but often while growing. Dry out after blooming to ripen until required for repotting.

Amaryllis hippeastrum (star Lily). Perhaps nothing will give the amateur greater pleasure than these lily-like, easily managed plants. It is essentially a window-garden plant, producing under the simplest conditions two to three spikes and three to six blooms. It is indiffer-

ent to house conditions and in later years many colored hybrids have increased its popularity.

Plant them as soon as received, usually during October and November, or any time before January, in pots one inch greater in diameter than the bulbs. They will not bloom if the pots are too large. Only the thick part is covered with soil; the long neck must be fully exposed. Use two parts good soil, one part rotted cow manure, and some bone meal, both fine and coarse. Turn the soil well and water sparingly until growth is well started and supply generously thereafter. Be careful of drainage. Keep them in a cool, shaded place but bring them into light at first sign of growth.

They need plenty of sunshine and liquid manure each week during the growing season. Flowers may form before leaves as the most of the foliage is produced after blooming. Take good care of the leaves after flowering if you want them to bloom again next year. They vary greatly in time of flowering, some buds appearing in January and others not blooming until spring.

Repot in summer if well established, using only slightly larger pots. Plunge the pots into soil in the open where they will get plenty of sunlight. When the leaves begin to turn yellow or frost checks them, gradually decrease watering and store the pots in a cool cellar. Look them over occasionally. Bring them to light and water them regularly when they show signs of life.

Tuberous begonia. They may be started from February to April. Pack them in peat moss level with the surface or on the surface, smooth side down (concave side up). Keep them damp, not wet, and place them in a warm, shady place until new growth starts. Then for rooting put each tuber in a four-inch pot of compost of garden soil (humus, dried cow manure and some sand) finely screened, rich and loose. Do not break roots when potting. Grow in temperature of 50° to 60°; protect them from too much sunlight, and change to pots six inches or better as soon as roots fill the smaller ones.

Soil for second potting is two parts fine leaf mould or leaf woods soil, one part humus, some sand, and a generous dusting of bone meal and dried blood. Have three-fourths inch of pot rim exposed for watering, which must be done often. Good and prompt drain-

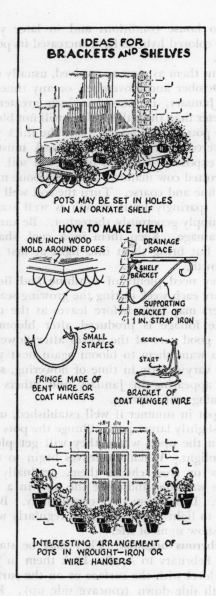

IDEAS FOR BRACKETS AND SHELVES

POTS MAY BE SET IN HOLES IN AN ORNATE SHELF

HOW TO MAKE THEM

ONE INCH WOOD MOLD AROUND EDGES

DRAINAGE SPACE

A SHELF BRACKET

SUPPORTING BRACKET OF 1 IN. STRAP IRON

SMALL STAPLES

SCREW

START

FRINGE MADE OF BENT WIRE OR COAT HANGERS

BRACKET OF COAT HANGER WIRE

INTERESTING ARRANGEMENT OF POTS IN WROUGHT-IRON OR WIRE HANGERS

age is necessary. Always plant tubers near surface. Pinch buds until plants are vigorous. Keep them protected from direct sun. Apply weak liquid manure when they are well established.

Semperflorens is the one type which always gives satisfaction for easy bloom. Beautiful semituberous begonias are featured by many florists (Melior, Glory of Cincinnati, and Mrs. Peterson are excellent examples) but these plants should be purchased as their propagation is difficult and exacting.

Calla or Richardia (*Tantedeschia aethiopica*). This so-called lily is a relation to the Jack-in-the-pulpit of our woods and is well known to amateurs. Use a six-inch pot of rich heavy soil, in the late fall, allowing about one inch of the root to remain above the surface. A compost of 2 parts good soil, one part cow manure (very old), and a little sand to open it up is best. Do not place in the dark but root them in a slightly cool place since they freeze easily. As soon as new growth is shown move them to a sunny window and water them plentifully and regularly. A saucer of water under them is sometimes used.

Frequent applications of sulphate of ammonia, one-half ounce to the gallon of water just before first bloom, make them continue freely. They stand a warm temperature. When the rest period approaches (June, July, and August), gradually dry them out in shade and place either plunged in soil or on their side. Repot in September.

White and yellow callas are recommended for house culture or out of doors. Spotted callas are usually reserved for outdoor culture. When in growing condition, warm water given several times weekly hastens the flowering period and the number of blooms, but may shorten the blooming period.

Cyclamen. One of the most deservedly popular house plants, it flowers from Christmas to Easter. Most plant lovers have found that new purchases each year make shapely specimens as the best blooms come from seedlings about 15 months old. Home propagation of seedlings is slow and difficult except in a greenhouse and last year's bulbs are very uncertain.

The young plants may be procured very reasonably in three-inch pots from August to November and repotted, as soon as received, in a four-inch pot. As fast as pots become filled with roots move into five- and six-inch pots. They do well in any soil that is not too heavy. Moisten them before potting. For fine blooms pinch out flowering stems that rise above foliage before November to conserve strength of the plant, and after this time give liquid manure or weak fertilized solution weekly.

They will continue to bloom for three months or more if flowers are pulled loose at the corm as soon as faded. Do not cut them; any parts of stems left will decay. Keep them in plenty of light but avoid noon sun. An even temperature is desirable; 40° to 50° will prolong the blooming season. Failure can usually be traced to neglect or constant exposure to hot, dry air.

Do not splash water on the plant when watering as the center of the bulb will decay if wet. Use water of room temperature and keep plant moist but not wet; sometime later empty saucer when watering. A fine spray with a sprinkler bulb is beneficial early in the day and the plant is kept shaded. Wash off leaves if dusty.

Gladioli. Most failure of gladioli, indoors, to bloom (coming blind) is due to attempts to grow them at room temperatures. Unless a temperature of 45° to 50° can be maintained, especially at night, do not attempt them. Use only early varieties and plant in December or January, using four-inch pots later to be shifted to six-inch containers or boxes six inches deep. Plant three inches deep and start in full light; use the same culture as that for freesia. Give water and drainage.

Gloxinia. Although they have the name of being difficult, these large, bell-shaped blooming plants are easily grown if understood. Colors are many and they get along well at a temperature of 60° to 70°.

They should be handled in the same general way as tuberous begonias except that the soil requires more sand. Take care in watering to keep the foliage absolutely dry. Keep soil moist but not muddy. The bulbs are on the market in February and March and bloom in March.

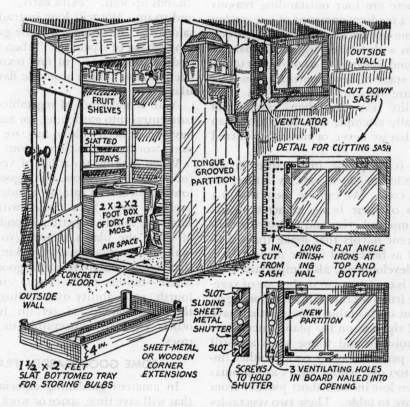

A cellar cool-closet can easily be made for wintering bulbs or for rooting them for forcing. It is also excellent for storing fruit or vegetables. A three or four by five foot cupboard gives a lot of storage. Use a corner so that the two concrete walls may help moderate the temperature. Cover the partition with wallboard if your cellar is hot. Bulbs, apples, etc., keep well in slat-bottomed trays but they keep better in boxes of dried peat moss and potted bulbs root well here also.

CHAPTER XVI

A Vegetable Garden

WHY GROW OUR OWN VEGETABLES?

NO MATTER how varied an assortment modern markets can offer nowadays, and no matter how high the quality of the frozen foods that are becoming increasingly available, there are four outstanding reasons for devoting a moderate amount of our garden space to home grown crops. First, a garden can supply us with fresher vegetables than we can buy; second, it can give us most vegetables in the finest stage of development, impossible when they are bought; third, we can grow higher quality varieties than commercial growers usually attempt; and, fourth, we can grow kinds that we never, or rarely, see offered for sale.

Freshness is of prime importance in all plants whose leaves we eat raw, as lettuce, endive, garden cress. We can use them within a few minutes of their being gathered, while they are plump and crisp and full of the delicate, evanescent flavors that make them delicious as well as beneficial in the menu.

Stage of development, also important with salad plants, is even more so in the case of vegetables whose fruits we eat. Only the home gardener can put on his table tomatoes that have attained full ripeness on the plant; cucumbers firm with moisture and whose seeds are still soft; garden peas and sweet corn, neither immature nor too old, whose sugars and aromas have not been lost in their short journey from garden to stove to table. These two vegetables especially lose their deliciousness rapidly between gathering and using, because their sugars change into starch and other tasteless compounds.

High quality is rarely found in commercial varieties because it is generally associated with fine texture and thin skin which do not make good shippers. We can well confine our selection of sorts to grow to those definitely suited to the small, amateur garden.

When seed catalogues do not specifically point them out, we can recognize the commercial kinds (and avoid them) by descriptive words and phrases that suggest business returns. Such, for instance, as "immense cropper," "highly prolific," "excellent shipper," "stands up well," "extra early," "long keeper," and so on. We will look instead for varieties said to be "ideal for the home garden," "with long season of ripening," "when served, everybody wants more," "of fine texture," "exquisite richness," "high aromatic flavor," and the like.

As to actual kinds of vegetables, here adventure enters into gardening, for among those we have never been able to buy, we may discover some worthy acquisitions to our diet.

When making up a list of vegetable kinds (*not* varieties) to grow, it is a good plan to follow a typical seed catalogue index so as not to overlook any. Your choice will depend on: First, the family appetite; second, the amount of space the plants require (you'll probably omit winter squash and pumpkin); third, those that you can obtain in just as good quality elsewhere—onions, potatoes and winter cabbage; fourth, your ability and willingness to meet the requirements of certain fussy sorts or others especially susceptible to pests or diseases.

SOME GOOD GARDEN PRACTICES

In amateur gardening especially, anything that will save time, space or work is well worth adopting.

In small gardens, the various distances between rows usually recommended by professional writers will cause more bother than benefit. Instead, the unit system of measurement between rows will save both time and space for you. It consists of using the narrowest recommended distance for small growing crops as the basis for all other distances. Radishes are often sown in rows only nine inches apart, so this distance, even though rather narrow, can be used. Crops that require more space are set twice, thrice or more times this basic distance apart. Perhaps the greatest advantage of this plan is that it avoids the necessity of changing the setting of blades and teeth on a wheelhoe in cultivating.

In large gardens it is often convenient and advisable to group the vegetables so the long season kinds are in one area, the short ones in another.

Companion cropping is a system in which two (or more) crops that reach edible maturity at different times are sown or planted out in alternate rows, or as alternate plants in the same row. For instance, lettuce plants can alternate with cabbage plants in the main rows with rows of radishes between. The radishes will all have been gathered within six weeks, and the last of the lettuce a week or two later, after which the cabbages have the ground to themselves.

The same plan may be used in late spring or early summer with tender vegetables, tomato plants or sweet corn alternating with bush beans, for instance; or a crop such as pepper or eggplant that would be killed by the first frost alternating with a hardy late one, as winter cabbage or brussels sprouts.

Succession cropping is the plan by which quick maturing crops are sown or planted in an area by themselves, and, after being gathered, are replaced by another crop. Spinach or early spring peas might be followed by bush beans sown in late spring or early summer, and these in turn by turnips or winter radish sown in midsummer for autumn and winter use. This would make possible three crops in one season from the same area.

GROUPING THE VEGETABLE KINDS

Before we can make a workable plan that will combine the advantages of these cropping systems, we must group the various vegetables according to the times their seeds must be sown or their plants (previously started in a greenhouse, hotbed, cold-frame or elsewhere) set out.

We must also bear in mind the time each will require to reach edible maturity, the amount of space each one will need, and the amount of watering and feeding it normally requires. All this is less complicated than it sounds!

Here is one grouping according to the time the crop occupies the ground:

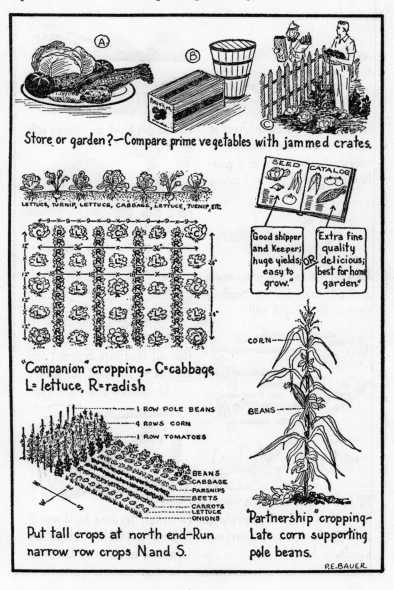

Store or garden?—Compare prime vegetables with jammed crates.

LETTUCE, TURNIP, LETTUCE, CABBAGE, LETTUCE, TURNIP, ETC.

"Companion" cropping— C=cabbage, L= lettuce, R=radish

"Good shipper and keeper; huge yields; easy to grow." OR "Extra fine quality delicious; best for home garden."

1 ROW POLE BEANS
4 ROWS CORN
1 ROW TOMATOES

BEANS
CABBAGE
PARSNIPS
BEETS
CARROTS
LETTUCE
ONIONS

Put tall crops at north end—Run narrow row crops N and S.

CORN
BEANS
"Partnership" cropping— Late corn supporting pole beans.

P.E.BAUER

Annual Crops: 1. *Early spring to late spring:* Forcing radish, early lettuce, onion sets, peppergrass (or garden cress), mustard, fetticus (lamb's lettuce, or corn salad), orach, spinach. 2. *Long season vegetables,* early spring to late fall: Parsnip, salsify, scorzonera, chickory, chard, celeriac, leek, parsley. 3. *Early spring to midsummer or early fall:* Beet, early cabbage, long rooted radish, carrot, onion, kohlrabi, early celery, pea, turnip. 4. *Late spring to early fall* (killed by frost): Tomato, okra, pepper, eggplant, sweet potato, bean, muskmelon, watermelon, pumpkin, squash, husk tomato (ground cherry), martynia, luffa, zit-kwa, gherkin. 5. *Midsummer to late fall:* Turnip, rutabaga, beet, carrot, kohlrabi, broc-coli, brussels sprouts, kale, cauliflower, endive, late cabbage, late celery. 6. *Late summer to late fall:* Lettuce, spinach, round seeded pea, winter radish, forcing radish, mustard garden cress, onion sets. 7. *To be sown in late summer or early fall for late fall or early spring use:* Dandelion, spinach, fetticus, sorrel.

Perennial Crops: Besides the annual crops mentioned there are several perennials, asparagus and rhubarb being the best known in home gardens. They belong in a separate class because they occupy the same area permanently. But, even so, they need not exclude quick maturing partnership crops which can be sown broadcast among them in early spring, and allowed to take their chances; these mature and are used before the perennials need the space.

THE VEGETABLE GARDEN PLAN

On narrow strips of paper write the names of the vegetables to be grown in each row; the number of days they will take to reach usable size, and the approximate dates they should be sown. When all are written, arrange and rearrange them on a table until you have worked out a feasible plan like those illustrated.

After testing the workability of the arrangement by studying each row in relation, first, to what it is to contain during the whole growing season, and second, to the row on each side of it, you can make an actual plan from the slips, either by rewriting the names or pasting the slips on a large sheet of paper or cardboard.

Crop rotation is less practicable in small gardens than in large scale farming. Nevertheless, whenever possible, group the plants that require similar cultural treatment and shift them about from year to year.

Laying out a garden—Sheet of paper on drawing or bread board—Use loose strips of paper to represent different crops.

Always firm soil well after sowing seed with board or by treading—especially in light soils.

How to dig light and heavy soils

Dig deep for root crops.

Simple way to store celery

THICK ROWS OF SEEDLINGS

SPACED 6" APART

Thin out seedlings to permit good growth. — Thinned out plants can be cooked and eaten too.

Tillage is essential—use wheel hoe with different interchangeable parts—or any of various kinds of hoes

For small gardens hand weeding is practical— Here are types of hand weeders.

P.E. BAUER

MAKING THE VEGETABLE GARDEN

The site. When choice is possible, this should be fully exposed to the sun and longer from north to south than from east to west. For if the rows can run north and south and the long way of the area, this will favor the even distribution of sunlight and also reduce the number of necessary turns with the wheel-hoe at the ends of the rows when cultivating. Always the plot should be well drained.

Soils. The best soils for vegetable gardens are loams, that is, combinations of sand, clay and humus. These hold moisture and fertility better than sands, and are more easily worked than clays.

Soil Preparation: Land that has been in sod for several years should be manured, plowed or dug in mid autumn and left rough over winter to break down the turf and destroy many insects. In spring, level the clods or furrows as soon as the soil is dry enough to work. The depth of the digging or plowing must depend upon the depth of the soil; avoid bringing up too much of the sub-soil at any one time.

SEASONAL VEGETABLE GARDEN ACTIVITIES

Seed Sowing. In spring seed can be sown about four times its diameter, then lightly firmed in with the head of a rake; later, in dry weather, sow deeper and press more firmly. Large seeds (peas, beans, etc.) will sprout well if, after tramping the rows firmly, you cover them with loosely raked soil to serve as a mulch.

Soon after sowing, use the steel rake very lightly over the entire bed; within a week repeat the raking *in the direction of the rows*, but preferably with a bamboo or metal broom rake. This is to kill millions of tiny weed seedlings and also to break the crust to let the vegetables through.

Setting Out Plants. In cold climates, some vegetables are always started under glass or in sheltered beds, and transplanted when they reach suitable size and when conditions in the open are favorable.

Cultivation of the soil between rows and plants should be carried on frequently to kill weeds and especially to maintain a dirt mulch which tends to prevent loss of soil by washing, to facilitate the entrance of water into the ground, and to prevent its loss by evaporation.

Until the foliage shades the ground, stir the soil after every rain (as soon as a crust has formed and dried) or, in dry spells, every week or ten days. For a garden 50 by 50 feet or larger, some form of wheelhoe is a great time and labor saver; for a smaller plot the Dutch or scuffle hoe (worked while walking backward) and other similar hand tools are excellent because they obviate walking on the freshly loosened ground.

Watering. If artificial watering seems needed, ordinary sprinkling with hose and nozzle is futile. Real watering should drench the ground a foot deep or more, and be followed as soon as possible by cultivation. Actually, an occasional such soaking will not call for as much water as daily sprinklings, but will make much better use of it.

Crop Protection. Control of plant enemies begins with "sanitation," that is, the disposal of weeds and crop residues that harbor plant diseases and insects between seasons.

Use repellents, such as naphthalene flakes or tobacco dust, in the soil around cucumber and melon plants to drive away cucumber beetles; hydrated lime and Bordeaux mixture to repel flea beetles on beets and potatoes, and so on.

The Harvest. When crops reach usuable size, gather the edible parts and remove the rest to the compost heap because, left in the ground, it only wastes plant food and water. Then prepare, plant, or sow the vacant ground to some other crop. Harvesting really starts when lettuce thinnings and peppergrass cuttings can first be used in early spring, and continues until the last turnips, cabbage, celery, etc., are gathered for winter use. As most crops of various kinds mature more rapidly than they can be consumed, a part of each can usually be canned or dried for use during winter.

Storage of home garden vegetables is generally limited to late fall crops that can, under favorable conditions, be kept for weeks or months. They fall into four classes: 1. Those that may be left in the ground over winter without injury, as parsnip, salsify, scorzonera, Jerusalem artichoke. 2. Those which, when dug, must be kept cold, dark and not too dry, as beet, carrot, turnip, potato, cabbage, cauliflower, brussels sprouts, celery, leek, eggplant, pepper, winter radish, rutabaga. 3. Those that must be kept cold and dry, onion, garlic. 4. Those that must be kept warm and dry, pumpkin and winter squash.

Name	Seed Required for 50 ft. Row	Time to Start Seed in Hotbed or Greenhouse	Time to Transplant Seedlings to Garden	Time to Sow Seed in Open Garden	Rows Apart (in feet)	Plants Apart in Row (In.)	Depth of Planting (In.)	Degree of Hardiness
Beans—(Bush)	½ pt.			April–May	1½–2	4	1½	Tender
Beans—(Pole)	½ pt.			May	4	36	1½–2	Very tender
Beans—Lima (Bush)	½ pt.			May 15	1½–2	4	1½–2	Very tender
Beans—Lima (Pole)	½ pt.			May 15	4	36	1½–2	Very tender
Beets (Early)	1 oz.	February	April	April	1½	4	½	Hardy
Beets (Late)	1 oz.			June–July	1½	4	½	Hardy
Carrot (Early)	½ oz.			April	1½–2	2–4	½	Hardy
Carrot (Late)	½ oz.			July–August	1½–2	2–4	½	Hardy
Chard (Swiss)	1 oz.			April	1½	6–8	¾	Hardy
Cress				April–May	1–1½	2–3	½	Hardy
Dill				April	1½	4–6	½	
Endive	¼ oz.			April	1½–1½	8–12	½	Tender
Lettuce	¼ oz.	Feb.–Mar.	April 15	April	1½–2	8–12	¼	Hardy
Mustard	1 oz.			April	1½–2	8–10	½	Tender
Onions (Sets)	1 qt.			April	1–1½	2–3	½	Hardy
Peas	1 lb.			April	6–8 Double Row	6	2	Hardy
Potato (Early)	4–5 lbs.			April	3	6–8	4	Hardy
Radish	½ oz.	Feb.–Mar.		April	1½–2	1–3	½	Hardy

Name	Seed Required for 50 ft. Row	Time to Start Seed in Hotbed or Greenhouse	Time to Transplant Seedlings to Garden	Time to Sow Seed in Open Garden	Rows Apart (in feet)	Plants Apart in Row (In.)	Depth of Planting (In.)	Degree of Hardiness
Artichoke, Jerusalem	4–5 lbs.			April	3–4	24–36	4	Tender
Broccoli	¼ oz.			April–May	2½–3	24	½–1	Hardy
Brussels Sprouts	¼ oz.	March	May	April	2½–3	18–24	½	Hardy
Cabbage (Early)	¼ oz.	Feb.–Mar.	May	April	2–3	24	½	Hardy
Cabbage (Late)	¼ oz.			May	2–3	24	½	Hardy
Cabbage (Savoy)	¼ oz.			May	2–3	24	½	Hardy
Cardoon	¼ oz.	Feb.–Mar.	May		3	18	½	Tender
Cauliflower	¼ oz.	Jan.–Feb.	May		2–3	15	½	Tender
Celeriac	¼ oz.	March	May	April	2	9	¼	Hardy
Celery	¼ oz.	Feb.–Mar.	May–June	April	2–3	6–8	¼	Hardy
Chicory				April	1–2	10–12	½	Hardy
Collards	¼ oz.	Feb.–Mar.		May	3	24–36	½	Hardy
Corn (Sweet)	½ pt.			May	3	24–36	1	Tender
Cucumbers	½ oz.			May–June	3–4	36–48	1	Tender
Egg Plant	¼ oz.	Feb.–Mar.	May		3	24	½	Tender
Kale (see Broccoli)	above)							
Kohl Rabi	¼ oz.			April	1½–2	8–12	½	Hardy
Leek	½ oz.			April	1¼–2	4–6	½	Very Hardy
Muskmelon	¼ oz.			May	3–4	36–48	1	Tender
New Zealand Spinach	¼ oz.			May	3	12–18	½	Hardy
Okra	1 oz.	April	June	May	3	12	½	Tender
Parsley	½ oz.			April	1	4–6	½	Hardy
Parsnip	¼ oz.			April	1½	4	½	Hardy
Peppers	¼ oz.	Feb.–Mar.	May	May	2	24	½	Tender
Potato (Late)	4–5 lbs.			May–June	3	6–8	4	Hardy
Pumpkins	½ oz.			May	4–5	36–48	1	Tender
Rutabaga	½ oz.			April	2½	8–12	½	Hardy
Salsify	1 oz.			April	1½	4	½	Hardy
Spinach	1 oz.			April	1–1½	6	½	Hardy
Squash	½ oz.			May–June	4–5	48–60	½	Very Tender
Sweet Potato	50 roots	March	May–June		3–5	14	3–4	Tender
Tomato	¼ oz.	March	May		2½–3	30–36	½	Tender
Turnip	½ oz.			April	1½–2	3–4	½	Hardy
Watermelon	1 oz.			May	8–10	80–90	1	Tender

Name	Seed Required for 50 ft. Row	Time to Start Seed in Hotbed or Greenhouse	Time to Transplant Seedlings to Garden	Time to Sow Seed in Open Garden	Rows Apart (in feet)	Plants Apart in Row (In.)	Depth of Planting (In.)	Degree of Hardiness
Artichoke, Globe	½ oz.	Feb.–Mar.	May		3–4	24	½	Hardy
Asparagus	40 plants			April	1½–3	14	4–5	Hardy
Dandelion	½ oz.			May	1½	8–10	½	Hardy
Horseradish	50 roots			April	2	8–12	2	Hardy
Rhubarb	25 roots			May	2½–3	24	¾	Hardy

By Permission of the American Fork & Hoe Co., Cleveland, Ohio.

PLANTING CHART

PLANTS

Successive Planting (Days Apart)	Days to Mature	Important Suggestions
14 days to July Season	60	Early plantings can be followed by Fall vegetables.
	60	Longer bearing than above. Use poles 6–8 ft. long, plant 6 seeds per pole and later thin to [three.
10 days to July Season	60	Cultivate as for Bush Snap Beans above.
		Plant and thin as for Pole Snap Beans above.
14 days	40–70	Late plantings for Winter use should use turnip varieties.
....	90	Before freezing, dig and store in cellar or pit.
14 days	100	Hoe deeply and frequently—keep clean of weeds.
....	120	Give plenty of water and keep soil well cultivated.
20–30	60–70	Can replant until September for Fall and Winter use.
14 days to Sept.	35	Easily grown in Winter in greenhouse, hotbed or window box.
Fall use in June	100–120	Tie outer leaves over center bud when 6 to 8 inches long.
August	70–90	Fertilize heavily—plant on rich soil and supply abundant moisture.
7 days	30–40	Can be grown in window boxes in Spring.
14 days	50–60	Till top soil frequently and keep free of weeds.
7–14 days	60	Do best in cool weather, so plant as early as possible.
June for Fall	90	Apply fertilizer between rows several times during season.
7–10 days	30	For Fall use long, white varieties.

PLANTS

Successive Planting (Days Apart)	Days to Mature	Important Suggestions
....	5–6 mos.	Plant 3 or 4 small tubers in a hill.
....	4–5 mos.	Winter crop may be started in May.
14 days	5–6 mos.	When small sprouts begin to appear—Cut large leaves off to favor sprouts.
....	4–5 mos.)	
....	4–5 mos.}	Fertilize and cultivate freely—Hill up slightly as growth progresses.
....	4–5 mos.)	
....	5–6 mos.	Leaves bunched for blanching in early Fall.
....	4–5 mos.	Never allow plants to become checked in growth.
....	5–6 mos.	Blanching not required—Roots remain in ground until wanted.
....	5–6 mos.	See "Vegetable Guide" for information on blanching.
....	6–7 mos.	Then raised and transplanted in trench and covered with manure—After 4 to 5 weeks ready [for use.
June	3–4 mos.	Stands hot weather better than cabbage or kale. Grown widely in Southern States.
10 days to June	2–3 mos.	Deep soil and frequent cultivation makes best crop.
....	2–3 mos.	Plant in low hills for perfect drainage while young.
....	4–5 mos.	Grow best in well drained, warm soil.
....	2½–3 mos.	Quite hardy and does well where cauliflower cannot be grown.
....	3–4 mos.	Plant in open furrow 5 or 6 inches deep—Draw in earth as plants grow to level of garden.
....	3–4 mos.	Plant in hills, 10 to 12 seed, thin to 4 plants.
....	3–4 mos.	Soak seed 2 hours in hot water.
June	3 mos.	Requires frequent cultivation until plants cover the ground.
May–June	3–4 mos.	Seed germinate very slowly—mark rows with radish seeds.
....	4–5 mos.	Better flavored if subjected to early frosts.
....	4–5 mos.	Top dress soil between rows when plants 6 inches high.
....	4–5 mos.	Dig before hard freezing.
....	4–5 mos.	Plant on hills and cultivate as for cucumbers.
....	4–5 mos.	Pull roots before freezing, cut off tops and store in cellar.
....	4–5 mos.	Dig roots in Fall or Winter as required.
....	3 mos.	Apply nitrate of soda between rows to stimulate growth.
....	2–4 mos.	Winter squash may be planted later and stored for use in moderately warm, dry place.
....	5–6 mos.	Dig when vines have been killed by frost.
June	4–5 mos.	Protect from frost when first set out in garden.
June–July	2–3 mos.	Crowding or weeds make poorly flavored roots.
....	4–5 mos.	Top dress with fertilizer high in nitrogen and potash.

PLANTS

Successive Planting (Days Apart)	Days to Mature	Important Suggestions
....	Aug.–Sept.	If crowns get too large after two or three years—divide and reset.
....	May–June	In northern states mulch asparagus to prevent heaving of the roots during winter.
....	Sept. (1st. yr.)	Blanch by covering with straw or leaves.
....	....	Tends to become rank weed—cultivate closely and root out volunteers.
....	2nd Spring	Keep blossom stalks cut back—flowers and seed exhaust plant.

CHAPTER XVII

Garden Fruits and Fruit Trees

ALL the reasons advanced for growing vegetables apply, and with even greater force, to growing fruits in home gardens. Moreover, fruit plants have other than food producing values. They cost no more, generally speaking, than shrubs, trees and vines that are planted solely for ornament. Yet, most of them are attractive enough in foliage and flower to deserve ornamental positions in the garden; they are as easy to manage, and their enemies are better understood and more easily controlled. And above all is the physical benefit and pleasure a family can take in "fruit from our own garden." Apricot trees are conspicuous with their glorious rose-pink flowers in early spring; the large-flowered varieties of peaches soon follow; then come the Japanese plums, the European varieties, sweet and sour cherries, apples and pears. All these can be used as specimen or shade trees except along the street front. The bramble fruits may serve as hedges along a fence or in place of it.

For an informal, unclipped hedge about five feet high the black raspberry is excellent because it "stays put," (whereas red raspberries spread to adjacent ground by developing suckers from their roots); it bears snowbanks of bloom in May and delicious fruit in July. Dwarf fruit trees trained as cordons or espaliers are excellent for beautifying unsightly walls or they can be grown on trellises like grapes. Grapes may replace such vines as kudzu, akebia and actinidia on verandas, pergolas and summerhouses. Even strawberries in well tended beds are pleasing to look at throughout the growing season.

The objection that one "must wait so long" before getting fruit can be answered two ways. First, no matter how long one waits he will *never* get any fruit from an elm or a spruce, a Dutchman's pipe vine, a forsythia bush or any other "purely ornamental" plant. Second, the waiting period is not "so long" after all. For instance, everbearing strawberry plants set in early spring will start to bear in July and continue more or less regularly until cold weather stops them. Regular varieties will bear abundantly the following summer. Bush fruits and grapes will start the year following planting and give increasing annual yields for several years. Nectarines, peaches, sour cherries, plums, apricots, and summer varieties of apples and pears generally bear fruit the third summer, while even sweet cherries and the slower maturing varieties of apples and pears usually begin the fourth or fifth, especially if on dwarf stock.

As a specimen for a prominent position few shrubs equal a well grown quince bush in full flower; none approach it in early autumn when laden with golden fruit. One bush is sufficient both as a specimen and as a source of fruit for a family of ordinary size. In soil naturally or purposely made acid, blueberries (huckleberries) may be grown in the garden. Their foliage is glorious in its autumn color and during winter the red branches are conspicuous. Some of the new, improved varieties developed by Miss Elizabeth White of New Jersey ripen successively over a period of about two months.

Choosing and Buying Plants. In choosing varieties for the home garden always select those of high quality and that are popular in the locality, even though the stock may have to be bought from a nursery some distance away. Choice varieties not obtainable in nurseries may be had by grafting or budding them on sturdy-growing commercial varieties or seedling trees. These processes are simple, so if space is limited one tree may be made to bear several to many varieties. Scions or buds of desired varieties may be secured through exchange or purchase from owners. Local experiment stations generally know who has trees of desired kinds and will gladly aid searchers. A few nurseries offer trees already grafted or budded with three to five varieties, but so far as I have learned, not sorts best adapted to an amateur's needs.

Among the most widely successful fruit varieties of high quality which can generally be bought from nurseries, even though the fruit is not often found in markets or stores, are those listed on page 121 as a guide to help amateurs in making their selections.

Good amateur practice dictates that one should almost never plant trees older than two years; in fact, one year trees are generally preferred because the branches can be developed where the planter wants them to be.

FRUIT GROWING PRACTICES

Building Strong Trees. When you buy a fruit tree, insist upon one whose straight stem has never been cut or broken. If its branches are far apart on the trunk with the three largest pointing in different directions, you will have no difficulty in developing a symmetrical, strong specimen. Next best is a "whip," or branchless, yearling tree on which, by suppressing undesired shoots and encouraging well placed branches, you can develop a symmetrical tree.

Always avoid a tree with a Y-crotch formation—two erect stems of equal size and vigor. If both grow, they will sooner or later split apart. But this fault can be corrected (1) by cutting back one branch severely and the other little or not at all; (2) cutting back one to a six-inch stub which is left for two or three years then removed cleanly (this plan is best with newly planted trees); (3) if the tree is a sapling with a well established root system, not a newly planted one, you can cut off one branch at once, at its base.

Most fruit trees, bushes and vines are dug in autumn and stored for spring delivery. It is well to order by January while stocks are complete. Before you sign for a delayed shipment of nursery stock insist on a "bad order receipt" from the express, freight or mail agent. Send it to the nursery company at once with a statement giving the facts and describing the condition of the plants. A month or six weeks later report on their performance and, if necessary, file a claim.

Unpack nursery stock in a sheltered, shaded place. Examine the roots and prune back to sound wood any that are broken or scraped.

In planting, make the holes amply large and even deeper than seems necessary. Throw the upper layer of good soil in one pile and in filling the hole put it in first, around the roots. Never place manure or chemical fertilizer close

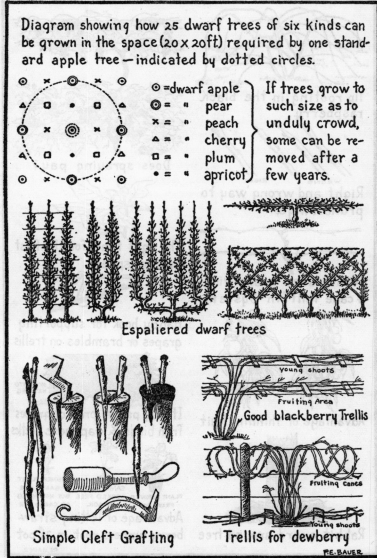

Diagram showing how 25 dwarf trees of six kinds can be grown in the space (20 x 20 ft) required by one standard apple tree—indicated by dotted circles.

⊙ = dwarf apple
◎ = " pear
✕ = " peach
△ = " cherry
☐ = " plum
● = " apricot

If trees grow to such size as to unduly crowd, some can be removed after a few years.

Espaliered dwarf trees

Simple Cleft Grafting

Good blackberry Trellis
young shoots
Fruiting Area

Trellis for dewberry
Fruiting Canes
Young shoots

F.E. BAUER

enough to burn them. Organic fertilizers—bone meal, cottonseed meal and dried blood—are safe to mix with the soil and damp peat moss will help the roots to start growth. Break the soil up so it will sift down among the roots and when they are covered, pack it thoroughly by tramping. When the hole is full, leave a bowl-like depression in which to apply water during dry spells.

After planting, cut back the top one half or more so as to create a balance between it and the root system. When doing this, loosen the wires holding any labels or hang them by large loops around the trunk or a main branch.

Here are proper distances (in feet) to allow between plants based on the space that will be occupied when the tree is full grown:

Apple, Standard, 30; Apple, Dwarf on Doucin roots, 20; Apple, Dwarf on Paradise roots, 12; Apricot, 20; Blackberry, 8; Blueberry, 8; Boysenberry, 8; Cherry, Hybrid Bush, 6; Cherry, Sour, 20; Cherry, Sweet, 30; Currant, 5; Dewberry, 6 to 8; Gooseberry, 5; Grape, 8; Loganberry, 8; Nectarine, 20; Peach, 20; Pear, Dwarf, 15; Pear, Standard, 25; Plum, 20; Quince, 15; Raspberry, Black, 6; Raspberry, Purple, 8; Raspberry, Red, 5; Strawberry, 2; Youngberry, 8.

Site. When planning a garden for fruit, choose the site—if choice is offered—with even more care than you would locate a vegetable garden. (See Chapter XVI). Exposure is especially important. Avoid eastern and southern slopes for apricots, peaches and nectarines because in such places the flower buds are likely to swell early and be injured by spring cold snaps. Or plant these trees on northern and western sides of buildings and walls. Other tree fruits, grapes and berry plants are hardier and blossom later.

Soil. Fruits can often be made to thrive in soil where a vegetable garden would fail. In such cases make the holes extra large and deep, cover the bottoms liberally with bones, and fill them at planting time with a mixture of equal parts good soil and damp peat moss, dusted with a handful of bone meal to each three or four shovelfuls.

Feeding. The first year after planting the feeding roots extend only a little way from the base of the plant, but thereafter they forage farther and farther in all directions, the main root branches becoming mere carriers of moisture and food. Hence, manure and fertilizer should be applied to an encircling zone that extends from about half way between the trunk and the limit of

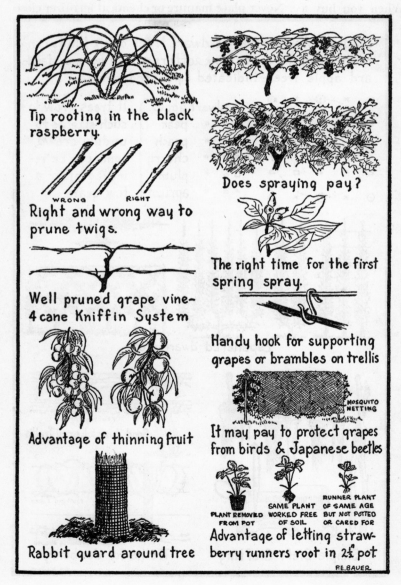

Tip rooting in the black raspberry.

Right and wrong way to prune twigs.   WRONG   RIGHT

Well pruned grape vine—4 cane Kniffin System

Advantage of thinning fruit

Rabbit guard around tree

Does spraying pay?

The right time for the first spring spray.

Handy hook for supporting grapes or brambles on trellis

MOSQUITO NETTING

It may pay to protect grapes from birds & Japanese beetles

PLANT REMOVED FROM POT   SAME PLANT WORKED FREE OF SOIL   RUNNER PLANT OF SAME AGE BUT NOT POTTED OR CARED FOR

Advantage of letting strawberry runners root in 2½" pot

R.E. BAUER

the branch spread to about twice that distance. Where the ground is kept cultivated or well mulched, the applications of manures and fertilizers recommended for the vegetable garden are satisfactory, but on sod land they should be doubled so both the grass and the fruit plants will be fed. Clean cultivation is preferable for tree and bush fruits grown in rows; but if they are planted along fences, heavy mulching is usually better as it conserves moisture, keeps down weeds, and adds humus.

How to Gather Fruits. Tree fruits should never be pulled off the trees so as to break the twigs or wound the fruits. Proper ways are as follows: *Apple.* Hold the specimen in the palm of the hand, the stem firmly between fingers and thumb, and give a twist. If it is ripe enough, the stem will separate from the twig without damage to either. *Pear.* Hold as described for apple but raise specimen through an arc of about 30°. If the stem does not separate readily at the point of union with the twig, it is not ripe enough; leave it on the tree.

PEST CONTROL IN THE FRUIT GARDEN

It has been demonstrated that scale and other insects that hatch in early spring from eggs laid on plants the previous fall can be most readily killed by spraying with a "dormant" or "winter-strength" lime-sulphur solution, or a miscible oil emulsion, just when the leaf buds begin to swell. At this time the shells of the eggs and the protective covering of hibernating scales become softer and more porous so the spray penetrates them more readily. Overwintering fungi can also be destroyed by lime-sulphur, so the one spray at the time specified will be doubly effective. Arsenate of lead can be added to poison the first to appear of the chewing insects which, somehow, seem to know just when the first tender leaflets are going to be ready for them.

FRUITS FOR HOME GARDENS

Before you plant even one standard apple tree, make sure you can spare the space it will need—a circle at least 40 ft. in diameter. If you can't, plan to use dwarf trees which are often planted 10 ft. apart. However, it is better to set apple (or pear) trees 20 ft. apart and put smaller growing, shorter lived kinds alternating in each direction between them—peach, nectarine, apricot, plum and cherry. In this way 25 dwarf trees can go in the space one standard apple tree would need, as shown in the illustration. As they become crowded, take out the shortest lived kinds first. In any case, it is advisable to devote the surrounding ground, while the trees are small, to annual vegetables or strawberries; or else to keep the ground in a two foot circle around each tree cultivated clean so as to reduce the danger of attacks by borers.

HIGH QUALITY FRUIT VARIETIES FOR HOME GARDENS

APPLES
Williams
Primate
Early McIntosh
Sweet Bough
McIntosh
Wagener
Fall Pippin
Delicious
Grimes Golden
Northern Spy
Esopus Spitzenberg
Newtown Pippin

CRAB APPLES
Transcendent
Excelsior
Hyslop
Whitney

PEARS
Bartlett
Tyson
Comice
Howell
Seckel
Beurre Bosc
Anjou
Lawrence

PEACHES
Greensboro
Rochester
Belle of Georgia
Elberta (canning only)
Frances

Morris White
Carman
Hiley
Champion
Fox
Fitzgerald

PLUMS
Abundance (Jap.)
Reine Claude (Eu.)
Italian Prune
    (Eu. Canning and Jam)
French Damson
    (Eu. Canning and Jam)
Burbank (Jap.)
Golden Drop (Eu.)

CHERRY, SWEET
Black Tartarian
Napoleon
Windsor
Sweet September
    (New variety well
    spoken of)

CHERRY, SOUR
Early Richmond
Montmorency
English Morello
Chase

APRICOT
Montgamet
Moorpark
Alexander (Russian)
Alexis

QUINCE
Orange
Champion

CURRANT
Perfection
Red Lake
Wilder
White Grape

GOOSEBERRY
Downing
Chautauqua
Whitesmith
Red Jacket
Columbus
Poorman

RASPBERRY
Bristol (Black)
Logan (Black)
Plum Farmer (Black)
Columbian (Purple)
Marion (Purple)
Sodus (Purple)
Chief (Red)
Cuthbert (Red)
Latham (Red)
Marcy (Red)
Newburgh (Red)
Indian Summer
    (Fall bearing, red)
Ranere or St. Regis
    (Fall bearing, red)

BLACKBERRY
Lucretia (Dewberry)
Eldorado

Early Harvest
Alfred (New)
Rathbun
Brainerd (New)

GRAPE
Portland (White)
Ontario (White)
Niagara (White)
Golden Muscat (White)
Agawam (Red)
Vergennes (Red)
Brilliant (Red)
Brighton (Red)
Catawba (Red)
Delaware (Red)
Moore's Early (Black)
Fredonia (Black)
Concord (Black)
Barry (Black)

STRAWBERRY
Premier
Fairfax
Big Joe
Ambrosia
Aroma
William Belt
* Mastodon
* Green Mountain
Dorsett
Catskill
Gandy
Orem
Chesapeake
Aberdeen
* Gem
* Wayzata

Everbearing varieties.

CHAPTER XVIII

Pest Control

There was a little robin, whose head was always bobbin',
Who remarked as he gobbled up a worm;
"I have eaten all his brothers and ninety-seven others,
But, Golly! how they tickle when they squirm!"

MATERIALS TO USE

Arsenate of lead. Arsenate of lead is the most-used and best-known material for killing leaf-eating insects. It can be combined with bordeaux mixture or sulphur to control both insects and diseases.

Barium fluosilicate. Barium fluosilicate is another stomach poison used for dusting in the same way as arsenate of lead. It is especially effective on beetles difficult to kill with arsenate of lead.

Bordeaux mixture. This is the most widely used spray for the protection of garden and truck crops against fungous diseases.

Calcium arsenate. Calcium arsenate (arsenate of lime) has slightly stronger killing power than arsenate of lead due to a higher percentage of arsenic oxide, but must be used with lime to prevent foliage burning on most vegetables and ornamental plantings.

Nicotine spray. Concentrated tobacco solution for spraying plant lice is sold under several trade names. The spray kills only when it comes in contact with the bodies of the insects, hence must be directed against the underside of the leaves. It may be combined with arsenate of lead for controlling both aphids and leaf-eating insects. It can also be used with bordeaux mixture.

Nicotine dust. A finely powdered material containing a small percentage of nicotine sulphate mixed with a sulphur, talc, lime, or other carrier is now sold under trade names or under the name of nicotine dust. This mixture is serviceable for killing plant lice and other soft-bodied insects.

Massey dust. Massey dust is about the most efficient dust to prevent black spot and rose mildew. You can make it by mixing nine parts of dusting sulphur and one part of arsenate of lead. Tobacco dust may be added to it to control aphids.

Miscible oil. Miscible oil is used for control of scale insects on dormant plants, also for summer spraying for scale and red spider.

Pyrethrum spray. Pyrethrum sprays are especially adapted for use on small plantings where expense is no item and on flowers where staining of the foliage or bloom would be objectionable.

Poisoned bran mash. Poison bait for cutworms and grasshoppers may be made of one-half teaspoon of Paris green or white arsenic, one pint of bran, one tablespoon of syrup, one-half pint of water, and one-fourth ground orange or lemon.

Mix the bran and Paris green dry, stir the syrup and finely ground fruit into the water. Pour the sweetened liquid over the poison bran and mix thoroughly so that it is crumbly, but not sloppy. Scatter this around the plants in the evening and keep away poultry or pets.

Sulphur dust. There are on the market, especially in fruit sections, a large number of sulphur dusts. They are excellent fungicides. Some can be obtained in a new form (colloidal). On evergreens it acts as a fumigant to destroy red spider.

Tobacco dust. Finely ground tobacco, sometimes called tobacco stem meal, may be safely worked into the soil around asters or other plants infested with soil pests or may be scattered upon the surface of the ground. It is excellent mixed with peat moss or domestic humus when used as a mulch.

PREVENTIVE MEASURES

Seed disinfection. Corrosive sublimate, which is a deadly poison, is used as a seed disinfectant, and also as a control for maggots and root pests.   Corrosive sublimate should be used only in wooden or earthen vessels, since it corrodes metals.

Soil sterilization.   Some soil fungi and bacteria which infect young seedlings can be best killed by soil sterilization.   Soil in larger quantities is disinfected by the use of steam or baking, but for the amateur, organic mercury compounds and formaldehyde dusts are best.

Dormant spray.   Dormant spray consists of

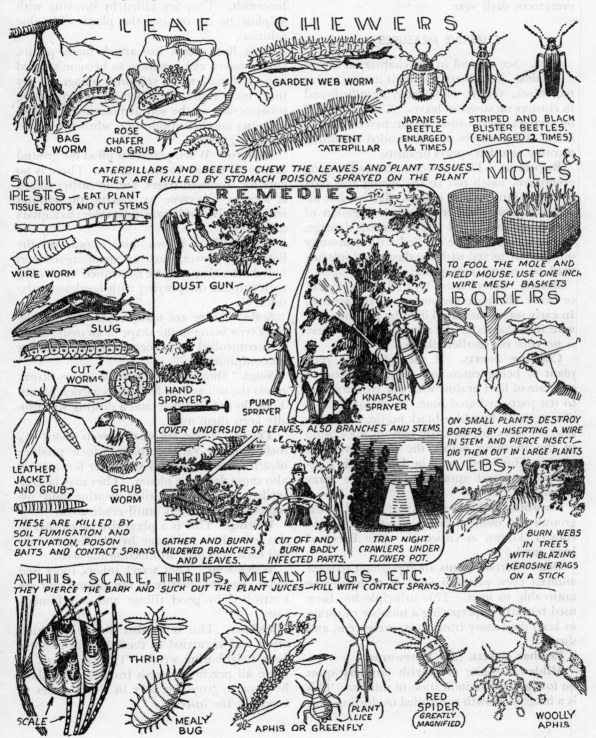

LEAF CHEWERS

BAG WORM

ROSE CHAFER AND GRUB

GARDEN WEB WORM

TENT CATERPILLAR

JAPANESE BEETLE (ENLARGED ½ TIMES)

STRIPED AND BLACK BLISTER BEETLES. (ENLARGED 2 TIMES)

CATERPILLARS AND BEETLES CHEW THE LEAVES AND PLANT TISSUES— THEY ARE KILLED BY STOMACH POISONS SPRAYED ON THE PLANT

SOIL PESTS— EAT PLANT TISSUE, ROOTS AND CUT STEMS

WIRE WORM

SLUG

CUT WORMS

LEATHER JACKET AND GRUB

GRUB WORM

THESE ARE KILLED BY SOIL FUMIGATION AND CULTIVATION, POISON BAITS AND CONTACT SPRAYS

REMEDIES

DUST GUN

HAND SPRAYER

PUMP SPRAYER

KNAPSACK SPRAYER

COVER UNDERSIDE OF LEAVES, ALSO BRANCHES AND STEMS.

GATHER AND BURN MILDEWED BRANCHES AND LEAVES.

CUT OFF AND BURN BADLY INFECTED PARTS.

TRAP NIGHT CRAWLERS UNDER FLOWER POT.

MICE & MOLES

TO FOOL THE MOLE AND FIELD MOUSE, USE ONE INCH WIRE MESH BASKETS

BORERS

ON SMALL PLANTS DESTROY BORERS BY INSERTING A WIRE IN STEM AND PIERCE INSECT— DIG THEM OUT IN LARGE PLANTS

WEBS

BURN WEBS IN TREES WITH BLAZING KEROSINE RAGS ON A STICK

APHIS, SCALE, THRIPS, MEALY BUGS, ETC.
THEY PIERCE THE BARK AND SUCK OUT THE PLANT JUICES—KILL WITH CONTACT SPRAYS

SCALE

THRIP

MEALY BUG

APHIS OR GREENFLY.

(PLANT LICE)

RED SPIDER (GREATLY MAGNIFIED)

WOOLLY APHIS

lime-sulphur or miscible oil. If the lime-sulphur is used it should be purchased in solution and applied as directed. Miscible oil is the cleanest and best for the amateur. It is well to spray all dormant trees, shrubbery, and evergreens each year.

CURATIVE MEASURES

Ants. See control in the chapter on lawns.

Aphids. Aphids are the small insects, green, red, black, yellow, and white, usually found in clusters on stems or leaves. They are killed by contact spray—nicotine or pyrethrum extract. They may be also controlled by adding nicotine to other sprays or dusts.

Bagworms. These worms, chiefly infesting evergreens, hatch out in the spring and start eating. Handpicking is most effective, but arsenate of lead (ten teaspoons to a gallon of water) applied May 1 will save much damage. The arsenate may be applied with a summer oil spray or mixed with the dusting of sulphur used to control red spider.

Borers. Borers cause tops of plants to wilt or break off above the surface of the ground. In early stages they are killed by inserting fine wire into the stalk. In advanced stages there is no cure on smaller plants.

Chewing insects. If the foliage of your plant is being eaten, use an application of arsenate of lead or dust with one part arsenate to ten parts hydrated lime. If the offender is discovered to be a blue-black beetle, which the arsenate does not kill, use barium fluosilicate in the morning before the dew leaves the plant. This beetle may be killed with a pyrethrum contact spray, provided the spray touches it.

Cutworms. When plants are cut off at the ground the most probable reason is a night crawler, known as cutworm. (See **Poisoned bran mash.**)

Dogs. Certain scents are repugnant to some animals even when so faint as to hardly be noticeable to man. This principle has been used recently in preparing a number of sprays to keep dogs away from trees, evergreens, and shrubs.

Leather jackets. See **Wireworms.**

Mildew. White or greyish powdery spots on foliage are the indication of mildew. This is a fungous growth controlled by dusting with

sulphur alone, or sulphur combined with materials to control other pests.

Red spiders. Red spiders infest evergreens, phlox, butterfly bushes, and many other plants, causing them to turn light grey and brownish. They are killed by spraying with sulphur or by coating the plant with glue solution.

Root lice. Root lice attack many plants, chiefly asters, causing them to become stunted in growth with weak, yellowish foliage. They may, most times, be killed by incorporating tobacco dust in the soil at planting time and by using another application when the plants are half grown.

Root rot. When plants rot off at the ground it may be caused by this disease. There is no cure for advanced stages, but, in earlier stages, it may be overcome by soaking the ground with corrosive sublimate (one tablet to a quart of water).

Rust. When brown spots appear on the bottom of leaves, such as snapdragons and hollyhocks, they may be controlled by dusting with sulphur or spraying with bordeaux mixture.

Scale. There are many types of scale, the chief type being in the shape of an oyster shell. It is controlled by a dormant spray of oil or lime-sulphur.

Slugs. Slugs usually leave a silvery streak across the soil as they feed upon garden plants. They do not like lime and a dusting will usually keep them away.

Thrips. These are small insects about $\frac{1}{16}$ inch long in various colors which produce bleach spots on gladioli and other flowers and also cause defective bloom. They may be controlled by spraying with nicotine and pyrethrum once a week until eradicated.

Wilting. This is a plant disease carried in the soil. It is overcome by planting in new soil each year and disinfecting the seed.

Wireworms. They attack tubers, roots, and other vegetable matter in the ground and are controlled by good tillage and soil fumigation.

Yellows. This is another disease of China asters and is carried to them by leaf hoppers from neighboring weeds. The cure is to remove all perennial weeds from the neighborhood or to grow the aster in cloth houses to keep out the insects.

THE CONTROL OF INSECT PESTS AND PLANT DISEASES

From Bulletin 76, Ohio State University by T. H. Parks and A. L. Pierstorff.
(Diseases are listed in italics)

Crop attacked	Insect or disease	Description	Remedy or prevention	When to apply
All or Most Garden Plants	White grubs	Large, white larvae with hard, brown heads. Live under the surface of soil	If grubs are discovered in the seedbed, sow more seed and thin out later Plow or spade deeply in October, garden soil known to harbor white grubs Grub-proof lawns with 5 to 10 lbs. lead arsenate per 1000 sq.ft. spread evenly and watered in.	(See remedy)
	Wireworms	Long, slender, yellow or brown larvae living in the soil	No remedy, except prevention Avoid planting potatoes, sweet corn, or root crops in soil known to contain these worms Rotate garden crops Spade or plow deeply in the fall	(See remedy)
	Grasshoppers	Need no description	Poisoned bran mash	When grasshoppers first appear
	Damping-off	Seedlings rot off at surface of ground	Sterilize seed and soil Plant seeds thin in rows Keep surface of soil stirred after seeds come up. Water thoroughly at longer intervals. Give as much sunlight and air as possible.	Before planting After seeds come up
Aster	Blister beetle	Black or gray elongate beetles ½ to ⅝ inch in length which frequently appear in large numbers and ruin the flower and buds	Spray beetles as soon as they appear with strong pyrethrum spray Strike insects with spray. Repeat as new beetles appear	When beetles first appear and as long as they are present
	Leaf beetle (12 spotted)	Greenish-yellow beetles, ¼ inch long, with twelve prominent black spots on wings. Eat holes in leaves	Spray plants with arsenate of lead 4 level tablespoons in 1 gal. (1 pint to 8 gals.) of water; or Use pyrethrum spray as for blister beetles to avoid stain on flower if asters are ready to cut for market or ornament	When beetles are first seen As long as beetles are present
	Root aphis	Bluish green plant lice attack the roots causing growth to stop and leaves turn yellow	Destroy ants which foster these aphids Work into the soil about the roots fresh tobacco dust, or Loosen soil about portion of roots and pour into it nicotine sulfate solution at strength of 1½ teaspoons to a gallon of soapy water	When insects are found
	Striped stalk borer	See Dahlia	See Dahlia	
	Leaf hoppers	Small yellowish-green insects that suck sap from under surface of leaves. Winged ones fly away upon least disturbance. Young run sideways across leaf Insects transmit "yellows" disease	Spray both surfaces of leaves with bordeaux mixture 3–5–50 and nicotine sulfate 1½ teaspoons to 1 gal. of soapy water or Spray insects with pyrethrum spray	When insects are first noticed. Repeat at 7- to 10-day intervals Repeat as above
	Wilt	Plants wilt. Lower leaves turn yellow. A ring of brown dots inside of stem just beneath the "bark."	Select seed from healthy plants or sow seed in sterilized soil Grow wilt resistant varieties which are now on the market Plant in new location	Before seed is sown
	Yellows	Plants turn yellow, are much dwarfed and the flower heads open unevenly or only partially and have a greenish cast	Pull up and burn diseased plants. Keep weeds down Spray at 7- to 10-day intervals with bordeaux mixture 3–5–50 to prevent leafhopper feeding of Grow plants under insect proof cheesecloth cages	As soon as diseased plants are noticed
Chrysanthemum	Aphis	Green or black plant-lice that cluster on stems and branches	See Aster	
	Blister beetle	See Aster	See Aster	
	Striped stalk borer	See Dahlia	See Dahlia	
	Wilt	Plants wilt and die. Lower part of stem turns black	Plant in new location	
Dahlia	Striped stalk borer	Borer enters stem through a round hole and tunnels the center, causing wilting	No effective remedy after infested Keep coarse weeds and grass cut near flowers Destroy wilted stems	Until August 1
	Blister beetle	See Aster	See Aster	
	Tarnished Plant bug	Brown plant bugs about ¼ inch long that fly away rapidly. Bugs puncture and deform flower buds	Difficult to control Strike bugs with pyrethrum spray	When first observed
	Leaf hopper	See Aster	See Aster	
	Rose chafer	See Rose	See Rose	
	Stunt (Mosaic)	Plants stunted, bushy, and foliage yellowish green	Dig up and discard infected clumps if the cause of stunt is not due to insects, rotted tubers or poor growing conditions	As soon as noticed
	Stunt (Insects)	Plants bushy and dwarfed. Foliage bears leaf hoppers	See Leaf hopper	
Evergreen (Arborvitae)	Bag worm	Brown larvae encased in a small conical bag or covering made of fragments of leaves. Feeds on foliage	Hand pick and destroy bags with larvae On larger plantings, spray with 4 level tablespoons of arsenate of lead or calcium arsenate in 1 gal. of water	When insects first appear
	Red Spider	Very small mites that feed upon foliage causing "rusty" appearance of same	Dust plants with powdered sulphur or Spray plants with 1 pound of glue dissolved in hot water plus dry lime-sulphur 2½ oz. and dilute to 10 gallons	When insects first appear

Crop attacked	Insect or disease	Description	Remedy or prevention	When to apply
GLADIOLUS	Thrips	Very small active, black insects that feed under leaf sheath, causing plants to be stunted and flowers deformed	Plant only sound, uninfected corms If plants become infested, spray with 1 tablespoon of paris green and 2 lbs. of brown sugar in 3 gals. water. Or tartar emetic spray. Frequent drenching of plants with a stream of water affords some relief Fumigate infested corms	Spring As soon as thrips are noticed and repeated weekly until flowers show
	Penicillium rot	Lesions brown outside, gray within. Causes a porous rot throughout corm	By avoiding injury through digging, this disease can largely be eliminated. Sort out all rotting corms in storage	
	Scab	At first small brown spots on leaves; later elongating and turning black. Base of leaf may rot off or entire top die	Avoid injuring corms at harvest time Remove all husks before planting. Discard all corms which show any spotting Plant in soil which has not grown gladioli Treat corms in a solution of corrosive sublimate 1 to 1000 for 2 hours	Before storing Just before planting
	Hard rot	Spots on leaves reddish brown sometimes with purplish margins. Minute black dots in center of older spots Lesions on corms in fall are minute, appear water soaked reddish-brown to brownish-black in color	Rake up and burn all dead tops left on ground. Also follow remedies suggested under scab	After harvest
	Dry rot	Stems may rot off below the surface of the ground Lesions on corms are minute reddish-brown circular spots later increasing in size with sunken centers, definite margins and the color deepening to black	Follow suggestions for *Scab and Hard rot.* In addition dig up and destroy any infected plants	During growing season and at harvest time
IRIS	Iris borer	Large cream to pinkish colored caterpillar spotted on sides. Tunnels through larger roots, causing them to decay and plants to die	Destroy old top growth in early spring Cut away and remove leaf fans showing early feeding work, which removes young borer with it and prevents root damage Reset plants every second year soon after bloom	Early spring May or early June
PEONY	Rose chafer	Long legged yellowish-brown beetles about ½ inch long that feed on blossoms and leaves	See Rose	
	Ants	Cluster on flower buds	These do no harm to buds but feed on sweet secretion	
	Botrytis bud blight	Blasting of young and old buds. Young shoots have brownish water soaked lesions at ground line	Remove and burn diseased portions Spray plants with 4-6-50 bordeaux mixture as soon as shoots show in spring	As soon as noticed
	Root rot	Crown and large roots rot	Dig up and destroy badly rotted plants. Slightly rotted roots may be cut away and healthy portion planted in new location	As soon as noticed
ROSE	Rose slug	Slimy, green slugs that feed upon the upper surface of rose leaves, skeletonizing them	Spray or sprinkle with hellebore, 1½ oz. to 1 gal. water or Arsenate of lead (pwd.) 3 level tablespoons to 1 gal. water (½ pt. to 5 gals.) Drench frequently with water from hose	When slugs appear
	Rose chafer (rose bug)	Long-legged yellowish-brown beetles about ½-inch long that puncture young buds and leaves	Spray with arsenate of lead (pwd.) 5 level tablespoons to 1 gal. water sweetened with sirup 1 pt. of arsenate of lead to 6 gals. sweetened water) or Spray beetles with strong pyrethrum spray or Spray or dust with fluosilicates	When beetles appear
	Leaf hopper	Small, greenish-white, active insects that suck the sap from underside of leaf. Cause leaves to have white speckled appearance	Spray with nicotine or pyrethrum solution as for rose aphis. Be sure to wet the underside of leaves or Dust insects with nicotine dust	When insects appear
	Leaf roller	Pale green caterpillar with brown head which rolls up and lives in fold of leaf	Collect and burn infested leaves containing these worms Spray with arsenate of lead (pwd.) 3 level tablespoons to 1 gal. water (½ pt. to 5 gals.)	When damage is first noticed
	Aphis or plant louse	Small, sluggish, green plant lice which mass upon the buds and stems, and suck the sap	Spray insects with nicotine sulfate 1½ teaspoons to 1 gal. soapy water or Pyrethrum spray directed against the lice or Dust insects with nicotine dust	When insects first appear
	Ants	No description needed	Ants on stems and buds do no direct damage to roses but feed on honey-dew secreted by aphis For control, see under Grass	
	Leaf cutting bee	Bee which cuts out circular pieces from leaf	No remedy known. Damage is not usually severe	
	Black-spot	Large, circular, black blotches on leaves	Dust thoroughly with 90-10 sulfur-manganar or 90-10 sulfur-lead dust or Spray with 4-6-50 bordeaux mixture	Before disease appears, if possible Repeat at 10-day intervals
	Mildew	Leaves covered with white powdery growth, often dwarfed and deformed	Same as for black spot	When disease first appears
	Brown canker	Small purple spots on stems or petioles of leaves. Later light colored in center, with purplish margin. Similar spots on leaves and petals.	Cut out and burn large cankers Spray 5 to 6 times with bordeaux mixture 4-6-50	As soon as noticed Start with new growth in spring

CHAPTER XIX

How to Attract Birds

BIRDS are so much a part of the garden that the coming of the robin in February or March seems to act as the gardener's first notice that spring is on its way. Almost everyone wants birds in the garden but few know how to attract them.

Food and water. Their chief need is food and fresh water. During the early spring freezes, the need for water becomes acute and frequently they are seen flying about in search of it. A pan of warm water in their accustomed drinking place will solve this problem. The water in ornamental bird baths is too often allowed to become stagnant and worthless. Anyone who has seen them in summer about an automatic lawn sprinkler will be impressed with their desire for fresh, cool water. Food, consisting of a piece of suet wired to a tree limb, combined with seeds or at least crumbs and table scraps, will keep them coming back year after year if they are supplied with water and suitable nesting places.

Nesting needs. A little knowledge of the various simple nesting needs of the more familiar types will keep them safe from their natural enemies. The size of birds, the distance from the ground, the surroundings they like best, and, most of all, the size and shape of home which they require must be carefully considered. Guards of metal 12 inches wide and six feet from the ground, tacked completely around the tree or pole, will keep a cat from climbing as the cat cannot get its claws into the wood.

Wood is the best and easiest material to use. One half inch poplar or pine is readily obtained at box factory or mill. Painting should be done several weeks before the house is to be occupied. Newly painted houses keep out the birds. Colors should be rather somber. They do not wish to attract too much attention to their nesting places. Provision must be made for cleaning each year as few birds will clean a dirty house. Do not place nesting materials in the houses but upon the ground

in the open near-by. A few strings, shredded rags, or fine short pieces of raffia may help.

Purple martin. The purple martin seems to be the one which does well in an apartment. He is the largest of the swallows and likes his house on top of a pole. Make a porch four to six inches wide on which the birds can rest in the sun. Do not have a railing upon it. This bird arrives in April, nests in May, and stays until September. Close the boxes until April 1 to keep the sparrows out.

House wren. The house wren will build in almost anything, but the entrance should never be larger than $7/8$ of an inch or the young birds may be destroyed by a cat. This size also keeps out the undesirable sparrow. A perch is not absolutely necessary but is a help.

Robin. The robin likes a sheltered shelf open on three sides. A board nailed under the eaves serves well. This gives the mother bird protection from spring rains while nesting. It is the best known and most sociable of native birds, building its nest where no other bird would venture. Its calls vary with the hour and season.

Give him pieces of apple, suet, scraped meat (no salt), and crumbs and he will soon be perched upon the porch rail or doorstep. Those who object to his raids upon the cherry tree should supply some easily grown wild fruits such as wild cherry, mulberry, dogwood, etc. He much prefers these.

Bluebird. A bluebird will build in a swinging house and a sparrow will not. As the sparrow is his worst enemy and frequently drives him from his home, this is important. The house should be in place by March 15 as the bird nests in early April. All houses except the martin's should have partial shade. All houses need a number of $1/4$-inch holes bored just under the eaves for ventilation.

Feeding stations. Almost every school child has at some time or other sprinkled a few crumbs outside the window hoping the birds would come up to eat them but this habit of

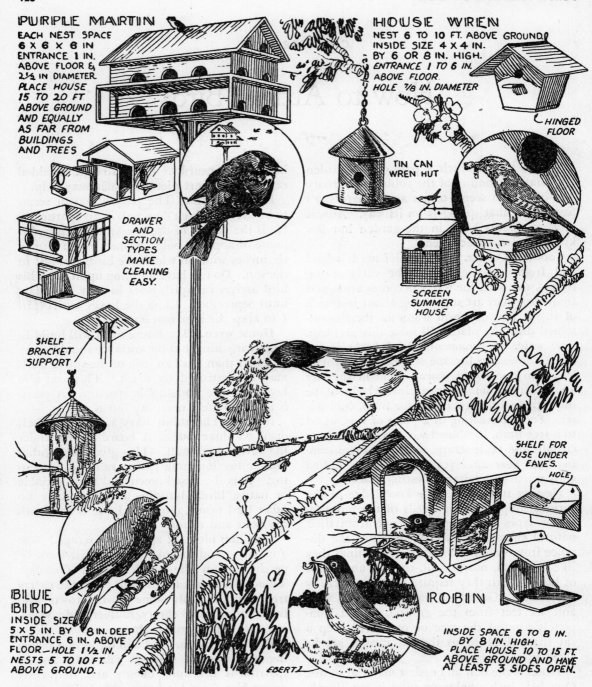

PURPLE MARTIN
EACH NEST SPACE
6 X 6 X 6 IN.
ENTRANCE 1 IN.
ABOVE FLOOR &
2½ IN. DIAMETER.
PLACE HOUSE
15 TO 20 FT.
ABOVE GROUND
AND EQUALLY
AS FAR FROM
BUILDINGS
AND TREES

DRAWER
AND
SECTION
TYPES
MAKE
CLEANING
EASY.

SHELF
BRACKET
SUPPORT

BLUE BIRD
INSIDE SIZE
5 X 5 IN. BY 8 IN. DEEP
ENTRANCE 6 IN. ABOVE
FLOOR—HOLE 1½ IN.
NESTS 5 TO 10 FT.
ABOVE GROUND.

HOUSE WREN
NEST 6 TO 10 FT. ABOVE GROUND.
INSIDE SIZE 4 X 4 IN.
BY 6 OR 8 IN. HIGH.
ENTRANCE 1 TO 6 IN.
ABOVE FLOOR.
HOLE ⅞ IN. DIAMETER

HINGED
FLOOR

TIN CAN
WREN HUT

SCREEN
SUMMER
HOUSE

SHELF FOR
USE UNDER
EAVES.

HOLE

ROBIN
INSIDE SPACE 6 TO 8 IN.
BY 8 IN. HIGH.
PLACE HOUSE 10 TO 15 FT.
ABOVE GROUND AND HAVE
AT LEAST 3 SIDES OPEN.

EBERTZ

kindness was attempted after the birds had acquired the habit of looking elsewhere for food and water. Establish your feeding stations early in the fall to have their companionship through the year. Then the birds may be seen scratching in the snow for the stones of fruits dropped from such trees as wild cherry and red bud and such shrubbery as cranberries and barberry.

We advise the retention of plants which will feed and shelter the birds that stay over the winter and also lend liveliness and interest to the home grounds. Seedheads of sunflowers, zinnias, cosmos, marigolds, and other common garden flowers are granaries quickly found and resorted to all winter by white-tailed juncoes, gold finches, chickadees, white-throated tree, song, and fox sparrows, and many others. The destruction, in autumn, of such natural food supplies is cruelly unkind to the birds.

CHAPTER XX

Gardening Round the Year

THE GARDENER'S JANUARY

GENERAL

Make an inventory of your garden supplies, tools, fertilizers, spraying material and other necessities. Order your seeds early and buy only the best quality. Old edge tools should be gone over and sharpened for the coming season. New handles should be placed and friction tape wrapped about that split place which always pinches your finger. Paint the handles a bright color to find them easily in the long grass and to help you remember to take them in at night.

Dig up your garden and expose the soil to the beneficial effects of freezing, which breaks apart the heavy clods, causing them to crumble. The turning also exposes the eggs of ground pests to the effect of sun, wind, freezing, and the food-hunting winter birds. Save coal ashes to dig into beds which need loosening. They do not have much fertilizing value, but are excellent for ground conditioning.

PESTS

During the mild spells of winter is a good time to go after the moles with calcium cyanide. Don't forget to spray for scale. Also burn out all of the webs from your trees with torches made of rags soaked in kerosene. Be sure to shake off the snow of the evergreens to keep the branches from breaking or bending out of shape and get ready to give them an oil spray some time before March 15 on a day when the temperature is over forty-five degrees, without much chance for a drop at night. You will be surprised how it removes the whitish scale and keeps down red spider and other pests.

FLOWERS

Rockery. Sunny days bring out life in the rock garden. A close watch should be kept, if the snow is absent as a protector, to see that the surface soil has not been washed away from the plant's crown. Press any lifted plants back in their pockets and sprinkle more stone chips or gritty soil around them.

Seeds. Seed-sowing time will soon be here. Have you all the material ready—soil which has been screened, sand, stones or broken flowerpots for drainage, moss, boxes, seed pans, label sticks, etc.? If not, you had better get them at once and have them in good order ahead of time.

Pansies. If the planting urge is already on, start in the flats on pansy seed and stock. Pansies take their time about growing. Drainage, fine soil, seed, more fine soil, all pressed down, is the procedure. Never let the soil dry out.

Bulbs. The bulbs outdoors sometimes poke through the ground during a warm spell; in such cases, cover them with soil or peat moss, or draw the covering of boughs or straw a bit closer. An excellent use for discarded Christmas trees is to cover such early adventurers.

HOUSE PLANTS

Soap and water work wonders with dust-clogged leaf pores of house plants. Don't forget to feed them. Sheep manure made into liquid manure (used only after a thorough watering) or dug into the top-soil; bone meal; and patent foods will do the trick if applied regularly.

CHRISTMAS PLANTS

Poinsettia. Protect the poinsettia from draft, keeping it in a temperature of seventy degrees in the daytime and not lower than sixty-three at night. Never give it cold water and never water it from below. Water it twice a day with tepid or slightly warm water from above.

Begonia. Christmas begonias last for a long time, in bloom, if given reasonable care and temperature conditions similar to those advised for poinsettias.

Cherry. The Christmas cherry is long-lasting and less delicate than either begonias or poinsettias, thriving well in a cooler temperature and withstanding greater variations of temperature.

Cactus. The Christmas cactus, also called lobster and crab cactus, uses a very small pot because the proportion of roots to the upper plant is very small. It often blooms as early as Thanksgiving and as late as Easter. After it blooms give it a complete rest with merely enough moisture to prevent shriveling, and plunge it into the garden for the summer.

Bulbs. If you have rooted bulbs, as previously instructed, you are now enjoying bloom aplenty but if you haven't, lily-of-the-valley pips may be obtained from your own garden or from your florist. Their preparation for bloom is simplicity itself. Hyacinths, Chinese sacred lilies, paper white narcissus, soleil d'or, etc., may now be forced in bowls of water for the house.

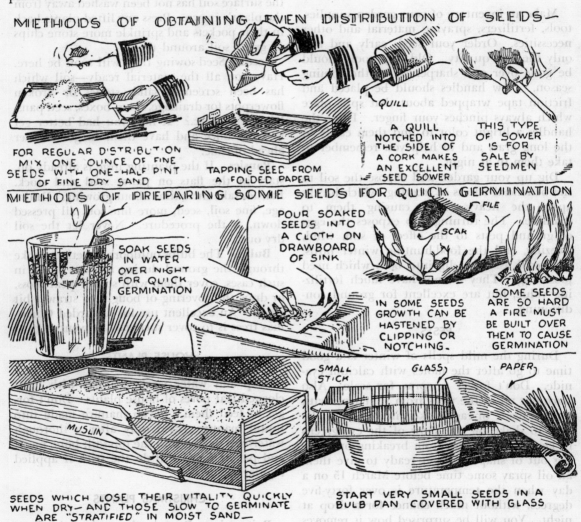

METHODS OF OBTAINING EVEN DISTRIBUTION OF SEEDS

FOR REGULAR DISTRIBUTION MIX ONE OUNCE OF FINE SEEDS WITH ONE-HALF PINT OF FINE DRY SAND

TAPPING SEED FROM A FOLDED PAPER

QUILL — A QUILL NOTCHED INTO THE SIDE OF A CORK MAKES AN EXCELLENT SEED SOWER

THIS TYPE OF SOWER IS FOR SALE BY SEEDMEN

METHODS OF PREPARING SOME SEEDS FOR QUICK GERMINATION

SOAK SEEDS IN WATER OVER NIGHT FOR QUICK GERMINATION

POUR SOAKED SEEDS INTO A CLOTH ON DRAWBOARD OF SINK

IN SOME SEEDS GROWTH CAN BE HASTENED BY CLIPPING OR NOTCHING.

FILE — SCAR

SOME SEEDS ARE SO HARD A FIRE MUST BE BUILT OVER THEM TO CAUSE GERMINATION

MUSLIN

SEEDS WHICH LOSE THEIR VITALITY QUICKLY WHEN DRY — AND THOSE SLOW TO GERMINATE ARE "STRATIFIED" IN MOIST SAND —

SMALL STICK   GLASS   PAPER

START VERY SMALL SEEDS IN A BULB PAN COVERED WITH GLASS

Some of our most prized blooming plants come to us from localities where the seasons are longer than ours and their seeds must be started indoors to secure an early start. Get good seed; it pays. The peculiar requirements of seeds form a source of interesting study. The seed of the soft acacia, growing in south Australia, is said to require the heat of a brush fire to prepare it for germination. Barbary, dogwood, and hawthorn must be soaked until the outer covering is removed. Japanese morning-glories, cardinal climber, and others must have a small cut in the outer covering (not deep and away from the scar or embryo) to let in the moisture. Japanese barbary, privets, viburnums, holly, etc. must be stratified in layers of cloth and sand in a cool place over the winter to be ready for spring planting.

GETTING STARTED IN FEBRUARY

GENERAL

This gardener must confess his greatest sin. He has a tendency to crowd too much into his garden. This is the reason that he repeats the advice against this practice so many times. Study some of the principles of planting in making your plan this year and don't attempt too great a variety. Don't let your garden become a collection of oddities no matter how great a temptation it may be to have something different from your neighbors. Resolve this year to make your garden plan something truly relative to gardening. Eliminate the center pieces of rock castles and interesting miniatures. Avoid over-ornamentation and, above all, get balance in an irregular and uniform manner.

FLOWERS

Beds. Beds which are to receive the annual plants should be prepared as soon as you are able to work them without puddling the soil. Work in the coarse-textured manure or dressing but use the fine-textured material as a top dressing.

Bulbs. All the summer-flowering bulbs, such as cannas, dahlias, gladioli, etc., are most likely to be damaged at this time. See that they have not been started into growth by heat or dampness. They should be stored in a thoroughly dry place at a temperature of about forty-five degrees to hold them back. If the tubers have shriveled, place them in slightly damp peat moss but keep them cool so that they will not start into premature growth.

Annuals. The time for selecting annual seeds is at hand. For all-round general use and beauty, nothing can equal petunias, nasturtiums, zinnias, snapdragons, etc. The zinnias come in so many sizes, colors, and shapes —from lilliput to the dahlia-flowered—that a large space might be devoted to their culture without monotony. They do best, of course, when intermingled with plants of softer foliage texture.

Winter bouquets. Now, while it is still winter, is a good time to appreciate the value of everlasting bouquets for winter decorations. Some of these may be brought indoors from the shrubbery border or the woods, but the majority of them require careful planting in the garden. A great many catalogs devote a special space to the descriptions of these plants. You will find some of them fit into your borders very well while others are too stiff or sturdy in their texture and must be grown to themselves. By all means include some of them in your seed order. Instructions for drying them will come in the May calendar.

Starting indoors. February 22 is the traditional time to plant the seeds which take a long time to germinate, such as lobelia, ageratum, verbena, petunia, pentstemon, scaboisa, pansy, etc. Read the instructions in Chapter V. These will also help you get ready for the sowing of many other seeds for March.

HOUSE PLANTS

Sponge the leaves of house plants every week with clean water. Give them plenty of fresh air, but not direct drafts. Now that the turn of the winter has passed, use a little fertilizer on any house plants which have begun to show new growth. Do not try to force these before they start.

Do not try to keep cineraria or poinsettias active after they have finished blooming. Keep Jerusalem cherry, cyclamen, erica, azalea, genesta, and heliotrope moist. Repot orange trees each season and keep them pot-bound. Feed house plants with bone meal once a month while growing. Put freezia in the cellar when flowering is over to repot it from August to February. Plunge genista in the ground in May.

Watch out for these pests inside: red spiders, aphids, white flies, mealy bugs, and scales. For aphids and mealy bugs use thick soapsuds and rinse the leaves after an hour, or wipe with a soft cloth dipped in soapsuds. Scale must be scraped off by hand with cloth or brush and the foliage rinsed later. Red spiders are very difficult to get rid of and very easy to acquire. Remember that they cannot live in moist, cool conditions and that the underside of the leaf is especially affected. Wash the leaves often with water as a preventive and keep the air moist and cool. White flies suck the plant juices. Use nicotine and soapsuds as for aphids or, if the flies are very prevalent, fumigate the window or room, using a nicotine fumigant from your seed store. This is a heroic treatment and may be carried on in a large box in your garage or cellar some warm day when windows can be opened to get out the fumes.

TREES, VINES, AND SHRUBBERY

Destroy insect eggs. February is an excellent month to get your trees in shape for the growing season. Get some miscible-oil spray from the seed store and get after the scale. Remember, this should be done before March 15. Brush cocoons off the bark but do not scrape so as to injure the trees. Collect and destroy the egg masses of tent caterpillars, which make rings of tiny gray cells or eggs around the small twigs of trees, especially of some of the fruits. Investigate anything that looks foreign to you on the tree and find out what it is so that you may destroy it, if necessary. Spray lilacs with lime and sulphur for scale if badly infested.

Care pays. Read Chapter VII and do the things necessary to get the trees and shrubbery off to a flying start. If you want rapid growth cultivate under the spread of the branches during the early warm spells when the ground is dry enough. Work lightly into the top soil some bone meal or manure (not hot), but don't use chemical plant food until the tree is coming out in leaf.

Trimming. Get all your trimming and shaping of shrubbery done as soon as possible. Avoid spring trimming of the trees which bleed, such as elms, maples, etc. This trimming is best done after the leaf is thoroughly established or it should be left until September. Be careful to trim only the flowering variety by pruning now. Pruning of shrubbery is largely to remove the oldest wood to induce new growth from the bottom.

Evergreens. Cultivation about your evergreens at this time is also an excellent plan as well as giving them a dressing of slow-acting fertilizer. Giving them a dormant spray now will help keep down the red spider as well as scale and other pests. It is one of the best health tonics known for coniferous types. Shake off the snow which clings to them, as the shape of the plant can be spoiled beyond remedy if snow is left on too long.

Grapes. Now is a good time to prune grapes. The fruit is borne near the beginning of shoots which will develop during the present season. These shoots come from last year's growth. In order to keep the strength of the plant from going into foliage instead of fruit, we must trim away the oldest wood, leaving only some of the principal stems. Each of these old stems should retain two to six of the canes which grew last year. These last year's canes must be cut back to three to ten buds each.

Berries. Cut back the canes of raspberries and blackberries which bore fruit last year. On currants, prune out the wood which is over three years old. Prepare supports of wire or tightly stretched wire fencing for the berries, so that the new canes may be fastened to them for the best exposure to sun and air.

Fruit trees. Fruit trees should be pruned now. Of course, they will bear if they are not pruned, but will do much better if given care at this time. Spray with lime and sulphur at dormant strength or use miscible oil if they are close to your house.

THE BUSY MONTH OF MARCH

GENERAL

While it is best not to remove the mulch, loosen it so that it will dry and allow the air to penetrate. When you do your early spring cultivation dig all the finer mulch into the beds. Rake off the rougher material to be burned or composted. It is well to let this matter rest until about April 1 in most localities, suiting the time to your location and climate. If you live south of Cincinnati, for example, you may remove the mulch a little sooner; if you live north, a little later. Always remember it is better to be too late with this removal than too early.

Fork over the compost pile. The rapidity with which it becomes compost depends a great deal upon the moisture and frequent stirrings.

PESTS

This is about your last chance to get after tent caterpillars and other webs on your trees

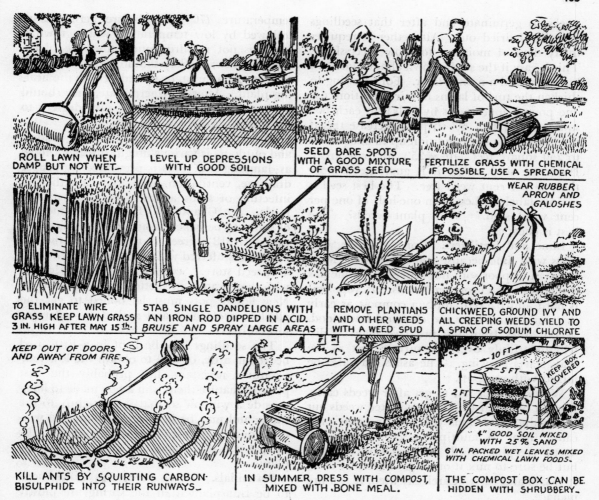

ROLL LAWN WHEN DAMP BUT NOT WET

LEVEL UP DEPRESSIONS WITH GOOD SOIL

SEED BARE SPOTS WITH A GOOD MIXTURE OF GRASS SEED

FERTILIZE GRASS WITH CHEMICAL IF POSSIBLE, USE A SPREADER

TO ELIMINATE WIRE GRASS KEEP LAWN GRASS 3 IN. HIGH AFTER MAY 15th

STAB SINGLE DANDELIONS WITH AN IRON ROD DIPPED IN ACID. BRUISE AND SPRAY LARGE AREAS

REMOVE PLANTIANS AND OTHER WEEDS WITH A WEED SPUD

WEAR RUBBER APRON AND GALOSHES

CHICKWEED, GROUND IVY AND ALL CREEPING WEEDS YIELD TO A SPRAY OF SODIUM CHLORATE

KEEP OUT OF DOORS AND AWAY FROM FIRE

KILL ANTS BY SQUIRTING CARBON-BISULPHIDE INTO THEIR RUNWAYS

IN SUMMER, DRESS WITH COMPOST, MIXED WITH BONE MEAL.

10 FT
5 FT
2 FT
KEEP BOX COVERED

4" GOOD SOIL MIXED WITH 25% SAND
6 IN. PACKED WET LEAVES MIXED WITH CHEMICAL LAWN FOODS

THE COMPOST BOX CAN BE HIDDEN WITH SHRUBBERY.

Some lawn work can be done in March to good advantage but much of the work is detrimental because it is started too early.

as directed in several previous calendars. Dormant spraying may be safely done in most localities until March 15. After that, the strength must be cut down considerably in order to keep it from injuring the swelling buds. The best time is a dull, still day when the weather is over forty degrees. Use lime and sulphur for fruit trees and lilacs if they are far enough away from the house to avoid splattering paint work. This material oxidizes white lead and spots it. It may also discolor brick or stucco. Miscible oil (from your seed store) is the best general-purpose dormant spray. It will not injure buildings, walks, trellises, etc. Refer to Chapter XVIII. Any plants subject to mildew should be sprayed or dusted with bordeaux mixture as they emerge from the dormant state. Roses, phlox, peonies, etc., benefit from this treatment.

LAWN DON'TS

Construction. Don't delay any filling or changes. Thawing will help settle the lawn and prevent more work in the summer.

Rolling. Don't be in a hurry to roll your lawn with a heavy roller. Heavy rolling when the ground is wet compacts the ground so that clay soil puddles into a sticky, puttylike mass that cracks and bakes in dry weather. It destroys soil texture. Light rollings are good to force the clumps of heaved sod back into contact with the soil but reserve heavy rolling, necessary to smooth the lawn, until a dry spell after the frost is definitely out of the ground. A water-weight roller is a great advantage in regulating light and heavy rollings.

Seeding. Don't wait until May to sow grass seed. Seed must be kept wet for at least two weeks to germinate and after that seedlings will die if dried out. Altogether it requires thirty days of moisture to grow successfully. This is easy if the seed is sown about March 15 but very hard a month later. For resowing to thicken the turf of lawns in fair condition, use one pound (one quart by bulk) to each 600 square feet (10' x 60' strip). Increase this if the lawn is in poor condition up to one pound to 250 square feet (10' x 25') for bare areas. Don't use seed unless it is guaranteed more than 98 per cent weed free. The best seed is plainly labeled "Less than one-half of one per cent weed seed." Why plant weeds? The best is cheapest.

Lime and fertilizers. Don't sprinkle your grass with lime because you have moss. Moss is a sign of poor soil, not sour soil. Lime has a tendency to encourage weeds. If your soil is hard and packed, apply a compost as early as possible and later use chemical lawn food. Wood ashes from the fireplace may be distributed thinly over the surface just as the grass starts growing. The ashes may also be mixed with compost.

Weeds. Don't fail to get after weeds early. Dig out plantain and shallow-rooted weeds but if you dig dandelions you will probably only cause them to multiply. See Chapter IV. Spray creeping weeds with sodium chlorate but be sure to mix it outside. Carefully used, it is safe and easy. Carelessly used, it is a fire menace.

Dressing. Don't fail to start some compost now for a summer dressing. Get a box or pit to compost soil and humus, peat mould with bone meal. *Don't use stable manure on your lawn unless you want to spoil it.*

FLOWERS

Equipment. At this time of the year a cold frame or forcing frame is almost a necessity. Plants may be started indoors by various means but many more can be started outdoors in a cold frame. Also the indoor plants must be hardened to the weather before being placed in permanent positions. A cold frame is excellent to protect them from late frosts or cold dank days. See Chapter II.

Seeds indoors. Many of us have become discouraged with seeds indoors because we have not understood their needs. Instructions for planting will be found in the first part of Chapter V. The chief requirement is a high temperature (70°–80°) before germination, followed by low temperature when growing. Light is not required until after the plants start to grow; so they should be well covered to keep them moist, or placed next to the heating plant. After they germinate, they should be kept at a temperature of fifty degrees to make them stocky and healthy.

The chief enemy of all seedlings indoors and outdoors is various fungus diseases known as damping-off. This is prevented by proper drainage, ventilation, and, above all, the disinfecting of seeds and soil before a start is made. See Chapter XVIII. Small amounts of soil may be baked in an oven at a temperature over 212 degrees for two hours or the soil may be disinfected with preparations obtained at a seed store. Seed flats can be scalded off with hot water, or better still, disinfected. New flower pots must be boiled to get the alkali out of them and soaked in water for several days.

The seedlings may be kept in a little-used bedroom, attic, or hall to obtain the low temperatures necessary, but probably the best place to mature them is in a box made to hang outside a window so that it fits tightly to the frame and may be heated by raising the window and ventilated by manipulating the hinged sash top, which lets in the light to the plants.

Perennials. Those perennials which need to be transplanted in the spring are mostly the ones which bloomed last fall. This is done as soon as the ground is dry enough to be readily handled. See Chapter XI.

Rock garden. Look it over often during the spring thaws to see that the tiny plants have not been heaved or washed out of the soil. When frost is past, see that they are firmly settled and well covered. Force some small stones about their crowns to hold them down.

Bulbs and roots. Daffodils will soon be in bloom and it is not necessary to do very much about them, but the results from tulips and hyacinths will be endangered by freezing if they start too early. Loosen the mulch to keep them well covered and add some more mulch to those over-valiant shoots which insist on coming through.

Cannas. These should be divided by cutting the eyes separately and rooting them in sharp sand or potting them in a light soil so that they may have an early start outdoors after all danger of frost is past.

WINTER PROTECTION

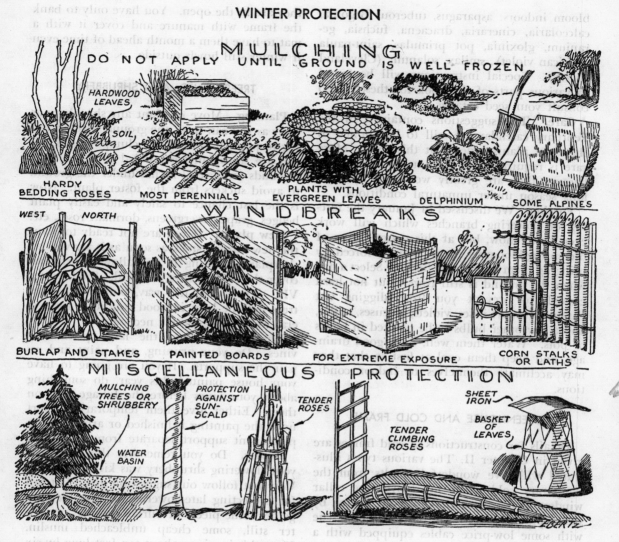

MULCHING

DO NOT APPLY UNTIL GROUND IS WELL FROZEN

HARDWOOD LEAVES
SOIL

HARDY BEDDING ROSES — MOST PERENNIALS — PLANTS WITH EVERGREEN LEAVES — DELPHINIUM — SOME ALPINES

WINDBREAKS

WEST NORTH

BURLAP AND STAKES — PAINTED BOARDS — FOR EXTREME EXPOSURE — CORN STALKS OR LATHS

MISCELLANEOUS PROTECTION

MULCHING TREES OR SHRUBBERY
PROTECTION AGAINST SUN-SCALD
TENDER ROSES
TENDER CLIMBING ROSES
WATER BASIN
SHEET IRON
BASKET OF LEAVES

LBERTZ

Dahlias. Roots of dahlias should be started into growth late in the month so that they may easily be divided or so that you may have cuttings made from them if you wish. Lay the roots upon a few inches of sand, and water freely to start them into growth. Do not do this too early or give them too warm a temperature. Be sure to burn over the iris bed by following instructions in Chapter X. Use care and judgment not to endanger the roots.

Sanitation. Look over the garden mulch when you remove it to see that it does not contain mildew or insect pests. Either dig it into the ground if it is fine enough, bury it in the compost heap, or burn it. Be sure to spray roses, phlox, and delphinium with bordeaux mixture before growth starts and dust thereafter at regular ten-day intervals, using Massy

dust (Chapter XVIII) or a similar formula.

Roses. In the rose garden, the hardy polyantha, hybrid perpetual, and rambler roses can be pruned of dead, broken branches the latter part of the month, but the tender hybrid tea roses should not be pruned or uncovered till later. If you prune too soon the freezing will enter through the tender cut and run down the stem. It is unable to enter through the tough bark or skin. The best time to prune or uncover roses is just before they start to bud out. By all means avoid spring fever with roses.

HOUSE PLANTS

Starting plants. The following plants should be started in February or March for bloom indoors: asparagus, tuberous Begonia, calceolaria, cineraria, dracaena, fuchsia, geranium, gloxinia, pot primulas, saint-paula (African violet), smilax, solanum (Cleveland cherry). Special instructions will be found in various parts of the book for these. Also consult your seed catalog.

Care. The suggestions contained in the February calendar are still to be applied to the tired plants indoors at this time. More care is required now than at any other time because they are greatly weakened by their long season under unnatural conditions.

Forcing. We discussed in January the forcing of flowering branches which will work even better now, but at this season many of the spring-blooming plants may be forced by bringing them indoors in clumps. Select a day when the ground is still frozen but not hard enough to prevent you from digging out clumps of dwarf irises, violets, crocuses, scillas, and a few other bulbs to be planted in bowls or pots. Water them well, have good drainage, and keep them cool at first so that they may acclimate themselves to indoor conditions.

GREENHOUSE AND COLD FRAME

Details for constructions of cold frames are given in Chapter II. The various types illustrated will give wonderful results from the temporary cold frame fitted over the cellar window to the more elaborate one heated by steam pipes. Electricity comes to our rescue with some low-price cables equipped with a thermostat, which maintain an even temperature in all kinds of weather.

The forcing of clumps of bulbs, violets, etc., is very easily done in a cold frame. If preparation is made in the fall you may have pansies, narcissi, primulas, wallflowers, and all the early spring bulbs in bloom long before they are in the open. You have only to bank the frame with manure and cover it with a mat to have them a month ahead of time even if winter still howls outside.

TREES, VINES, AND SHRUBBERY

Planting. Move or plant any shrubbery as early as you can work the ground without trying to plant it with frozen clumps of soil. If you are transplanting budded stock, see that the buds are several inches under the ground to avoid suckers from the foster plant. Now is the last chance to safely and easily plant hedges, grapes, evergreens, dormant roses, etc.

New plants. If you are not ready to plant the new nursery stock as soon as it arrives, lay the plants slanting in a shallow trench and cover the roots deeply with soil. See Chapter VII. Treated in this way, both shrubs and trees may be kept in good condition for several weeks if absolutely necessary.

Vines. Look over the large permanent vines. Do your pruning, and paint and repair the supports. If you are going to have your house painted this year, do something about your vines before the foliage is upon them. Either give them temporary support until the painting is finished or arrange for a permanent support separate from the house.

Covers. Do you remember the years that your flowering shrubbery was killed by frost? Why not follow our suggestion given last fall for protecting late-flowering plants? Sew together some pieces of burlap sacking, or, better still, some cheap unbleached muslin. Have this in pieces about ten feet long by six feet wide. Throw the pieces over the bushes on the nights that frost threatens, and preserve the bloom for future enjoyment. Preserve the covers to use upon chrysanthemums, zinnias, dahlias, asters, etc., later in the fall season.

PLANNING AND WORKING IN APRIL

GENERAL

Mulches should be removed with care, a little at a time. All beds should be carefully raked over, working the finer parts of the mulch into the ground and putting the balance in the bottom of the compost pile so that disease may be retarded while it is rotting.

Get at the bottom of the compost pile and remove the oldest and most rotted parts to mix up for soil compost. These parts, forced through a screen, make the best dressing for covering seeds. Early in the month begin to prepare the seed beds by digging them and letting them settle. Turn under the cover crops which you planted last year. Be careful to do all digging when the ground is fairly dry so that you will not destroy its structure. Break up all clumps so that they will not dry out and bake, causing you trouble later. See the March calendar for illustration and read Chapters III and V before doing your planting.

PESTS

Get a supply of spraying materials on hand for the bugs and diseases which are sure to make their appearance even in the best of gardens. Supplies of bordeaux mixture, arsenate of lead, nicotine sulphate, dusting sulphur, and tobacco dust should be on hand. See that your sprays and dust guns are working.

As previously instructed, look over your trees and shrubs before they come out in leaf. Destroy any caterpillar egg clusters before they hatch. Use a cloth soaked in kerosene and get them out of inaccessible places by a light touch of a blowtorch flame. Do not wait for them to hatch as it will cause more trouble later. If your cedars develop brown balls, destroy them at once as they are said to spread disease to fruit trees.

Wrap the trunks of newly planted trees (especially the smooth-bark type) with burlap to prevent sun-scald. The trunks of elms and maples which have been infested with borers should be wrapped with several thicknesses and securely fastened with twine at the top and bottom. The burlap should be removed about once a month to check up on the operations of these pests.

Spray phlox, delphinium, larkspur, aconites, foxgloves, hollyhocks and roses with bordeaux mixture before the foliage starts and then dust them with Massy dust at least twice a month all summer, to prevent mildew. Get the bagworms this year by spraying the evergreens with arsenate of lead during the latter part of the month. For red spider on juniper and arborvitae start dusting with Massy dust, using a dust gun. Be sure to get the underside of branches and repeat in about thirty days. If you have used miscible oil for a dormant spray as previously suggested, wait until about the first of May before using sulphur. For the blood louse on pines, spray with nicotine sulphate and some arsenate of lead mixed with mild soapsuds as a spreader. Oak and elm trees should be sprayed early with arsenate of lead solution for canker and leaf rollers.

Watch your elms if the leaves were badly eaten last year. Another infestation this season may kill them.

LAWN

The care of the lawn was covered in the March calendar but we show another picture this month. Read the chapter on lawns completely, as many of the things which apply to lawn-making also apply to the care of an established lawn. Roll the surface of your lawn when it is fairly dry and springy to smooth it out.

HOUSE PLANTS

Many of the house plants need repotting at this time. Place them out of doors during the day and help them recuperate from the hardships of the winter. Palms, rubber plants, dracaenas, and all other foliage plants usually need renewal, especially if they have outgrown their pots.

STARTING THE FLOWERS

Preparation. Prepare to dust all plants which are subject to disease as described under "Pests" in this calendar. Be sure they are free from old leaves, stalks, and rubbish, which are usually a sure source of disease. Search out and remove all dead foliage around them. Don't forget to spray at ten-day intervals with Massy dust.

Cultivation. All borders or open spaces around plants should be kept loosened with a fork or cultivating hoe. Loosened soil is extremely beneficial to the soil because it admits the air and also forms a dust mulch which prevents rapid evaporation of moisture and nitrates.

Perennials. When you have uncovered the border you may count your losses and order plants to fill the voids. Dig under some good manure and give the bed a good dressing of raw crushed bone. Annuals should be planted between the younger clumps which are yet to fill out. You may now divide such plants as delphiniums, helenium, anemone, japonica, fall asters, ceratostigma, and shasta daisy. Divide the chrysanthemum as early as possible. Each small division will make a blooming plant by autumn if planted in good location and soil. Phlox and Michaelmas daisy should be divided by using only the live parts of the outer ring. When weather becomes settled, set out the plants which have been wintered in a cold frame: pansies, forget-me-nots, daisies, Canterbury bells, aquilegias, foxgloves, etc. Rampant plants which try to overrun the garden, such as achillea, goldenglow, boltonia, etc., should be weeded out so that they will have room for new growth.

Bulbs. Uncover the spring-flowering bulbs carefully and get ready to plant the summer flower varieties. Gladioli may be planted about the middle of May for early-flowering effect. Continue the plantings every ten days.

Delphiniums. Apply plenty of bone meal and plenty of humus after they start to grow. Any division of the plant may be made now. Three-year-old plants should be divided as soon as growth appears. Set out new plants in a loose, sandy loam, moderately limed. Be sure it is well drained. Dust around the plant crowns with dry bordeaux mixture. Remove all dead or weak shoots and water abundantly.

Iris. Use bone meal and wood ashes on iris but do not overdo. The bearded varieties profit from a dusting of lime. Do not use lime on the beardless or fibrous-rooted varieties. Use leaf mould or humus mixed with a little tankage.

Herbs. Small, fragrant herbs used for flavoring, such as thyme, dill, sage, marjoram, etc., should be sown in open spots in the border.

Roses. Wait until the buds are about to appear and then prune the hybrid-type roses to three eyes but leave about four inches of wood on the teas. Prune to buds which point towards the outside of the plants. The new wood will grow from these in the right direction. The weaker the rose, the more it needs pruning. The first of April is about the best time in spring to plant dormant roses. Heap soil or peat moss around the newly planted bushes and keep it there for about two weeks. Remove it on a cloudy day. This prevents the bottom of the canes from drying out until the roots have a chance to take hold.

Japanese morning-glory. It is best started indoors in pots. Lightly notch the seed (away from the scar) with a file and soak it overnight until the outer coating is softened. Keep it well watered until four leaves are formed and then transplant it into a large flowerpot. Stake each plant and leave in a sunny window until it grows a foot and a half.

In most localities the seeds may be planted directly outside about the middle of May (earlier in the South) in soil dug to a depth of 18 inches and made light with sand and fertilized with bone meal and cow manure. After they are up, set them eight inches apart and fasten them by soft string to the permanent support. About the first of July, cover the bed with several inches of peat moss and every day or two spray the vines until they are dripping wet. While they require a great deal of food and moisture, they do not like chemical fertilizer.

TREES AND SHRUBBERY

Early planting. Early planting is best for most kinds of woody stock. Try to get all deciduous trees and shrubs planted before foliage starts. The exception is the magnolia, which should be transplanted during May while it is in leaf. Evergreens should be set early so that there will be plenty of rain while they are establishing themselves. Stake and wire all newly planted trees to prevent them from swaying in high winds. Don't neglect new stock; liberal watering once a week in the dry weather is essential and a heavy mulching of manure a little later is excellent. Do not remove stakes or guy wires until the plant is thoroughly established.

Pruning. If you have not already done so, prune grapevines and orchard fruits at once. Box and privet hedges should be trimmed before they start into growth. Young dogwoods that have died back are fairly sure to send up new growths, if cut back to the ground. Prune them and train them as shrubs. Evergreens in need of shaping and thickening may be sheared advantageously as the new growth gets under way. Fertilize all trees and shrubbery while they are coming out in leaf and see that they do not lack for water. If pruning on your early-flowering shrubs is necessary, prepare to do it soon after they have bloomed. Forsythia is probably the earliest one. Rub water sprouts from fruit trees and other trees.

Fertilizing. Roses and all other shrubs will benefit from a top dressing of bone meal applied now and scratched in lightly. See that trees have a plentiful supply of water and nitrates.

Fruits. Begin to care early for your fruit plants. Watch the currant bushes and spray with arsenate of lead to kill the currant worms while they are small and first appear on the leaves. It is almost impossible to raise currants without spraying. The roots of grapevines are close to the surface. Be careful in cultivation at this time of year. Scratch in lightly some bone meal and mulch with cow manure.

Pussy willow. If you have sprays of pussy willow in the house, they will probably have made roots in the water. Later in the month plant them outdoors in a damp spot and they will eventually form bushes.

GREENHOUSE AND COLD FRAME

Repair. Late April is a good time to start repairing. Broken glass should be replaced and loose glass reset. All wood frame-work should be painted now.

Hardening. Start hardening-off the bedding plants in the greenhouse or frame now.

It is certain death to set out coleus, geraniums, etc. unless they have been gradually accustomed to the marked change in temperature. Give more and more cool, fresh air to them each pleasant day.

Individual pots. Many flowering plants, as well as vegetables, are easily started indoors in individual paper pots sold for the purpose. These are made square to fit into trays so that they may be set outside without disturbing the roots by merely unfolding the bottom of the plant.

New plants. Root chrysanthemums need cutting now. Sow China asters in a cold frame. This is the proper time to start some plants from seed for flowering next winter in the greenhouse. Primula, cyclamen, snapdragon, and many others come under this head. Keep the young plants growing along without check and transplant them or set them in pots when needed.

THE HOME GARDEN IN MAY

GENERAL

We hope you have your tools ready and on hand to keep up the appearance of your garden during the summer. A one-wheel lawn mower is an excellent thing to use around the garden beds and close to the walls, while a grass whip swung like a golf club and cutting both ways allows us to get close to the fences and shrubbery without stooping. If you have a vegetable garden, investigate the wheel hoe. Flowers which are staked early in the season are easy to train and also make disease more easily detected. Weed killers, used on walks and drives while the weeds are young, will prevent a great deal of damage and hard work later.

It is always well to have a supply of straw or other mulch handy as a guard against late killing frosts. Investigate the cloth covers mentioned in the March and April calendars. They come in handy almost all season.

Everything that is being transplanted, from tiny seedlings to young trees, must have its roots protected against drying while out of the ground. Unless this is done, these highly sensitive and vital parts will be severely injured if not killed. Transplant them on cloudy days.

Have a supply of liquid manure readily accessible for use on weak plants and to increase the size of blooms. If you use a barrel, see that it is carefully covered with fine screen or it will be a breeding place for mosquitos.

PESTS

Currant bushes, gooseberries, elms, cherries, and, in fact, all trees and shrubbery should have at least one application of arsenate of lead as soon as they are out in leaf. With the exception of tall trees, a small pump-sprayer with various nozzles and an extension rod will enable you to do the work single-handed. Keep up the use of Massy dust on evergreens, roses, and perennials which are subject to mildew—delphinium, hollyhock, phlox, Chinese larkspur, etc. Should the mildew get out of hand, spray it every ten days with bordeaux mixture.

LAWNS

Good lawns are the result of liberal fertilization and frequent care. We have covered this subject thoroughly in the past two calendars but its appearance will be kept up only by constant attention. Seed the bare spots as soon as they appear. In hot weather cover them with a cloth, as shown in the April calendar. Do not sprinkle the lawn. Frequent sprinklings cause much loss. Newly seeded lawn should be cut high until the grass begins to grow vigorously and thickens.

The prevention of crab grass should be started in the middle of the month. Shading is the only successful method. Fairly short mowing in the spring is beneficial to the plant. After May 15 the grass should be kept mowed at three inches high. It makes a better appearance; shades the crab grass seed to keep it from germinating; retards the evaporation of moisture and nitrates by keeping the surface of the soil cool during the hot weather; and crowds out the growth of weeds which flourish in hot soil.

HOUSE PLANTS

Read carefully the directions for repotting in Chapter XV. Examine your plants to see if they need attention before being set outdoors for summer recuperation.

Tubbed plants of all kinds may be taken from their winter quarters and moved into place now that danger of real frost is past. They should be given liquid manure. As growth becomes active, loosen the surface of the soil in their containers. Keep them well watered. Bring out the poinsettias to start them into growth and dry out the callas for resting on their sides in the shade during the summer.

FLOWERS

Marking. The importance of proper labeling is important often in the spring. The areas in the perennial border in which the late maturing plants are placed are often dug up, ruining the plants.

Planting seeds. Plant seeds only when the ground is workable. Read the March and April calendars. Consult the plant lists in Chapter XI. If you have not already done so, there is still time to plant out many of the favorite annuals, but do not delay it, for summer will soon be here. Prepare the ground thoroughly, although annuals do not need the deep cultivation which must be given to perennials. Continue to sow sweet alyssum and candytuft for edging. Seeds of all the tender annuals may be sown now: impatiens, amaranth, gomphrena, celosia, gaillardia, browallia, petunia, portulaca, torenia, vinca rosea and alba, zinnia. These will replace the pansies, English daisies, lobelias, and other very early annuals, now growing shabby. Thin and transplant those already set out and do not let them dry out or suffer from late frosts.

Gourds. Sow the seeds of gourds in late May or early June in the sun and in light loam, enriched with very old stable manure. Plant them ten seeds to the hill, where they are to grow, for they do not transplant well. Provide some support, for they grow ten feet high.

Flowering vines. Plant vines to cover fences and garages. See Chapter VIII.

Potted annuals. To transplant seedlings from flat or pot into the open ground, loosen carefully the rootlets which have made tight little wads, so that they will be in condition to take up food and water. Dig a hole the full length of the plant's roots, then fill the upper half of the hole with dry soil, and water no more. By this method there will be no moisture on the surface of the ground for the sun to bake or steam. For a few days keep the plants covered with flowerpots or strawberry baskets during the day to prevent evaporation from the leaves by sun or wind, removing the protection at night. To insure a stocky growth remove the central bud at the top of the plant when it is six inches tall. Calendulas, ageratum, snapdragons, stocks, marigolds, drummond phlox, alyssum, and petunias are types needing such treatment. Poppies, asters, and nicotiana are best left alone.

Perennial replacement. You can see what you need in the way of replacement. Secure hardy clumps and select a cool, cloudy day for planting. Hold the plants for a day or so rather than plant them in heat and wind. A newly set plant must first have its roots developed before it can support top growth. Keep the plants shaded if the weather is warm. Newspapers may be used, but all shade should be removed at night. Do not overcrowd. Plant firmly. Press the soil around the edges of the plant, rather than the top of the plant itself. Spread the roots naturally and fill the spaces between them. Each root must be surrounded with soil free from air pockets. Set the crowns as they were in the nursery. Cultivate often. Never walk on the soil or cultivate it when it is wet. Newly planted perennials must be watered regularly, in early morning or just before sundown.

See Chapter X for culture of peonies, dahlias, and gladioli.

Asters. Before planting asters of any kind apply wood ashes to the soil. Contrary to popular belief they do not thrive well in poor soil. Manure it well and dig it deeply with a finely raked finish. Plant seed in the rows two inches apart with the rows ten inches long. Planting half an inch deep will give later flowers but better plants.

Lilies. Plant lilies in May. Summer planting is best for most lilies but regal lily (regale), gold-band lily of Japan (auratum), and any of the show lilies (specosium) do very well with spring planting.

Columbines. Aquilegia is one of the most popular plants in the garden but many of us become discouraged with it because it dies out in a few years. It is a wise gardener who keeps a supply of them coming along from seed sown in a propagating bed in spring or early summer. April and May seem the best months for sowing seed as it is easier to keep the seed bed moist. All hardy clumps should be divided in September, much as perennials.

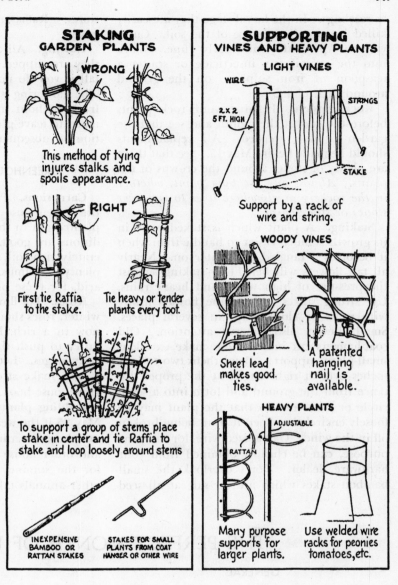

STAKING GARDEN PLANTS

WRONG

This method of tying injures stalks and spoils appearance.

RIGHT

First tie Raffia to the stake.

Tie heavy or tender plants every foot.

To support a group of stems place stake in center and tie Raffia to stake and loop loosely around stems

INEXPENSIVE BAMBOO OR RATTAN STAKES

STAKES FOR SMALL PLANTS FROM COAT HANGER OR OTHER WIRE

SUPPORTING VINES AND HEAVY PLANTS

LIGHT VINES

WIRE

2 X 2 5 FT. HIGH

STRINGS

STAKE

Support by a rack of wire and string.

WOODY VINES

Sheet lead makes good ties.

A patented hanging nail is available.

HEAVY PLANTS

RATTAN

ADJUSTABLE

Many purpose supports for larger plants.

Use welded wire racks for peonies tomatoes, etc.

Lupines. For years these beautiful candle-like blooms were gently admired but though they would grow readily and lustily in some locations, they refused to repeat under similar culture in others. For such plants special bacteria is necessary. Your seedsman should be able to obtain them for you from concerns dealing in legume bacteria. The plants are well worth the small effort needed to get them started, and, once established, are sturdy growers, with colors rivaling the rainbow. They make fine companions for delphiniums.

The best start comes from plants rather than seed. Improved strains of perpetual-flowering varieties start blooming late in April in warmer sections. If seed is used, sow it early in spring so that the long tap roots may become established. The deep root is the way the plant combats extreme midsummer heat. Do not wait until the ground warms up to sow seed. They will not rot while waiting for germination. September sowing followed by winter protection gives blooming plants the following season.

Roses. You may take the protection completely off roses by the last of the month. A last-minute rose garden can be made even now if you buy pot-grown plants. They can be transferred without much harmful root disturbance. Cultivate the rose beds daily to kill the rosebug larvae which are just below the soil surface until June, when they emerge as rosebugs. In the larval stage they are easily killed by any disturbance of the soil. Cultivate in April, May, and early June. Work into the topsoil any insecticide or scatter a teaspoon of iron sulphate on the ground around each plant.

Rock garden. Fertilize your rock plants before the end of the month and see that the garden is well weeded. All replacements should be made before May 15. See that there are plenty of stones around the crowns of the plants. *Almost any creeping plant, whether in the rockery or elsewhere likes to run over stones or stone chips.*

Staking. A plant which is staked early in its growth is much easier to handle than when it becomes a tangled mass later on. Nearly all tall flowers will benefit by staking against the pressure of high winds and heavy rains. Use strong stakes and tie the flowers firmly with raffia or cloth strips in several places. Small flowers also deserve attention. Old coat-hangers cut into sections make excellent small-plant supports. Bend them two to four inches over at right angles at the proper distance from the ground and form into a semicircle or corkscrew so that the plant may be loosely encircled to keep it from being broken off in the wind. Galvanized wire, for the same purpose, can be cheaply obtained from your hardware dealer. Don't overlook the small bamboo stakes which are for sale at all seed stores. Raffia may be purchased and dyed green.

Cutting. All annuals will bloom longer if they are clipped. Snip them off and let them fall if you do not need them for cut flowers. The flowering stalks of the iris can be cut freely without injury to the plants if care is taken to leave plenty of foliage for the promotion of subsequent growth.

GREENHOUSE AND COLD FRAME

Carnations. Plants intended for forcing in the greenhouse next winter can now be planted out in the garden where growing conditions are good. They should have a moderately rich soil, well drained and containing plenty of humus. It should be alkaline, not acid, for these plants.

Roses. For flowering in the greenhouse next winter, roses should be planted in the benches now in a rich, heavy soil. Do not be in a hurry to push their development during the early stages. Let them take their time about it and make strong wood. Consult a good greenhouse book.

Bedding plants. They are usually out by May 25 if the weather appears settled: geraniums, begonias, cannas, salvia, coleus, etc. Ferns and other house plants may also be removed for the summer and petunias, cosmos, and other annuals taken from the cold frames.

THE PERFECT MONTH OF JUNE

GENERAL

Among the most important things in June is cultivation. It is often better than watering. It is a good insecticide and greatly aids fertilization. Work the soil deeply and often. Be careful not to injure plant roots. In the straight rows of the vegetable garden, use a wheel hoe. Do not let the soil between the plants remain packed very long after a hard rain. Don't neglect mulching your acid plants. The wild garden should also have slightly acid soil and be permanently mulched with needles from beneath your evergreens and last year's oak leaves. These yearly mulchings with new material early in the summer helps get them ready for next year's bloom.

PESTS

Fungus. Don't wait until disease has weakened your plants before attempting the cure. Delphiniums, hollyhocks, phlox, roses, and many others are subject to fungus; therefore, dust them several times each month. Aphids may seem inconsequential on your plants but they are sucking the juices and should be removed with a nicotine spray.

Rosebugs. Rose beds may harbor the beginning of a rosebug nest. Frequent cultivation until July 1 is the answer. A tablespoon of sulphate of iron scattered around each bush and worked into the soil will help. The same treatment helps peonies and magnolias. When you have the brown beetles, which mutilate rose and magnolia blossoms, do not use poison sprays. Eradicate them by knocking them into a can of kerosene.

Black spots. Black spots on roses and other leaf blights on perennials are difficult diseases to cure. Started off right and dusted as previously instructed, your plants will not have them unless they come from new additions to your garden. Such infection is not incurable if plants are sprayed with bordeaux mixture and all foliage is kept off the ground.

Ants. Don't think that ants in your garden are harmless creatures. They harbor ground pests which they use to produce food. Drive them away by cultivation, spreading poison or any of the other things previously suggested.

Leaf chewers. Arsenate of lead is the general remedy for leaf chewers. Mix it with mild soapsuds to make it spread. The leaves of all trees and shrubbery should have at least one application of it after they come out in full foliage. Use it on the evergreens to prevent bagworms, but do it as early as possible. Bordeaux mixture is the general cure for disease. It is absolutely necessary on fruits at the producing stage.

Moles. Moles disfigure lawns and are blamed for eating bulbs and roots. The truth is that these little animals go through the ground searching for earthworms and in so doing make runways which mice and other pests use to do the damage which is often attributed to the moles. Eradication of moles is described in Chapter IV.

WITH THE FLOWERS

Thinning and staking. Thinning of all kinds of seedlings should be done when the plants are very small and before the roots are interlocked. Thinning of rampant-growing plants to keep air in the center of the clumps, as well as around the outer edges, must be done all season. Do not confine your staking operations to dahlias, peonies, and the plants which seem to cry for it. Attend to the little fellows also.

Clipping, marking, and budding. Clip the blossoms of all flowers as they are about to fade. We have already spoken of pinching off the tops of many plants to make them branch out. Cosmos are among the plants which need it this month but many others also benefit from it. Previous calendars have

given you lists. Try pinching some of all plants so that you may learn which will do best. An expert may do it with his fingernails but for beginners a very sharp knife or a scissors is best.

Mark the areas occupied by such plants as bleeding-heart, trillium, small bulbs, mertensia, etc. which are going dormant now. You will need the marking next spring. Continue this process all summer.

Perennial propagation. Sow seeds of perennials for next year's garden. The process is described in Chapter VI. Sow the seed late in June and soak in warm water for a couple of hours. For softwood cuttings take the first shoots that appear when they are three inches high. Cut them with a heel and place them in sand as described in Chapter V.

Miscellaneous culture. Watch the roses for suckers. Dress with liquid manure for larger blooms. Cultivate the areas until July 1 to destroy the rosebugs. If infested, look over the plants each day and shake the bugs into a can of kerosene. If your roses are healthy, you may save a lot of cultivation during the summer by mulching them with peat moss after July 1. Don't forget successive plantings of gladioli. Watch for thrips. Train the dahlias to one stalk and be sure they are staked firmly.

Do not overlook the smaller varieties which grow in the flower borders. Look into the merits of some English singles. Fertilize when first buds form, unless growth is rank. Water the delphiniums well. Cut down the stems as the bloom ends. Watch the iris for the borer (soft and slimy leaves) and remove or burn affected plants. Plant chrysanthemums before the end of the month. The first part of June is about the deadline for summer-flowering seeds.

Late flowers. The flowers which endure early frost should not be overlooked now. That beautiful late season is an interesting period in the garden if you provide it with bloom. Some of the perennials, such as delphiniums and achillea, should be cut down immediately after flowering in June or July, watered well, and given a deep treatment of plant food. There will be a second flowering in September and October. Perennials for late bloom are anemone, asters, boltonia, ceratostigma, chrysanthemum, cimicifuga, coreopsis, delphinium (second blooming), lilies, and phlox. Annuals may be sown now but should be planted a little deeper than three or four times the seed diameter.

A garden bank account. Over a long period of years this gardener was in the habit of having some two hundred fifty people entertained on his grounds each summer. Of course, he wanted the grounds to be at their best and invariably there was some failure of some particular fine bloom whether the party was given in spring or fall. So came the idea of preparing a "borrow garden" which is to be used much as a savings account for the proverbial rainy day. Every garden has annuals to throw away when the beds are thinned. Some of these are placed in small pots and plunged into the corners of the vegetable gardens or into a space set aside for the purpose. Gladioli were planted in the same manner. When the bare spots came and any part of the border showed lack of bloom, it was only the work of a minute to slip these out of the pots and into the places needed where they would be well watered and take hold at once. If height was needed they could be set upon the ground in pots and soil heaped about them.

When it becomes necessary to thin the plants in your border, pot them up and keep them shaded for a few days with plenty of water and some wise pruning. Bring them gradually into the full sun and then sink them in a sunny secluded spot where they will not be neglected. Petunias, marigolds, and faithful geraniums fit beautifully into this idea. Every size and shape of handy receptacle has its use. Old butter tubs, nail kegs, and soapboxes bound with wire may be painted green and filled with well-composted soil, enriched with plenty of rotted manure. These will house about five plants apiece. Trailing petunias which have been pinched back to form leaders come in all shades and sizes. Aztec marigolds, if planted now, will be a mass of pale-yellow bloom four or five feet high in October. For a gay, quick vine plant squash—three plants in a fourteen-inch wooden tub. Place them on the terrace or some place where you can give them attention. Then don't overlook the second or even third sowings of such plants as alyssum, California and Shirley poppies, baby's-breath, and mignonette.

TREES, VINES, AND SHRUBBERY

Cutting and pruning. As soon as the spring-flowering shrubbery has finished blooming, cut out all unnecessary wood to the ground as illustrated in Chapter VI. All hedge cutting should be done now and frequently thereafter, until August. Frequent trimming of hedges makes a thick, green surface growth and avoids unsightly open spots. Break or cut all seed pods from azaleas and lilacs but be careful with the lilacs because next year's blooming buds are being formed now.

Watering. Care should be taken with newly planted materials so that they receive a thorough soaking each week. Soak; do not sprinkle. Mulch them and wash the leaves carefully.

Climbing roses. They should be looked over carefully and any heavy growth should be firmly tied into the proper position. Prune them after blossoming according to illustrations and instructions in Chapter IX.

GARDENING IN JULY

GENERAL

Watering-time is again at hand and we must call your attention to the difference between watering and sprinkling. For the most part, sprinkling is harmful, especially upon lawns. Watering means *soaking*. Soak the soil to the bottom of the roots, then cultivate the topsoil to keep it from evaporating and to kill the revived weeds. Do it thoroughly and less often. Investigate automatic watering devices. Now is the time to begin to sow cover crops between rows and in vacated beds. Sow clover, rye, and vetch. These, dug under later, will return humus and nitrates to the soil. See "Green Manuring" in Chapter III.

LAWNS

This month, we mow, water, and weed. If our previous work has been wise we need not worry about our lawn. High mowing, deep waterings, and weed watchfulness are still necessary. Don't let the weed seeds form, and, above all, try to influence your neighbor to do the same.

THE SUMMER FLOWERS

Cultivation and mulching. To kill various ground pests as well as to increase soil porosity, it is well to cultivate diligently until July 1. Cultivation does not take the place of watering, but it does conserve the water in the soil. After July 1 much of this labor can be avoided by mulching. Under a summer sun the soil often goes over this maximum for long periods, thus starving the plants. Moisture is the great temperature regulator. The mulch acts as a parasol and an insulated seal. It keeps the soil cool and moist. It must be light to admit air but in turn its air spaces keep out excess heat.

First cultivate well, water thoroughly, and cover with an inch, or better, two inches of peat moss, domestic humus, straw, leaf mould, or thoroughly rotted manure. It is well to give a ration of lime, thoroughly worked in, to all except the plants inclined to prefer acidity. The mulch is slightly acid and, unless your soil is strongly alkaline, may retard some growth. Rake off the mulch in late fall for cultivation or winter protection. It may be saved for soil conditioning or in compost.

Do not mulch irises, dahlias, or any of the plants requiring special care. Mulching goes well around newly planted shrubbery. It is also good upon the flower border and if your roses are healthy and free from rosebugs, it improves both foliage and bloom after July 1.

Miscellaneous culture. Cut back viola cornuta, forget-me-not, and nepta to four inches and dress with sheep manure for August bloom. Phlox, veronica, and hollyhock will bloom again if kept from seeding. Pinch back pink and white boltonia and New England aster to five inches, early in July, to keep them bushy. Make cuttings of centaurea, coleus, alternanthera, artemisia, torenia, impatiens, etc. Set out coleus, begonias, and geraniums to enliven the borders.

Now is the time to sow vines along fences and near garages. It is too late to plant any annuals except portulaca, torenia, balsam, vinca, zinnia, annual lupines, Shirley poppies, and mignonette. Cut back chrysanthemums and poinsettias, disbudding and removing surplus shoots. Order colchicum (autumn crocus) for August planting.

Spray nasturtiums, sweet peas, and goldenglow with nicotine. Examine aster roots for insects and dig in tobacco dust. Spray with nicotine for tarnish bugs which attack growing aster tips and spray with bordeaux mixture on the underside of leaves of young plants to act as a rust preventive. If the sweet peas are heavily mulched, their roots will be kept cooler and their season prolonged. Use rough litter or grass clippings. If aphids appear, spray them with nicotine. A little shade at midday will help to maintain the quality of the flowers and prolong the season.

Rock garden. A few good late-blooming rock plants are *campanula* (family lasts into July); *Erigeron alpinus* (dwarf purple daisy, blooms all summer); *Coronilla cappadoccia* (blue-green trailer racemes, blooms in July); *Dianthus knappi* (dainty yellow-pink); *Wahlenbergia tasmanica* and *W. dalmaticus* (like dwarf platycodons); *Anemone narcissiflora* (white flower heads); and *Allium thibeticum* (waxy lilac flowers six inches high).

Dahlias. The main stems of the dahlias should be reduced to one or two stems. In larger varieties, a single stalk is the best. Keep the lateral shoots pinched out on the flowering stems and remove half the buds. Some sort of adequate support must be provided to prevent storm breakage. Water them well and follow feeding directions.

Iris. Bearded iris should be divided if over three years old and if roots are crowding. Replace the more common ones with some new specimens. Top dress the existing borders with bone meal. Do not use manure. Water the oriental iris well before flowering and withhold water afterwards. Divide every three years after they have flowered, lifting and separating carefully with a sharp knife. Set much deeper than bearded kinds and water sparingly after transplanting.

Peonies. They are now making ready for next year's bloom. Care for them. Maybe they need division in September. Get them ready.

Gladioli. Continue to plant until January 10 for late bloom. Try planting five inches deep to avoid staking. Dig up and burn every stunted yellow plant. They will not flower, so you lose nothing and yet prevent infection spreading in your soil to other bulbs.

Flower boxes. Soil in the porch boxes must be kept in a state of richness. A good stimulant is nitrate of soda, one pound; phosphate, one-half pound; and sulphate of potash or wood ashes, one-half pound. Use one quarter of a teaspoonful in a quart of water every two days, being careful not to touch the leaves. Never depend on rains, but water daily. Plant tablets are convenient.

WATER GARDEN

If you do it regularly, the care of the water garden should not average five minutes per day after the pool is cleaned and ready. Pests are very few and treatment is seldom necessary.

Late in the season, lilies may exhaust the food supply in the tubs. Plant food may then be inserted about four inches away from the crowns.

Aphids may be washed into the overflow with a hose or sprayed with nicotine. Authorities say fish do not eat them, as is claimed by some writers. Dusting with arsenate of lead kills leaf chewers. Don't overdo the use of it. Keep it out of the water as much as possible.

Wash off the leaves after sundown by the use of a fine spray, but avoid any large quantity of cold water.

THINGS TO DO IN AUGUST

GENERAL

Now is the time to locate some manure for rotting to use next spring. The wise gardener who wants bulbs for fall planting orders them early. The stock of some species and varieties is limited and only the early comers can be served. Order alpine seed to plant late in autumn in an uncovered frame. Now that you can see your garden in bloom, start your seed list for next year.

Uncultivated ground that you intend to plant next year ought now to be plowed or spaded, raked, and planted with some green cover crop like Canada peas or vetch. The cover crop, in turn, is to be turned under in the fall and left to rot away in the soil during the winter. Several years of this will work wonders.

Every weed that ripens and spreads its seed means more trouble for you next year. Get weeds out of the ground before they mature. Surface cultivation two or three days after a rain or watering will kill innumerable seedling weeds.

Thorough cultivation of the surface soil after every rain or watering will prevent caking and do much to conserve the moisture where it is needed in the region of the roots. Furthermore, such cultivation will destroy the young weeds before they get a start and begin to do damage.

Keep the birds' bath filled, especially if a drought comes. The contents evaporate rapidly in such weather, to say nothing of what the birds themselves spatter about. It is a great convenience, of course, to have the water piped direct from the regular house supply.

Remember water evaporates at this time of year. Water deeply and thoroughly. Use a mulch where it is specified and don't forget to water compost heap.

LAWN

August is the time to go over your lawn, destroying insects and keeping weeds from seeding, weakening the stand so that winter will do the rest. Look carefully after crab grass to keep it from seeding. Follow Nature's tip and do your seeding to the best advantage. A dressing of lawn food late in the month will be very beneficial if it is well watered down or applied with a hose syphon.

When sprinkling the lawn, do the job thoroughly so as to wet the ground several inches deep. Indeed, this principle is one which should be applied to all watering. A mere surface sprinkling does more harm than good, for it encourages shallow rooting, easily injured.

AMONG THE FLOWERS

Care. Don't let your flower garden run down, as so many people have a tendency to do at this season of the year. Keep tall flowers well staked and cut out all your dead stalks. Keep the edges trimmed, and stir the soil on the surface to prevent weeds and to conserve moisture. Use a mulch to save labor and moisture. Use humus, peat, straw, or decayed leaves at least two inches thick. Water well once in a while.

Gladioli. Taller varieties of gladioli should be staked to protect them from breakage by wind. For individuals and small clumps, single stakes will suffice. For rows, use lines of twine on both sides of the row, stretched tight between stakes set ten feet or so apart, forming an alley. Apply manure water.

Lilies. Lilies like to have their roots fairly cool, especially during the hot weather. Unless foliage of some sort shades them and produces this result, mulch the ground over and around the roots with grass clippings or some kind of rough litter that is free from weed and grass seeds.

Dahlias. Feed and disbud the dahlias now. Just before they are ready to bloom, apply about a pint of special dahlia plant food. Keep the cut blooms away from windows and doors. They do not like drafts.

Oriental poppies. Do not mulch oriental poppies. They prefer hot sunbaked ground when resting.

Peonies. Feed and cultivate peonies now for next year's bloom.

Helichrysum. Strawflowers intended for winter bouquets ought to be cut before the blossoms are fully open. Dry them in the shade, hanging them head downward in small, loose, uncrowded bunches. In handling, be especially careful not to crack the stems near the blossoms.

Manure water. Use manure water on plants ready to bloom (especially on heliotrope) and to hasten the second blooming of delphinium, etc.

Wood ashes. Use wood ashes around phlox, aster, and cosmos. In using wood ashes, do not pile on too much at one time. The goodness leaches away and is wasted. Sprinkle them on the ground near the roots, allowing a little brown earth to show through.

Phlox. There is nothing which will give such definite and beautiful mass effects in the garden in August as hardy or perennial phlox, provided it is well grown.

The secret of phlox culture lies in these four essential conditions: full sun; deep preparation to make them grow tall; plenty of moisture at their roots, especially during droughts; and preventing the flowers from going to seed. Plants must be divided also as soon as they get too thick, every three years or oftener. Never leave more than four or five stalks to a plant. Keep plants sprayed with bordeaux mixture or dust them every ten days from the time they appear above ground, to prevent mildew. They should be grown in groups of no less than five plants to a group. Phlox may also be successfully propagated

from stem cuttings taken in late summer and rooted in a cold frame. Protect the cuttings over winter and set them out in spring when they are six inches high. Propagation from root cuttings is made from clumps taken in the fall and protected in a cold frame until spring. These cuttings, two inches in length, are laid in flats of sandy loam and covered with one-half inch of soil. Transplant them when they are from two to four inches high.

Window boxes. Use plant tablets on porch boxes, and keep the plants well watered.

Cut flowers. Pick exhibition blossoms the night before they are to be shown and keep them in a cool dark cellar in water up to their necks. It is well to keep on hand at least one ordinary florist vase in which to keep flowers overnight or until they can be arranged.

Roses. Use care to avoid adding any quick-acting plant food to roses at this time. A light dusting of bone meal raked in is good just before a mulch is applied. Though this fertilizer does not necessarily improve the quality of the fall flowers it is sure to give the plant more vigor and will strengthen it for blossoming the following year. The mulch is best applied in July, but if you have not used it, do so now and save water and cultivation. Don't forget to add some tobacco dust to it. Pick up and burn all fallen leaves, as they may be infested with black spot.

HOUSE PLANTS, GREENHOUSE, AND COLD FRAME

If you have a greenhouse make a compost heap of discarded plants. Use topsoil with a sod growth, adding manure and bone meal for enrichment. The material will decompose and form the finest sort of soil for repotting or direct use in the greenhouse benches.

Cuttings. Cuttings should be taken of bedding plants such as coleus, geraniums, etc. If these are carried in a cool greenhouse through the winter they will make good stock for setting out next spring. Some of the modern varieties of geraniums are especially worth while.

Annuals. Sow annuals for winter forcing. Calendulas bloom well and keep long. Browallia, mignonette, sweet peas, lupine, ageratum, marigolds, stocks, snapdragons, and many others are good subjects. One professional grower specialized in dandelions for table decorations and made them a success.

Bulbs. Bulbs intended for forcing into bloom in the greenhouse should be ordered at this time. Boxes, pans, soil, and other materials needed for them should be made ready as some bulbs are available now. Successive plantings, of course, mean an extended period of bloom.

Chrysanthemums. Buds will be forming on most of the greenhouse chrysanthemums by this time and strong feedings will be necessary if you want highest quality flowers. Unless you are experienced in their culture it will pay you to get a good book on hothouse chrysanthemums.

Garden plants. If you are planning to take some garden plants indoors to provide for early fall bloom, use a sharp knife to root-prune them now to a size a little smaller than the pot. Remove all buds and flowers and cut back the top growth severely. Water them well until they are ready to lift.

House plants. Look over house plants which are summering outdoors to see that they are not suffering for want of water. Be careful not to disturb those now going through their rest periods.

Cold frame. If you do not have a cold frame, now is the time to plan one. You can see how it will fit into the garden plan.

TREES, VINES, AND SHRUBBERY

Hedges. Hedges of all types, including evergreens that have been confined to a form and plants that are clipped, should be gone over now, because growth for the season is about to cease. One of the secrets of success with such plants is never to let them get unkempt and out of hand. Be careful not to fertilize to start new growth which will winter kill.

Evergreens. Evergreens, both broad-leaved and coniferous, should be planted from now to September 15. They need a great deal of water, so it is advisable, when resetting them, to saturate the soil. Where possible, too, let them be protected somewhat from the sweep of drying summer winds.

Vines. It is as necessary to prune vines as it is to prune other plants. All unproductive wood should be removed. This will give room for the more vigorous shoots and promote the general welfare of the plants. A fall top dressing of manure is advisable also, for best future results.

Transplanting. Ornamental stock, woody as well as herbaceous, can be transplanted if it is well soaked several hours before lifting, reset quickly and firmly, and thoroughly watered. Where feasible, it is good to provide shade and wind protection for a few days in a very hot weather. If you plan to move them after freezing, root-prune them now; see the illustrations in Chapters VI and VII.

Shrubbery. The scholartree (*Sophora japonica*) is the tree found around temples and pagodas in Japan. It is one of the four most beautiful flowering trees, useful especially for its creamy-white flowers in large panicles in August, when few trees are blooming. The flower is liked by the bees. It is a graceful tree, low-branching where it has room. The foliage is similar to that of the locust and turns yellow in the fall and persists late. It is slow-growing and does not flower when young. The old trees flower freely, especially in the hot season in August and September. It will stand drought. Use it in well-drained, sandy soil.

Our common summersweet bush (*Clethra alnifolia*) makes the hedge rows fragrant in August with its white flowers in upright panicles, and its crisp leaves. It likes a moist peaty or sandy soil, but will thrive in ordinary garden soil.

The arnold hawthorn (*Crataegus arnoldiana*) is one of the earliest among the hawthorns to fruit and is popular on that account. It flowers in May. It has a bright red fruit, about an inch in diameter, in August, which falls early. The tree grows twenty feet tall. It is easy to transplant if pruned severely, all over, at the time. It likes lime, in common with other hawthorns. Use sandy loam enriched with well-rotted manure.

PROPAGATING, SEEDING, AND PLANTING

Iris. If you have not done so, divide iris now when it becomes crowded. Japanese iris which has grown in the same spot for three or four years should be divided at once.

Seed sowing. Pansies, forget-me-nots, English daisies, etc., are sturdier plants if sown this month. Parsley seed should be sown now for the green garden. Many perennials should be started this month. However, unless one has time and patience to keep them watered and shaded until well established, it is useless to plant them. While many perennials can be started in a shady spot in the yard it is almost necessary to have a cold frame in order to winter them over.

Biennials, such as foxglove, can be started from seed now. It is inadvisable to set out any of the young plants in the border, for the winter would probably kill them.

Seedlings. About this time of the year we will discover many self-grown seedlings of hollyhock, larkspur, columbine, sweet william, etc. If the parent plant is worthy, these should be carefully guarded, for here is a way to stretch your garden budget. Tag these seedlings carefully for transplanting. Remember, phlox seldom comes true to color from seed.

Woody plants. Cuttings of various woody plants can be started in a shaded cold frame which can be covered with sash as cold weather comes. In most cases, use ripe new wood with most of the foliage removed. Various combinations of sand, sand and soil, or sand and peat moss are used.

Narcissus. Transplant narcissus that have become crowded, using directions given in Chapter X. Get some variety. There are now over six hundred varieties of daffodils.

Madonna lily. Transplant as soon as basal leaves wither.

Oriental poppies. Don't limit yourself to reds; get some fine ones in pink and white. Now is the only time to buy and transplant.

They require full sun and perfect drainage. They come easily from roots and will grow again if a small piece is left. To propagate, cut two-inch lengths as thick as a lead pencil. Cut straight across at top and slanting at bottom. Set straight up and down and cover one inch deep. Water well and cover with peat moss. Do not cover old established plants.

CLIPPING AND PRUNING

Clip off the dried heads of last spring's lilac blooms. Cut seed heads off the phlox and all annuals if you want continuous bloom. Do not let them go to seed. It will not be much of a job if you use shears and let the dried flowers fall where they may.

For the finest dahlias, disbudding should be continued to the end of the season. Generally speaking, the two side buds in every group of three are the ones to be removed. Watch chrysanthemums to keep them from bearing too many buds or growing too tall.

Deciduous trees that need only moderate pruning may receive it now. It is easier to gauge such work while the foliage is on than after it has fallen in the autumn. Large limbs, of course, should not be removed until the sap has receded from the branches in the autumn.

WHAT TO DO IN SEPTEMBER

GENERAL

Even if you do have occasional rains, remember that the soil dries out quickly now. See that propagating beds and newly planted or transplanted items are kept moist. They are getting their first root growth now and need constant water supply. Don't forget to water the compost heap. Do not neglect to sow down freely with rye and vetch the vacant patches of ground in the garden. When dug under next spring these cover crops will benefit the soil decidedly. Sowing can also be made between the rows of crops that are well spaced.

Wire grass, rye grass, and other heavy-growing grasses and weeds, if allowed to overrun your garden now, will be a serious factor to contend with next spring. Better haul them out, roots and all, for they are persistent pests and seem to have at least nine lives when once well started.

THE LAWN

Keep cutting the grass until all growth has ceased. Failure to do this will result in a long growth, which will turn brown in spring and be hard to eradicate. Do not, however, cut as closely as you did in the spring, for now the roots need more surface protection than in the early season.

This is about the last chance for properly seeding down lawns; most weed growth is over and the grass will get sufficient start to carry it through the winter. You must be prepared, however, to water it abundantly in case the fall rains fail to put in an appearance, as often happens.

AMONG THE FLOWERS

Sanitation. The flower garden should be given a final clean-up for the season: the walks properly edged, all weeds and old stalks removed and burned. Thus will you not only create a more pleasing setting for the fall flower display, but also prepare for next season's best results. Disease germs and pests lurk in dead stalks and leaves left around all winter. All dead matter which harbors them should be collected and completely destroyed by burning. Do not stop using Massy dust on the perennials. Delphinium is especially subject to fungous growths in September.

Frosts. Watch for early frosts and cover tender plants with newspaper or muslin. A few strips of unbleached muslin sewed together and kept for this purpose is inexpensive and prolongs the blooming season. It should be in every garden toolkit.

Bulbs. Get your bulb orders in now and carefully plan for the planting season. This means better results next spring. See Chapter X. Don't let the narcissi go into the winter in a crowded condition; get them in as early as possible. By all means, visit your bulb store and get a few crocuses, scillas, and chionodaxes. Plant them either in the rockery or at the edge of the foundation planting. It is not good practice to plant them in the lawn, for most gardeners start mowing before the leaves of these little flowers have completely ripened, thereby ruining the bulb. Prepare beds now for bulbs to be planted later.

Field mice that roam through the burrows made by moles destroy thousands of tulip bulbs annually. This can be prevented by planting in baskets made of one-half-inch mesh wire.

Seeds and roots. You never know just what forms you will get from flower seeds gathered from your own plants. That is what makes the experiment so interesting. Collect the seeds when ripe and keep them till spring in a dry, cool place. Both annual and perennial flowers are interesting subjects to try. However, do not limit your garden to home-gathered seeds. It is always best to remember that new flower seeds each year come from selected flowers grown by experts under ideal conditions.

When the first bloom of the delphinium has withered, keep a few seeds of the choicest specimens on the stalk until ripe. Then plant them at once in a garden seed bed. They will grow into husky little plants that winter well where they are, ready to transplant into permanent quarters in the spring.

Hollyhocks respond in the same manner to the sowing of fresh ripe seed. If the color of the variety is one especially liked, protect the bloom with a glassine or cellophane bag, while the seed is forming, to keep off marauding bees.

Sometime this month when growth has stopped and vanished foliage indicates a dormant condition, dig up a good root each of bleeding heart, anchusa, and oriental poppy. Cut these long roots into inch pieces and plant them where the soil has been made of a mixture of sand and rich loam. Keep the area fairly moist. Soon tiny leaves will shoot up. They will be ready for permanent quarters in the spring. If you want to have annuals early, try sowing some of the hardy varieties this fall. Some of these are larkspur, poppies, sweet alyssum, ageratum, calliopsis, cornflowers, and petunias.

Late-blooming plants. Chrysanthemums, fall perennials, the second bloom of delphinium, and other similar plants that are in bud should be fed freely with liquid manures of different kinds until the buds show definite signs of opening. It is important that all of this material be kept well watered, lest it become dry and woody and flower poorly. If fresh manure is not obtainable, substitute the dry product which is sold by the garden supply stores. Spray chrysanthemums for black aphids, using nicotine sulphate. If your plants are bothered by grasshoppers spray them with arsenate of lead.

Hardy asters. Practically all asters need constant division in order not to deteriorate in the garden. Clumps should be divided every year, leaving not over four or five stalks to a plant. All asters should be staked early in the season. Later on, when the larkspur is cut down a few branches of aster staked to grow horizontally will help fill up vacant spaces.

Phlox. This is the last chance to tag phlox for division later. The flowers fade quickly toward the end of the month. Mark them for both height and color, so that you may plant them for proper display in the border.

Roses. It will not be necessary to feed the roses from now on, but they should be sprayed after each rain with a rose dust (Massy dust) to prevent black spot. Also, keep them well watered or mulched. Late fall planting of hardy garden roses is becoming popular as its advantages are better understood. You will do well to prepare the bed now so it will have time to settle before actual planting time. In general, try to get the plants in just before hard freezing weather. Order the new plants now.

Peonies. Try transplanting your peonies in rotation, a few each year. In this way you will not risk loss of bloom on all of them. Remember September 15 at 9 A.M. the clock strikes for transplanting peonies. Order roots at once and get ready for planting. Four to five years in one spot is about the limit of sure success with them.

Iris. Last chance to successfully divide irises this year.

Cosmos. Transplant late cosmos to boxes on the porch to keep them blooming after frost. Securely stake exposed plants.

Gaillardia. Divide gaillardia clumps over two years old. They stop blooming after three years. Late this month they revive for an overgrown bloom. They do not come well from seed, but can be propagated from cuttings even as late as this if they are grown inside for a few weeks and potted for the spring.

Pansies. Pansies may be wintered outside if covered with straw just before frost. If leaves are used be sure to have a poultry wire fence to hold them in place but not to pack them down. Transplant the August sown pansies and order more seed for earliest spring sowing.

Lilies. They may still be planted. Madonna lilies should be in by September 15.

Now while they are in bloom or have just finished is the time to make a list of fall blooming flowers to plant next spring. The following are two to consider:

Spirea. The spirea is a herbaceous plant that should be in every border. This is one plant that cares little about soil, but usually does best in a soil composed of good loam, sand, and manure, equal parts.

Anemone japonica (Japanese windflower). This hardy garden perennial revels in the strongest sunshine. Its colors range from pure white to deep pinks. This dainty little flower begins to unfold its lovely buds in early August, when there is a dearth of bloom in the garden, and continues its good work until late September.

Harvesting tender bulbs. Harvest the gladioli as soon as the foliage turns brown. Lift and store dahlias, cannas, and caladiums as soon as they are blackened by frost. Tuberous begonias should be taken up before the first light frost. Retain a large clump of dirt and place them in a frostproof but well-ventilated cellar that is not too hot. Wait until the foliage wilts and then cut it loose from the clump. Dry out bulbs for a few days and store in dry sand at about 50°.

Four-o'clock roots can be lifted and stored in a dry cellar or packed in sand. The temperature should be low (a little above freezing). Cut off and burn the dead tops but leave some soil on the roots to avoid breaking them. Planted in your garden, they will bloom several weeks earlier than those raised from seed.

Biennials. Any left-over hardy biennials may be gathered in a corner and easily protected with a loose mulch for planting next spring.

HOUSE PLANTS

Hardening. Start bringing in your house plants while the windows may still be left open so that the plants will gradually become inured to the dry house air. Dwarf asters and other small plants of annuals may be taken from the garden and set in small pots to flower in the house.

Bulbs for bloom indoors. Those who want early bloom indoors should start hyacinths, etc., now, following directions in Chapter X.

GREENHOUSE AND COLD FRAME

The greenhouse should be thoroughly overhauled before starting it into active operation for the cold season. Now is the time to do any necessary painting, glazing, or repairing of its heating.

Soil for winter potting ought to be obtained and stored somewhere under cover. The best kind is light and moderately rich, containing plenty of humus and some sand. Chopped sod and garden loam, allowed to compost for several months, are ideal as a basis for the mixture.

Get the cuttings of the outdoor bedding plants, such as chrysanthemum, coleus, etc., before they are destroyed by frost. These may be grown along and developed in the greenhouse or even on a glass-enclosed, heated sun porch. Each variety should be marked and kept separate.

FOUNDATION PLANTING

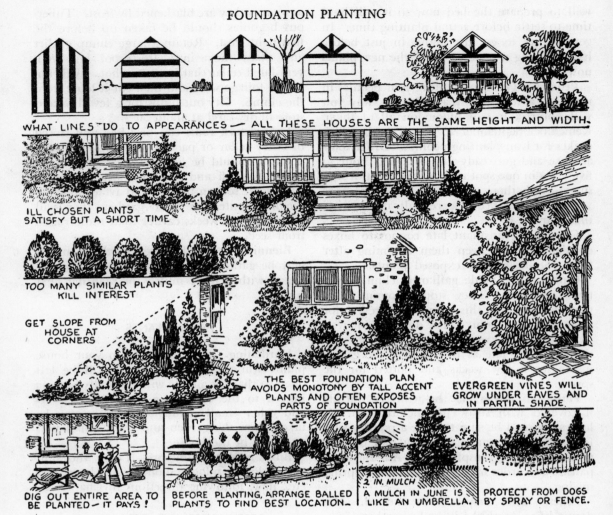

WHAT LINES DO TO APPEARANCES — ALL THESE HOUSES ARE THE SAME HEIGHT AND WIDTH.

ILL CHOSEN PLANTS SATISFY BUT A SHORT TIME

TOO MANY SIMILAR PLANTS KILL INTEREST

GET SLOPE FROM HOUSE AT CORNERS

THE BEST FOUNDATION PLAN AVOIDS MONOTONY BY TALL ACCENT PLANTS AND OFTEN EXPOSES PARTS OF FOUNDATION

EVERGREEN VINES WILL GROW UNDER EAVES AND IN PARTIAL SHADE.

DIG OUT ENTIRE AREA TO BE PLANTED — IT PAYS!

BEFORE PLANTING, ARRANGE BALLED PLANTS TO FIND BEST LOCATION.

2 IN. MULCH A MULCH IN JUNE IS LIKE AN UMBRELLA.

PROTECT FROM DOGS BY SPRAY OR FENCE.

Proper planting can help overcome many of the architectural shortcomings of a house, making it look wider and less top heavy. Choose the plants carefully so that they will not sprawl all over your walks and hide your house after a year or two.

Carnations that were planted out may now be put in the greenhouse for the indoor season, before the frost has a chance to catch them. The glass should be shaded slightly until the roots again become active, after which normal light is again allowed to enter the house.

Take in hydrangeas.

Start freesias and set them where they are to grow.

Buy shrubs for forcing.

Keep roses from developing buds as yet.

Plant Spanish iris in flats.

Transplant biennials, such as pansy and English daisy, in the frames for the winter to give early bloom.

Sow pansy seed in frames.

Propagate Japanese anemones by cuttings in the frames.

Sow annual lupine, snapdragons, sweet peas, schizanthus, annual larkspur, gypsophila, stock, and calendula.

Plant violets and lilies.

Propagate by cutting geraniums, coleus, heliotrope, verbena, chrysanthemums, etc.

TREES, VINES, AND SHRUBBERY

Do not fertilize trees or shrubbery at this time of year. It may start new growth which will winter kill. Do not prune your spring-flowering shrubs now or you endanger next year's bloom by removing the flower buds.

Evergreens. This is really the season when

evergreens (including rhododendrons and other broad-leaved types) are nearest dormant. Transplant them now for best results. See the August calendar. Pick off all bagworms and determine to spray at the proper time next year. Treat now for red spider.

Pruning. Shape up trees and shrubbery now while the foliage is on them and you can see what they will look like. Deadwood is easy to distinguish now. If you haven't followed directions under "Clipping and Pruning" in the August calendar, do so now.

Transplanting. As soon as the foliage turns on deciduous plants it is safe to transplant; transplant early so that the roots will have a better chance to take hold before cold weather.

Watering. A great deal of our so-called winter losses, especially with evergreens, is the result of these plants being allowed to become bone dry at this season. They should always

be well watered right up to the time the ground freezes hard, because they hold their leaves and evaporate water during the winter. When unable to take it from the frozen ground they go through great hardship. Water them in fall for health and for safety during the dry spells of winter.

Planting. Prepare the ground for planting new trees and shrubbery in October and November.

Vines. When other vines begin to fade you can really appreciate the virgin's bower (*Clematis paniculata*) which remains green until November. Give some lime and a mulch of manure this fall and follow with a ration of bone meal next spring. It will repay you.

Climbing roses. Those who have not pruned the ramblers after they finished blooming should do so now. Now is the proper time to prune all other kinds of climbing roses.

WHAT TO DO IN OCTOBER

GENERAL

The time for raking leaves is at hand. It must be remembered that they are a source of humus and if you have space enough by all means start a compost pile. Do not allow weeds to seed. This will save much trouble next year. Burn the dead stalks of perennials to help control insects and disease.

Any changes in the borders should be made now. Be sure to fertilize well.

This is also a good time to apply soil conditioners such as manures and forms of commercial humus. The manure does not need to be well rotted at this time if you are careful to keep it away from the plant roots. The freezing and thawing of winter will take a lot of the heat out of it before the spring growing season. Do not use manures on bulbs unless it is specially directed.

Small evergreens can be planted in the window boxes and if kept watered will do for replanting next spring or, with proper care, will last in the boxes all summer.

PESTS

The falling of the leaves marks the beginning of the season for spraying scale insects. Lilacs, fruit trees, Lombardy poplars, and ash trees should be examined for scale and sprayed

sometime while they are dormant, using miscible oil or commercial lime sulphur. This is also an excellent time to spray white pines and other evergreens with nicotine if they are subject to aphids. Watch the chrysanthemums and other late-flowering plants for aphids which flock to the tender new shoots and even devour the flowers. Spray them with nicotine.

THE LAWN

Lawn mowing is to be kept up as long as new growth continues to be apparent. This policy not only keeps the turf looking well, but also improves its condition next year. Long-matted grass that has lain on the lawn all winter means trouble in the spring when mowing begins. Keep the lawn free of leaves and other litter during the winter. The grass smothers easily at this time.

AMONG THE FLOWERS

Lilies. Many lily bulbs get into the market late. If you intend to plant later, prepare the bed and mulch the soil with manure to keep it from freezing. Don't forget to mulch the lilies already planted. Follow instructions in Chapter X.

Frosts. Don't forget the hint contained in

the September calendar concerning muslin covers for late-blooming flowers. If they are injured by frost you may be able to revive them by a very fine spray of cold water from the hose. This may be done in the morning before the sun strikes them. A light wooden scaffold or some stakes help in this protection. Do not put the cover in place until evening and be sure that you remove it when the sun is fairly up next morning. Chrysanthemum-lovers who have no greenhouses may keep their plants in bloom far into the fall weather by using a few light frames, covered with cheese cloth to form a little house. These may be made by any handy person from lath and lattice and easily fastened together with a few screen-door hooks. A temporary stake or two will aid in keeping then upright.

Spring-flowering bulbs. Few gardeners are sufficiently impressed with the necessity of setting out fall-planted bulbs at the proper time. Only tulips should be held until after October 15. The narcissus, while much planted in October, should go in as early as possible as it takes three months of warm weather to properly develop their roots. Many of the smaller bulbs may or should be planted in September or early October. This also applies to hyacinths. Some gardeners state that hyacinths should go in when the maple leaves begin to color. However, a little earlier is better, and they will also do fairly well if planted a little later.

Tender bulbs. Dig up and store all tender bulbous plants, such as gladioli, dahlias, etc. The dahlias must be stored in sand or in boxes and kept in a cool, dark cellar that is not too dry. One of the best packing materials for dahlias is peat moss. Packing is not needed for gladiolus corms.

Tender plants. Hydrangeas, bay trees, hibiscus, oleander, orange or lemon, crepe myrtle, etc., which have been used to decorate the porch or terrace, must be brought into a cool, fairly light cellar before freezing weather. Look over your garden for plants you wish to save or mature indoors; these would include cineraria, geranium, lobelia erinus, nasturtium, petunia, sweet alyssum, ageratum, etc.

Rockery. Stone chips used as top dressing will not only minimize erosion in the rock garden, but will also help to prevent soil's heaving and its resultant damage to roots. Work them up close around the crowns of the plants. Get them in place now and let them remain there permanently. Pine needles also make a good mulch for the rockery. Where plants are grown which do not care for lime, use marble or granite chips which may be obtained from the manufacturer of monuments.

Roses. The time for winter protection comes about the end of the month. Carefully study the directions in Chapter IX so that the plants do not suffer. The best time for fall planting of roses is just before freezing weather. Prepare the beds as early as possible and carefully follow instructions.

If your climbing roses are in an exposed location, tie them up firmly with broad strips of rags so that the wind will not beat them against the trellis and bruise the bark. We hope you have observed the pruning rules so that there will not be a mass of useless foliage to catch the wind.

Fall planting. In many instances autumn planting of perennials is greatly to be preferred to spring planting. It is essential, however, that the transplanting be done early enough in the fall to allow the plants to become well established before the ground freezes for the winter. As a general rule perennials which bloom in early spring benefit by autumn planting, while perennials which bloom in late summer or in autumn should be planted in the spring. Remember general rules are dangerous. Phlox and oriental poppy are best divided shortly after blooming, while chrysanthemums, lupines, anemone, etc. must wait until the approach of warm weather. The only satisfactory way is to ascertain the needs of each plant.

Sweet peas. Insurance for good sweet peas next year is to dig the trench now (two to three feet deep) and mix the soil well with plenty of manure. They are planted so early in the spring that there is hardly time to do it then.

Renovate the flower bed. Now is a good time to get ready for spring. Beds renovated or newly prepared now will be settled and ready for spring transplanting. See Chapter XI.

HOUSE PLANTS

Herbs. A plant or two of parsley, taken up from the garden and reset in a pot of good soil, will do well all winter if kept watered and

FALL PLANTING AND CARE

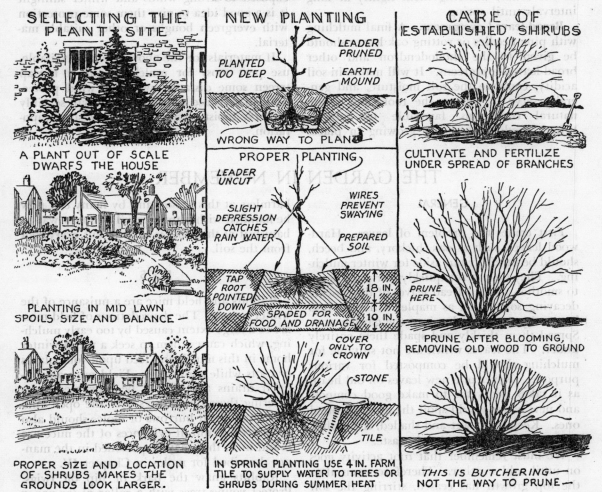

SELECTING THE PLANT SITE

A PLANT OUT OF SCALE DWARFS THE HOUSE

PLANTING IN MID LAWN SPOILS SIZE AND BALANCE

PROPER SIZE AND LOCATION OF SHRUBS MAKES THE GROUNDS LOOK LARGER.

NEW PLANTING

LEADER PRUNED
PLANTED TOO DEEP
EARTH MOUND

WRONG WAY TO PLANT

PROPER PLANTING
LEADER UNCUT
SLIGHT DEPRESSION CATCHES RAIN WATER
WIRES PREVENT SWAYING
PREPARED SOIL
TAP ROOT POINTED DOWN
18 IN.
10 IN.
SPADED FOR FOOD AND DRAINAGE

COVER ONLY TO CROWN
STONE
TILE

IN SPRING PLANTING USE 4 IN. FARM TILE TO SUPPLY WATER TO TREES OR SHRUBS DURING SUMMER HEAT

CARE OF ESTABLISHED SHRUBS

CULTIVATE AND FERTILIZE UNDER SPREAD OF BRANCHES

PRUNE HERE

PRUNE AFTER BLOOMING, REMOVING OLD WOOD TO GROUND

THIS IS BUTCHERING— NOT THE WAY TO PRUNE—

in a sunny window of the kitchen. This is one herb whose appearance, odor, and flavor are all welcome through the cold weather. Chives, rose geranium, garden sage, and thyme for seasoning can also be maintained in this manner.

Care. The first few days in the house are critical for indoor plants. Use great care in watering and be sure to keep the foliage sprayed lest the plant dry up too quickly. There is a lot of difference between outdoor and indoor conditions, which must be considered.

TREES AND SHRUBBERY

Coniferous evergreens. Don't forget to water the evergreens just before they go into the winter, if the weather is at all dry. All your evergreens will grow better if they are mulched with strawy manure after the ground freezes.

Fruits. Dwarf fruit trees, now available in excellent quality and variety, are highly desirable features for the home grounds, large or small. They can be planted successfully now. The espalier types can be grown against walls, trellises, or fences.

Transplanting. The planting of new trees and shrubs may be attended to at this time. Fall plantings usually give better results than spring plantings, except with a few sorts which have soft fleshy roots, such as rose of Sharon, magnolias, tulips, birch, and dogwood.

Grapes. Grapevine cuttings can be taken when the leaves fall. Let them be of the past season's growth, with two joints each. Bury them outdoors, butts up, for callusing. An often better plan is to cover them with sand in the cellar, watering them lightly at long intervals until spring.

Broad-leaved evergreens. A final mulching with pine needles or rotting oak leaves should be given to the rhododendron and other broad-leaved evergreens. It will maintain soil acidity, conserve the soil moisture, and generally serve to protect the roots and create natural conditions favorable to growth. Where rhododendron are growing in places exposed to strong winds and winter sunlight it is a good idea to give them some protection with evergreen boughs or other suitable material.

If materials for the above are not available, use peat moss for mulching and a burlap screen some distance away for wind protection; in fact, use anything which will sensibly conserve moisture and retard excessive evaporation.

THE GARDEN IN NOVEMBER

GENERAL

First comes the problem of leaves. Hardwood leaves, such as oak, hickory, and beech, should be carefully put aside for winter mulching. They do not rot quickly nor pack down to smother plants. Dead leaves of the quickly decaying sorts, such as maple, will turn into humus by spring if dug into the garden now. Spread them thickly and spade them entirely under. The leaves which are not suitable for mulching should be composted for various purposes. Never pile new leaves on old heaps as it takes two years to make good compost and new leaves would spoil the already rotted ones. Keep them wet and shaded, if possible. Never burn them, for that is waste.

We must remember that root activity goes on until cold weather. Therefore, even after the top growth has ceased, stirring the soil surface between the larger plants is a distinct advantage. In most gardens this is neglected with resulting loss. Frost penetrates it more easily, helping to kill insects and causing the plant to become dormant more gently.

Ill-kept gardens breed disease and insects. Clean up all refuse and burn the stalks and other material likely to decay. Thoroughly sterilize the ground by consistent cultivation. Some gardeners use the stalks of garden flowers for winter mulching. This is extremely poor economy, as it offers disease an opportunity to take charge of your garden. The best preventive of disease is to remove all dead flower stalks. All peat which has been used for mulching during the summer should now be raked off and put aside to be used as ground conditioner, using new peat next season. This removes all dead and diseased plant leaves, allowing for a fresh clean start next spring.

Poison ivy, that gardener's bane, is relatively harmless at this season and by many can now be handled with impunity. The surest way to banish it at this time is to grub out every root from the soil.

PESTS

Rabbits and field mice are a nuisance of the winter season. The depredations of field mice are to a large extent caused by too early mulching, which causes them to seek a warm winter home in this mulch and feed upon your plants or roots while snowed in. Field mice also inhabit drains and should be prevented from entering these by gratings over the open end. The abandoned burrows of moles should also be destroyed and, if evidences of the mice are found in it, they may be poisoned in the manner described for moles in Chapter IV.

Rabbits gnaw the bark or nip off twigs. Protect young trees with a collar of tar paper or a fence of poultry wire.

Lilacs, Lombardy poplars, most smooth-barked trees, and practically all fruit trees are subject to the attacks of San José scale. These trees should be sprayed with one of the soluble oil mixtures which can be purchased from seed stores. The reason that sprays sufficiently strong to kill scale on shrubs and trees can be applied only from now until March is that at any other time they would injure buds or bark. During the winter these insecticides are applied at "dormant strength" with entire safety to the growth.

THE LAWN

Low spots or irregularities in the surface may be top-dressed now to overcome these troubles. Use good soil, and when not more than two inches of it is applied, the grass has a chance to come through again.

If you have not done so, you may still apply a fall compost dressing as directed in Chapter IV. It is especialy good for grass if applied at this season. Be sure to keep all leaves and all other heavy matter off the grass as it smothers very easily during extremely cold weather.

AMONG THE FLOWERS

Perennials. The early days of November are the last call for the transplanting of herbaceous perennials. Firm the clumps well after watering them. Water which collects upon the surface of the garden during the winter may become stagnant and dangerous to perennials. Little ditches will carry this off. See that the beds drain well.

Chrysanthemums. When they are through flowering, remove the stalks at once within a few inches of the ground. This will help out development and make them send out vigorous sprouts in the spring. Some may be lifted and heeled into the cold frame. Pot plants can be taken from the side sprouts which will develop next May.

Bulbs and roots. This is a good time to work lime around the iris. Tulips may be planted until December, if the weather is mild. Ask your seedsman about the varieties in the rock garden. If any outdoor bulb planting remains to be done, do not forget to apply a mulch that will exclude the frost for five or six weeks so that proper roots can form. Otherwise next spring's flowers will probably be unsatisfactory and the bulbs themselves will suffer subsequently. Some of the hardy lilies are late in getting into the market. Be sure to get them into the ground as quickly as possible and mulch the ground heavily to keep it open.

Roses. Hybrid teas and hybrid perpetuals, shrubs, hardy climbers, etc. will winter well in most localities if heeled up with soil six or eight inches and covered loosely with leaves. The more tender varieties are more trouble. Tea roses must be covered with straw and heeled up around the base to help shed the water. Standard roses are about the hardest to protect. The stems should be laid down for the winter and the tops covered with soil. Dig away the soil from one side of the crown, taking care not to expose the roots, and then lay the canes in a trench covering them with the excavated soil. Hardy climbers, of course, do not need this attention.

While the more severe pruning of roses should be left until spring, shortening the branches will keep them from being blown about by the wind and make them easier to protect. Be sure to remove all leaves from the ground and burn them. Remove all summer mulch as previously described. Do not be in too big a hurry to cover them as it is best to have a freeze first.

Mulching. Late this month or early December is the time to put on this perennial border mulch for the winter, after the ground first freezes a couple of inches deep. Applying it earlier means the chance of harboring destructive field mice which are still on the lookout for comfortable winter quarters.

Heavy mulching of peonies is not desirable. Winter protection is seldom needed after the first year, and when too thick a layer is applied, the result is flowerless stalks. At most, apply a light mulch of manure over the root area, but not on the crowns. For this, wait until the leaves die.

Do not use old stalks for your flowers as it may help to carry disease. Be especially sure to burn the stalks of peonies, delphiniums, hollyhocks, etc. Don't forget to apply a shovel of ashes about the delphiniums. Read instructions for winter protection in Chapter XI.

HOUSE PLANTS

Care. Winter house plants need particular care to help them weather the generally adverse conditions. Feeding them every month with concentrated plant food will help. They benefit by moist air. To secure it indoors try setting each pot in a tray of pebbles which is kept filled with water almost to the top level of the stones. Of course, the real remedy for too dry air lies in the use of one of the modern house humidifiers. Sponge the foliage with soap solution and scrub the green scum off the pots. Complete instructions will be found in Chapter XV.

Forcing. If you are planning to have some hyacinths indoors, November is the time to pot them. Hyacinths and many others respond especially well to various easy treatments and will bloom until April.

GREENHOUSE AND COLD FRAME

Vegetables. Do not neglect to make successional sowings in the greenhouse of vegetable crops such as beans, beets, carrots, lettuce, etc. The secret of success is sowing in small quantities and frequently. Clumps of rhubarb and asparagus can also be taken with a sharp spade, using care to get a large clump. Plant them in deep boxes, kegs, or other receptacles and they will give excellent winter results.

Flower seeds. It is not too late to start seeds of some of the more rapid growth annuals in the greenhouse for winter flowers. Of these may be mentioned calliopsis, candytuft, and the ever-popular mignonette.

Perennials. There are a number of popular perennials which force well. Clumps of coreopsis, bleeding-heart, shasta daisy, dicentra, etc., may be lifted, potted, and then plunged in a sheltered bed outside to ripen properly before forcing.

Sweet peas. Sweet peas in the greenhouse should be fed freely with liquid manures. The first flowers to appear should be pinched off to conserve the plants' strength. Keep the atmosphere dry at night.

Christmas flowers. Poinsettias, limes, and other heat-loving crops intended for Christmas bloom must be forced rapidly. A temperature of 75° or even 80°, when plenty of moisture is available, will be beneficial to them.

Shrubs. At this time all hardwooded forcing plants, such as lilacs, cherries, wistaria, etc., should be lifted from their places about the grounds and placed in tubs or boxes for winter forcing.

Carnations. Carnation plants should be kept supported and properly disbudded. Never allow the branches to accumulate green mould. The surface of the ground should be kept stirred. Top-dress with sheep manure.

TREES AND SHRUBBERY

Planting. Where circumstances are such as to necessitate very late planting of trees or shrubs, it is well to remember that heavy mulching will keep frost out of the ground. Thus the soil both around the stock and on the proposed site can be kept workable until December at least. Newly planted trees (even small ones) require some sort of steadying support against wind and storm. Stakes or guy wires are effective for this purpose, depending on the tree size. These should be securely placed at the time of planting and left for a year. Newly planted shade trees are often

injured by the sun during the first winter. This is called "sun scald" and is prevented by wrapping the trunk with burlap. It is especially necessary on smooth-barked trees. A collar about 18 inches high fastened about the base of the tree will keep its bark from being injured by mice or rabbits.

Shrubs which have been transplanted from the wild will come up much more compactly if they are cut down to the ground and thereby forced to send up new growth. Before replanting, trim off all broken roots, cutting them cleanly with a knife or pruning shears. Berry-bearing shrubs are most appreciated just now.

Fruits. Dwarf fruit trees have a double purpose in furnishing flowers in the spring and fruit in the fall. They are particularly fitted to the small lot. Early in November is a good time to plant most of them, especially if a light mulch is applied to the roots. Apples and pears are among the most satisfactory kind. Cherries and peaches are also available. Don't forget to protect them at the ground with a tar paper collar.

Evergreens. Late fall planting of evergreens is risky. This class of plant should always be given plenty of time to re-establish its roots before the advent of really cold weather stops undergrowth. Furthermore, the top growth needs to be well supplied with moisture. Don't forget to thoroughly supply even old evergreens with plenty of water before freezing weather.

Pruning. November and December is a good time to clean out the tangle of overgrown vines. Cutting out the old diseased wood will send the strength into the remaining branches. It is much better to prune the flowering vines now, rather than to risk disturbing the tender shoots after they have started in the spring. Besides, there is the saving of valuable time.

The peegee and agee hydrangea are trimmed back to two to four buds on each shoot. The dwarf pinkish spirea (anthony waterer) should be cut back about two thirds and deadwood removed. Remove the suckers which spring up from the roots of the lilac bushes and the snowberry. Cut out the oldest stems of the mock orange (philadelphus) to the ground. Take out the oldest parts of the privet hedge and shape it up. Cut down the butterfly bush (beddleia) to within three or four inches of the ground. After freezing cover with soil several inches deep.

DRAINING WITH TILE

Drainage of any considerable size requires expert installation or much labor will be wasted, but many small problems can be solved by the amateur. Where the lot is small and

catches the drainage from surrounding land, a single line down the lowest spot will usually serve the purpose. Where there is a larger area or a more thorough saturation of the soil, a herringbone or gridiron plan is best. See the illustration.

GARDEN HINTS FOR DECEMBER

GENERAL

If you have made any new plantings they should be heavily mulched with manure. This not only serves to protect the plants by reducing the penetration of the frost, but increases the fertility and protectiveness of soil.

Low spots in the walks and drives that are invariably wet should be raised to shed water; or if the earth is taken out and the road bed filled with cinders it will help to make them dry and passable in bad weather.

Now is a good time to do any filling or grading about the ground so that it may have the benefit of settlement due to freezing in the coming cold months.

All of the ashes from the open fires this winter ought to be saved for garden use in the spring. They are a fertile source of potash, an essential plant food. Store the ashes in watertight containers over the winter and keep them dry, as their strength easily leaches away. When applying them in the spring use them thinly, especially on lawns. They are said to help save asters from blight and are sure to help loosen the soil if used consistently. Hardwood ashes can be bought by the bag.

Rhubarb may be forced in the cellar or attic of the dwelling by planting it beside the furnace or chimney. The soil should be kept moderately moist. Chicory is one of the best winter salad plants. It can be forced in any ordinary cellar by planting the roots in boxes and keeping them dark.

If you expect to secure any landscape service this year do it now as the man you select will have more time to give you now than later in the season, and while your grounds are bare he may get a better survey of your problems. Be sure that you have made the final cleanup of your grounds, removed all plant stalks, turned off the water, and drained the hose. Especially be sure that any garden ornaments, such as urns and jars, are turned over to keep them from collecting water and being broken by freezing.

CHRISTMAS FOR THE BIRDS

Why not a Christmas tree for the birds? Trim the branches with dried fruit, suet in pine cones, and as a special plum pudding tie on some packages of bird treat, so loved by the canaries. Be sure to keep water for them in pans that may be brought inside to be thawed out. This is one of their chief needs when everything is frozen. Grit or sand is another, so have a little fine poultry grit mixed with sand accessible to them.

A supply of sunflower, hemp, and millet seed supplemented with table scraps will take care of the food material very nicely. Suet wired to a branch is welcome to several species. A secluded fence corner facing south makes a good feeding station. A platform located in an open position in a hemlock, spruce, or pine tree is also very good. Protect these stations from cats by a band of tin twelve inches wide, tacked around the post or tree about six or eight feet from the ground. See Chapter XIX.

PESTS

Seeds which you have collected may be placed in dry paper packets and put in a tin box or a glass jar so that they will be kept dry and protected from mice.

Conduct a monthly examination of stored roots, bulbs, and tubers to see if they are being injured by mice. Look for signs of shriveling from being too dry or of rotting from too much dampness. If they are sprouting remove them to a cooler place.

Asbestos torches, or torches made of burlap and soaked in kerosene to make them inflammable, should be used to go over all the trees and destroy wintering-over nests of caterpillars and other pests. Do not scrape the bark on trees to destroy insect pests. Use a stiff brush or broom to remove the cocoons of various sort found attached to the bark and in sheltered recesses of the tree. Close examination of apple and wild-cherry twigs may disclose small, dark amber collars or clusters of insect eggs. These will hatch into husky colonies of tent caterpillars if not destroyed. They can be broken away from the bark or the twig may be cut off and burned.

LAWN

Poor lawns may be top-dressed, using a compost made of screened top soil compost or other humus with about 20 per cent bone meal and wood ashes added. This may be applied to the lawn liberally now.

Get after the chickweed with a spray described in Chapter IV. If you prefer to pull it, it can be best done now. Start early, because it grows and spreads every warm day all winter.

Clean off the rest of the leaves as they may smother patches of grass. Dig out any weeds which are hardy enough to grow. These are to go through their hardest season now, and, if weakened, will have the least chance to survive.

AMONG THE FLOWERS

Peonies. Peonies seem to flower best after a heavy continual freezing during the winter. Do not mulch them or protect them unless they are newly divided and then only with a very light mulch of manure. Never let it cover or even contact the crowns of the plants.

Roses. By the latter part of December there have been sufficient ground freezes to place manure for rotting between the hills of roses. Do not cover the hills with new manure.

Rockery. Some of the more tender rock plants may be protected with a thin mulch of hay; salt-marsh hay is better and evergreen boughs are best of all. These should be applied to act as windbreaks and the plants should be clearly visible through the mulch. Now is a good time to collect odd stones for extending the rock garden.

THE GARDEN INDOORS

General care. Much common failure of house plants is due to overwatering and poor drainage. They must have both food and drink but wet soggy soil is not to their liking. A good soaking once a week is better than a little water every day.

Ferns. Ferns, palms, and other house plants should be top-dressed occasionally with some of the concentrated plant foods sold for the purpose. Keep the surface of the soil loosened so that no green scum forms. They do best at a temperature of 60° to 70° with a weekly spray from above, using a plant syringe.

Bulbs. It is not too late to pot some bulbs in soil or to force them in water. Ten or twelve weeks seem a long time for them to root but the time soon passes and properly handled they are easy and sure of bloom. Don't let the idea of plunging bulbs outside frighten you. It is quite easy and once tried will become a yearly habit.

Indoor decorations. An outdoor flavor can be brought into your living room by the addition of branches kept in water. Small laurel branches will last all winter; the common Japanese barberry, with its attractive berries; and euonymus and other evergreens make an excellent bouquet. Try table decorations consisting of small boughs clipped from evergreens.

Christmas decorations. It is surprising the amount of Christmas decorations which can be done in a few minutes with material from your own yard. Clippings from your evergreen trees and the broad-leaved evergreen plants such as bittersweet (euonymus), myrtle, mahonis, holly laurel, and berried shrubs lend themselves well for this purpose. For wreaths fasten them to wire coat-hangers bent to proper shape with thread or short pieces of fine wire. Every gardener should have in his toolkit a bundle of tag wires, useful for many purposes, which can be purchased by the thousands from a stationer. The sprigs of white pine, hemlock, or pfitzer juniper make nice soft wreaths but the hemlock can only be used outside because it drops quickly in the heat. Garnish these ornaments with sleighbells, red ribbon, and silver tinsel.

Winter foliage. A welcome touch on a bleak winter day is the verdant vine of a common sweet potato growing in a jar of water. Hold it suspended in the water using some toothpicks stuck into it if necessary.

TREES AND SHRUBBERY

Planting. The planting of deciduous trees and shrubs may be continued just as long as the weather permits. Mulching heavily immediately after planting will prevent the penetration of frost if it should come soon. Trees that are to be moved with a ball of frozen earth around their roots may now have trenches dug to encircle them and facilitate the final diggings later on. To guard against drying out these trenches may be filled in with dead leaves or any rough litter.